MICROFINANCE

MICROFINANCE

Evolution, Achievements and Challenges

Edited by Malcolm Harper

PUBLISHING

London

SAMSKRITI

New Delhi

Published by:
ITDG Publishing
103–105 Southampton Row, London WC1B 4HL, UK
www.itdgpublishing.org.uk

Published in India, Nepal and Bangladesh by:
Samskriti
C-9020 Vasant Kunj, New Delhi 110070, India

First published in 2003 by ITDG Publishing

ISBN 1 85339 557 9 hb (ITDG Publishing)
ISBN 1 85339 561 7 pb (ITDG Publishing)
ISBN 81 87374 21 7 pb (Samskriti)

© ITDG Publishing 2003

A catalogue record for this book is available from the British Library.

ITDG Publishing is the publishing arm of the Intermediate Technology Development
Group. Our mission is to build the skills and capacity of people in developing
countries through the dissemination of information in all forms, enabling them to
improve the quality of their lives and that of future generations.

Typeset by Dorwyn Ltd, Rowlands Castle, Hants, UK
Printed in India

Contents

Preface

THE FIRST ISSUE of the *Small Enterprise Development* journal was published in March 1990. The journal has been published four times a year since that time, and something between three and four hundred articles have appeared in its pages. This book contains a selection of those papers, which are about financial services for small businesses, and in particular what is now known as microfinance, or financial services for businesses that are very small indeed. Perhaps half of the material that has appeared in the journal has been related to microfinance, so there has been a great deal from which to choose.

The first issue of the journal carried an article about the World Bank's lending to SME, but the 'M' stood firmly for 'medium', and the average loan size was $35 000; this was not microfinance. From the second issue onwards, however, microfinance has rarely been absent from its pages, except when we deliberately chose to focus an issue on a non-financial topic, partly in order to remind our readers that we were not only a journal of microfinance. Much excellent material has of course appeared in other publications, increasingly in electronic form, but *Small Enterprise Development* has from its first issue been regarded as one of the more significant international fora where new ideas on microfinance are presented and new views on enduring issues are put forward.

This collection has been assembled in order to provide a broad and varied set of material on the field in one convenient and accessible place. There is certainly no shortage of writing on microfinance, and one might be forgiven for wondering sometimes whether some of the effort and resources devoted to studying and writing about the field might not have been better spent if they had been directed towards extending and improving the availability of financial services to poor people. The actual market penetration is still very small indeed in relation to the need in all but a very few countries. Perhaps we can hope that this book will enable some people to learn more quickly what they need to know, and then to go and apply their knowledge in a practical way.

I should like to thank the writers whose material has been included for kindly allowing it to be used in this way. Nobody has ever been paid to write for *Small Enterprise Development*, and the reward to the writers whose material has been included in this book is the same 'warm glow' that they presumably felt when their contribution originally appeared. We can only reiterate our gratitude to them, and also to the far larger numbers of other authors who have over the years submitted papers to the journal, some of which were published but most of which were not. I hope that our sometimes harshly critical responses were not too discouraging to those whose submissions were not accepted.

I must also thank Toby Milner, Helen Marsden and their colleagues at ITDG Publishing for accepting the suggestion that this collection might be worth publishing, and for doing all the work that has been necessary to put it together.

The book itself has actually been printed in India; I hope that this has not only generated some income for the employees who produced it, but that it will also make the book more accessible to readers in India and South Asia. These countries are probably the world's main source of inspiration and innovation in microfinance, but they are also home to the world's largest numbers of poor people. It is to be doubted whether any of these people have the interest, the time, the education or the money to read this book, but I hope that some of them will benefit indirectly from its publication.

Introduction

This book provides a general overview of microfinance. The papers have been chosen in order to illustrate some of the major developments and changes that have occurred in the field during the period since 1990, to revisit some of the concerns that have continued to preoccupy practitioners, and also to remind us that there are still many unanswered questions. This selection does not pretend to include only the most seminal writing that has appeared on microfinance since 1991. We do feel, however, that the book provides a comprehensive overview of the field, and it includes material that looks broadly at general topics as well as other more detailed papers about specific programmes that effectively exemplify issues that affect microfinance everywhere.

It is perhaps odd that microfinance is still in many ways regarded as a subset of the broader field of small and micro enterprise development. Most business owners and managers, whatever the scale of their businesses, spend only quite a small amount of their time thinking about how to raise finance, or dealing with bankers, moneylenders, family members or others who may be able to provide it. On a day-to-day basis they are more concerned with making or buying things, and then marketing and selling them. And their longer-term decisions are more likely to be about what to make and sell, how and where to make and sell it, what prices to charge, how to balance the conflicting demands of household survival, whom to hire, how to conform to or evade regulations, and, in a broad strategic sense, what business they are in. Decisions and negotiations about acquiring finance, other than by reinvesting profits, tend to depend on and to follow decisions on other things.

One explanation for the continuing link in the literature between microfinance and enterprise development may be that material of this sort is not often written for or read by the owners and managers of small businesses. It is designed for people who work for institutions that try to assist small businesses. Some of these institutions devote some of their efforts to various forms of non-financial assistance, which have now been 're-merchandized' as 'business development services' or BDS, but finance remains a major concern for most national and international small business assistance agencies, and for those who fund them.

This is perhaps inevitable, particularly if they are concerned to assist microenterprises, which are usually the income-generating activities of the poor. External advisers, trainers and so on can contribute very little to the day-to-day management of such businesses. Each business is too small to justify the costs of the individual attention that is often needed, and the skills required for success are not those that outsiders know about.

Marketing may in fact be a more serious problem than finance for most microenterprises, particularly as microfinance institutions achieve greater outreach and serve larger numbers of the vast numbers of people who need the services they offer. Now that so many millions of households have access to finance for investment in microenterprises, more markets are becoming saturated. Good marketing is the key to survival in a competitive world, whether it is the world of globalized business or the world of a village market place.

It is, however, much easier to sell something to a business, such as a loan or savings product, than it is to assist the business to sell its products to others. It is particularly easy to sell credit if there is little competition apart from over-priced moneylenders who cannot use the law to get back their loans and may therefore have to use illegitimate means of recovery. If a generous government or donor pays the costs of lending money, and of the money itself, it is even easier. This is not to suggest that microfinance is simple; if it was, there would presumably be no need to write articles about it. It may, however, be the more obvious way for outsiders to help microenterprises.

Some major changes

From enterprise microcredit to household financial services

Seibel and Parhusip of the German agency GTZ write about some of the earlier attempts to link formal and informal financial institutions (Chapter 1). These experiments in Indonesia with bank loans to self-help groups foreshadowed and indeed paved the way for later developments in India, where some 400 000 such groups, with almost eight million women members, are now doing business with thousands of bank branches throughout the country.

We have included this as the first item in the selection partly because it goes beyond the early perception that microcredit, as it was then called, was the only financial service that people needed for microenterprise, and that they did not need, or perhaps should not have, loans for other purposes.

Maria Otero of ACCION wrote in 1991 about savings and microenterprises (Chapter 2). At that time microfinance was still firmly linked to microenterprise. Self-help group linkage, however, is based on the principle of 'savings first'. These savings are not only a way of creating group solidarity and testing people's willingness regularly to keep some cash aside, but they also create a loan fund from which the group can borrow. It was clear that no outside agency could or should try to control the way in which the members used their own savings. These savings, and the accumulated interest the members charge themselves on loans, may even make it unnecessary for the group to borrow from outside at all. This genuinely 'empowering' approach to microfinance, which is now rapidly gaining ground in India and elsewhere, was pioneered in Indonesia with German assistance. Seibel and Parhusip's and Otero's articles are thus important milestones in the development of microfinance.

The clients of microfinance institutions have always used some of their loans for purposes other than microenterprise investment. This may still be known as 'misuse' by some agencies, but most providers of microfinancial services are coming to realize that money is fungible, and that their customers probably know better than they do how best to use their money. Most articles about microfinance say less about how microloans are used for business, and more about the microfinance institutions themselves, or about new services that have little or nothing to do with business, such as life assurance. Ten years after Seibel and Parhusip's contribution, Stuart Rutherford of *Safe*Save in Dhaka writes of the transition of microfinance to the 'financial services era' (Chapter 3). Microfinance has thus in some sense come of age, as it has become more like the banking services that the non-poor have always enjoyed.

From 'Charity' to 'Sustainability'

Banks are businesses. Institutional microfinance started not as a business, but as a means of alleviating poverty and helping poor people to create sustainable livelihoods for themselves. The pioneers of microfinance, in the 1970s and still in the 2000s, were and are motivated by a desire to help the poor, not to make money. But, as Jackelen and Rhyne, from the UNDP and USAID, showed in their paper which was published at the end of 1991 (Chapter 4), microfinance seemed to have squared the circle; this was an intervention that could not only alleviate poverty, but that could and should also pay for itself, be 'sustainable' and even make profits. Only in that way, it is argued, can it reach the millions who need it.

Since that time, the issue of how to define 'sustainability', and how to achieve it, has received a great deal of attention. There is still no agreement on the issue of whether it is possible to have a sustainable microfinance programme which at the same time reaches and assists very poor people. The very fact that it may be possible, however, has had an important impact on the way the provision of non-financial enterprise services, or BDS, is regarded. Until relatively recently, it was felt that such services had to be provided by 'projects', with donor or government support, and that they should be evaluated by reference to their cost-effectiveness: did the benefits justify the costs? Now, however, BDS providers have to answer the same questions that confront microfinance institutions: are they sustainable? how can donors create genuine markets in BDS, so that they will continue to be provided by a number of competing institutions after external assistance has been withdrawn?

We can therefore identify three major shifts in microfinance: it has moved from charity to business, from microcredit to microfinancial services, and from enterprise investment to household money management. In all three cases, the shift has made the field broader, without, one hopes, losing the original narrower focus. Poor people can still take loans for investment in microenterprise, and thus become less poor. They can also make savings and take loans for other purposes, and the service itself can perhaps be genuinely 'sustainable', or profitable, for its providers as well as its customers.

Continuing issues

Microinsurance

A number of other issues have continued to preoccupy practitioners and observers of microfinance. One of these, which has only quite recently been explicitly recognized, is poor people's need for insurance. Slowly, it seems, we are starting to realize that the poor are not so different from 'us'. Savings can of course be a form of insurance, but a number of microfinance institutions have started themselves to offer life, health and other insurance products.

This is a natural continuation of the evolution from microloans to financial services that Rutherford observes, but Warren Brown of ACCION warns us (in Chapter 5) of the dangers of moving too fast into uncharted areas. A weak institution can make loans at no risk to anyone but itself. It must be much stronger and more durable before it can start to take savings, particularly those of the poor, and insurance requires skills and financial strength of a quite different order. Fortunately, microfinance institutions are also coming to realize that they can act as intermediaries between other institutions and their clients; they can act as middlemen, or agents, and they need not themselves provide all the financial products that they sell.

Supervision and regulation

As soon as microfinance institutions start to move beyond giving loans, and even if they take savings only as a pre-condition for loans rather than as a service in itself, there is a need for some sort of regulation. This is all the more necessary because their customers are poor; they cannot afford to lose their savings, and they are unlikely themselves to be able to assess the strength of the institution to which they are entrusting them. Poor people have always been the main prey to exploitation by bogus savings institutions. There is a very real risk that the growth and acceptability of 'formal' microfinance will enable unscrupulous or incompetent people to injure the vulnerable poor even more.

Effective supervision and regulation are the obvious answer, but Christen and Rosenberg of CIGAP show that this is not easy (Chapter 6). Poor countries, where microfinance is most needed, tend also to be the countries with the weakest banks and other formal financial institutions, and with the least ability to supervise and regulate them. If the authorities are not adequately supervising the existing banks, and the regulations governing their performance cannot be enforced, it is unrealistic to expect the same authorities to take on the task of supervising a new and unfamiliar set of institutions.

Many of these institutions may require very intense and sensitive supervision; their management are unfamiliar with formal banking requirements, and may even resent what they see as unnecessary official interference. Many would indeed be closed forthwith if they were subject to normally prudent banking standards, but this would be impractical and would also damage the interests of their clients, who have no alternative sources of financial services. If the existing supervisory system has to take on a large number of institutions of this kind, the net result may be an even further lowering of standards across the whole financial sector.

There are various different ways of addressing this problem. It may be possible to create a new supervisory body, either as a department of the existing authority or as a separate entity, but this is a slow and expensive process. Alternatively, the microfinance 'industry' may be able to regulate and supervise itself. Many professions and trades do this quite effectively; the individual institutions recognize that it is in their joint interest to maintain standards, even if this costs money and means that individual members will sometimes suffer. This does require a strong and more or less universally accepted 'industry association', however. If there is no single body that speaks for all the institutions, and is accepted and supported by them, it is very difficult to introduce any form of self-regulation.

Specialized institutions, or commercial banks?

The problems of supervision and regulation lead naturally to the issue of institutions: is there actually any long-term need for specialized regulation for microfinance at all? Some of the 'new generation' microfinance institutions will themselves become regulated commercial banks through internal growth and merger, and the existing banks may use their strength to move into the market and displace the weaker new institutions. Specialized microfinance institutions may be unnecessary in the long term.

Older-established institutions are rarely the innovators in any field. They have the experience, the resources, the market contacts, the skills and the legal position to recognize new market needs and to pioneer ways of serving them, but they are constrained by institutional inertia and the weight of their investment in yesterday's ways of doing things. There are many well-known cases of this failure, such as the introduction of personal computers, or 'no-frills' low-cost air travel, but microfinance provides a further classic example.

The commercial banks in many countries have large and often under-used branch networks, and their traditional urban-based corporate business is being threatened by the entry of multinational banks and other specialized financial institutions. Many large commercial banks are also still publicly owned, so that they have an obligation to serve social as well as financial goals. They are also allowed to offer a range of savings products, and some banks are already mobilizing large volumes of savings from poorer communities. The un-banked rural and urban poor are an obvious market opportunity for lending.

In spite of their need for new business, and the needs of the market, very few banks have been pioneers in microfinance. The National Bank of Indonesia (BRI) is of course a well-known exception, and the commercial banks in India, after a slow start, are now becoming quite heavily engaged in microfinance. Gloria Stemper, of the Inter-American Development Bank, described in her 1996 article (Chapter 7) how a number of commercial banks in Latin America were already then serving large numbers of women microentrepreneurs. These are still exceptions, however, and only a small minority of banks, anywhere, are starting to follow the example set by the new microfinance institutions. Ten years from now, the institutional landscape may look very different.

Impact assessment

Microfinance practitioners are under pressure to make their operations more 'sustainable', that is, less dependent on subsidy and more able to cover their costs and earn a return on the money invested in them. If microfinance is an integral part of a commercial bank, the pressure for profits will be all the stronger. This can dilute or even totally eliminate the original welfare objectives that prompted the founders and funders of the institution.

The accounting tools that enable us to judge the financial performance of an institution are fairly familiar, and a whole range of specialized financial indicators have been developed to measure and compare the sustainability of microfinance institutions. It is all too easy to apply these, and to neglect the far more difficult task of finding out how the services have affected clients' lives. A great deal of effort is being devoted to attempts to develop impact assessment tools which are both informative and institutionally feasible to use. Many writers have dealt at great length with various aspects of this topic, but in 1991 Chowdhury, Mahmood and Abed of BRAC in Bangladesh demonstrated a fairly simple and common-sense approach to the evaluation of microfinance (Chapter 8): they compared a group of clients with non-clients, and found out how much less poor the clients had become. Few microfinance institutions assess the impact of their services so rigorously, even today.

Worrying questions

In spite of all the research that has been carried out, there are still a number of vital questions that continue to worry microfinance practitioners and those who support them. We have chosen to include a number of papers which address these questions at the end of the collection, in order to demonstrate that microfinance is still very much unfinished business. The 'industry' is still young, and only in one or two countries have formal microfinancial services reached a significant proportion of the people who need them. The level of market penetration is still low.

Structural adjustment and microfinance

Microfinance has evolved during the era of liberalization, structural adjustment and reinforced belief in the virtues of markets. It was preceded by years of heavily subsidized and generally ineffective government and donor-financed credit programmes. These usually failed to benefit the poor to any significant extent, and they also destroyed many of the financial institutions that were forced to deliver them, along with the natural 'credit culture' of the poor.

The theory of microfinance, if there is such a thing, could be said to be based on the principle of free markets, where resources are allowed to flow to those who can make best use of them. There are as yet very few examples of microfinance institutions that are totally 'sustainable', in that they receive no subsidy at all, in cash or in kind. There are even fewer examples of institutions that pay their original investors any return on their investments. The initial set-up costs, or the equivalent of the 'risk capital' which funds the start-up of commercial firms, are often unknown, and most have been set up by donor organizations that would be most surprised if anyone tried to repay their grants.

If microenterprises are genuinely more efficient users of capital than other sorts of firms, more investment should flow to them when financial markets have been liberalized. Peninah Kariuki, of the Central Bank of Kenya, showed that this did not happen in Kenya (Chapter 9). Her research was carried out during the early 1990s, when microfinance was even less well established in Kenya than it is today, and the apparent market failure may have resulted from institutional constraints and information problems. Her conclusions should remind us, though, that liberalization is in itself not a sufficient condition for improved financial services. Existing institutions need to be reformed, and new ones may need to be established; the policy environment is also fundamental. Governments still have a vital role to play, possibly with donor assistance, and free markets and microfinance institutions alone cannot eliminate the barriers to investment in enterprise.

Can microfinance reach the poorest?

The debate on poverty outreach will never end. Most authorities seem to agree, however, that microfinance generally does not, and probably should not, directly reach the very poorest people. Practitioners use phrases such as 'the economically active poor' to describe the clients whom their institutions actually do reach, and perhaps also to excuse their failure to match the exaggerated expectations that some enthusiasts and publicists for 'microcredit', as they still call it, have created.

People who work in microfinance have generally accepted that it is not a panacea for poverty, and that it does not reach the 'poorest of the poor'. In Chapter 10, Graham Wright and Aleke Dondo, from Kenya, argue that a mix of clients is in any case appropriate, and they remind us that the boundary between being poor and very poor is a fine one; microfinance can significantly reduce vulnerability, and thus prevent people from slipping into extreme poverty. They also accept that the very poorest need relief, and possibly special savings facilities, rather than loans.

It can also be argued that the poorest are also the most profitable clients. Their only alternative is to take distress loans from moneylenders at totally extortionate interest rates, and they can absorb only very small sums of money; they can and will pay a high price for loans and accept low rates of interest on their savings. They are also usually more willing than people who are better off to work in groups, which makes them cheaper to deal with, and they are less 'empowered', so are less likely to default on repayments. These factors in part explain why women dominate the client profile of most microfinance institutions. Their needs conveniently coincide with those of the institution that serves them.

This issue takes us back to the debate between the proponents of 'sustainability' (that is, profits) and welfare. Christopher Dunford of Freedom from

Hunger is an articulate proponent of the view that the two aims are fundamentally inconsistent (Chapter 11). Profitability and growth are more likely to be achieved by offering more services to the same clients, rather than by reaching out to new and unserved clients. The client profile will inevitably drift upwards and away from the poor, and what started as a businesslike activity with charitable goals will become no more than another profit-seeking business.

Do the poorest clients benefit?

It can be argued that microfinance does not reach the poor, but in Chapter 12 David Hulme of The University of Manchester goes further. He shows that the poor benefit much less than the less poor when they are reached, that many do not benefit at all, and that many are also very severely injured by microfinance. He draws evidence from a wide range of countries and institutions, and leaves us with the disturbing conclusion that a development intervention that is trumpeted as an effective and sustainable way to alleviate or even eliminate poverty does not often reach the poorest, and that when it does it can make them even worse off than before.

It is tempting to dismiss Hulme's 'horror stories' as isolated and atypical instances, but there seems to be enough evidence from other sources and from our anecdotal field experience to make us pause. We may be doing more good than harm to most of our clients, but are we perhaps doing more harm than good to those who are most vulnerable? If microfinance is to remain true even to a small remnant of its original welfare objectives, its practitioners must be aware of the dangers and must regularly monitor their impact on the full spectrum of their clients. They must not only collect success stories, but must rigorously undertake the far more difficult and less rewarding task of searching for failures.

Can donors ever go away?

In spite of all the talk of sustainability and even of profits, there are few signs that microfinance has evolved into a real business that will grow and reach more people without further subsidy, whether it is given by foreign donors, national governments or charities. This is partly because it is perceived as a subsidy-dependent activity, and the continuing flow of donor funds 'crowds out' profit-seeking finance. There is little sign that start-up capital is flowing to microfinance, apart from the continuing presence of moneylenders.

Johnson, Mule, Hickson and Mwangi, however, describe a phenomenon in the Central Province of Kenya, which has emerged as a result of the withdrawal of donor assistance (Chapter 13). Ex-employees of microfinance NGOs have created jobs for themselves by managing accumulating savings and credit associations, and others are joining them. The associations pay them, the rate of membership growth is well over that being achieved by much longer-established and generously subsidized institutions operating in the same area, and they appear to be reaching poorer people. The fierce competition forces the independent managers to maintain repayment standards and to expand to new areas.

The donors who withdrew did not envisage this development, but it does seem to show that in places where there is a continuing need for microfinance, market forces can encourage entrepreneurial individuals to apply what has been learned from donor-supported initiatives. This may not be good news for donors whose existence depends on the continuing demand for donations, but it suggests that microfinance has a life of its own.

How long will it last?

Finally, Shahin Yaqub of BRAC warns us in Chapter 14 that microfinance may be nurturing within itself the seeds of its own destruction. Poor people save and repay as instructed and work within the often inconvenient group mechanisms that microfinance institutions demand, because they are weak. They have no alternatives. When microfinance helps them to become less poor, they become empowered. People who are empowered are able to resist and change unjust social, political and economic structures, but they are also more able to resist the legitimate claims of the microfinance institution that helped them to overcome their earlier weaknesses. Empowerment and virtue are not the same thing.

Yaqub's evidence is from Bangladesh, and it may be too early to judge whether the same process is taking place in other countries where microfinance is younger and less developed. It does convey a warning, however, that microfinance clients cannot and indeed should not be expected always to be as obedient and trustworthy as they have generally shown themselves to be thus far. If microfinance succeeds, its clients will become less dependent on it, and they will be able to access more alternatives. It will no longer be possible to demand that clients meet, save and borrow according to the convenience of microfinance institutions. There is already severe competition in many locations, and 'empowered' clients may also be increasingly able to access financial services from the commercial banks as they reach down to the new customers that microfinance is creating for them.

In the long term, as poorer countries become less poor, there will be less need for microfinance. There are some institutions in deprived areas of North America and Europe, but they tend to be small, heavily subsidized, and in many ways much less 'advanced' than their equivalents in poorer parts of the world. Microfinance practitioners must recognize that if they are genuinely successful, they will destroy their own institutions and their own jobs. This may, sadly, take many years or even several generations, but microfinance is at best no more than an effective and perhaps largely self-financing long-term sticking plaster for poverty. It will be judged to have succeeded only when it has disappeared.

1 Financial innovations for microenterprises – linking formal and informal financial institutions

HANS DIETER SEIBEL and UBEN PARHUSIP

This paper was first published in June 1990.

In the past, credit programmes including subsidies and neglecting savings mobilization have undermined rural finance. In recent years, the number of countries has been growing in which banks mobilize savings and practise commercial banking; but the rural poor still have to rely on informal financial institutions, which are better adjusted to local conditions. During the early 1980s, a novel approach entered into the debate: linking informal and formal financial institutions, with financial self-help groups acting as intermediaries between microentrepreneurs and the banks. This reduces transaction costs substantially, for the benefit of both. Within APRACA (Asian and Pacific Regional Agricultural Credit Association), Indonesia has been the first to implement such a pilot project. In a favourable policy climate, a project was designed which incorporates the major features of sustainability, such as reliance on institutional capacity, co-operation between governmental and private voluntary bodies and pre-existing grassroots organizations, domestic resource mobilization, market forces, flexibility and socio-cultural adjustment. In 1989, 30 bankers, 30 private voluntary organization (PVO) staff and 815 self-help group staff were trained. From May to September, a first set of some 20 bank units, 10 PVOs and 100 self-help groups entered into their initial financial transactions.

IN MOST DEVELOPING countries, policies for rural financial development have been based on three fallacies concerning their target groups: rural microentrepreneurs are unable to organize themselves; they are too poor to save; and they need cheap credit for their income-generating activities or small enterprises.

Three financial policies resulted from these assumptions: credit-oriented development banks and special programmes were set up which ignored savings mobilization; credit was subsidized; and generous credit guarantee schemes were set up to cover anticipated losses. The consequences of these policies did not contribute to the self-sustained growth of rural finance, nor did they sufficiently benefit the rural poor:

o Subsidization meant that the scope of credit remained severely restricted. There was no built-in growth factor which would have resulted from internal resource mobilization. The level of credit was directly tied to the amount of subsidies available. Small numbers of relatively large loans went to medium and large enterprises; and the masses had no, or little, access to institutional finance.

11

○ Banks were not motivated to give their customers a thorough screening and to recover their losses, while borrowers felt little motivation to repay their loans. This resulted in high default rates and in continuous programme decapitalization.
○ Subsidies led to the misallocation of production factors.

Around 1980, a reorientation among rural financial policy makers began. Mounting international debts, increasing shortages of internal and external credit supplies and a growing dissatisfaction with state-nurtured and seemingly ineffective credit programmes led to a rethinking, centring around such concepts as self-help, self-sustained growth and institutional viability. In terms of financial systems, this meant an emphasis on savings mobilization in particular, as a prime mechanism of internal resource generation. Development assistance was intended to promote, not to replace, self-help and personal effort.

It was then found that although microentrepreneurs in developing countries may be poor, they are able to save, and they are capable of forming their own self-help organizations. However, they usually face a number of problems:

○ Institutional finance is inaccessible to the majority of microenterprises.
○ Concessionary financial programmes for microenterprises have largely failed. They are not viable economically; in terms of impact, they reach only a minute proportion of their target group.
○ There is a wealth of human, organizational and institutional resources which, as long as it is not mobilized and appropriately linked, may remain untapped. Such resources include microenterprises, informal, semi-formal and formal financial institutions, private voluntary organizations and governmental agencies and programmes.
○ Conventional approaches to rural microenterprise finance face high transactional costs for both lenders and borrowers. At low interest rates they are unviable for banks; at market rates, they may be unviable for most of the potential borrowers.
○ Credit programmes without a savings component ignore savings as a means of internal resource mobilization; at the same time, they ignore the savings habit as a psychological basis for investment and repayment behaviour.
○ Confined to their own resources and membership, and barred from access to banks, most self-help groups of microentrepreneurs have been unable to make the most of their potential. Operating outside the formal sector, they have tended to keep the economy near stationary, and to contribute more to its stabilization than to rapid development.

The APRACA programme

APRACA (Asian and Pacific Regional Agricultural Credit Association) is an association of central banks, rural development banks and rural commercial banks, and is one of four Regional Agricultural Credit Associations (RACA) originally promoted by the United Nations Food and Agriculture Organization

(FAO). Established in 1977 with an emphasis on agricultural credit, it subsequently broadened its scope towards rural finance. At a workshop held in May 1986 in Nanjing, China, the member countries adopted a novel programme of access to formal financial institutions for the poorer sections of the population. This involved a financial system built around self-help groups as grassroots intermediaries between banks and rural microentrepreneurs.

Subsequently several APRACA members carried out surveys in their respective countries. They found that what stands in the way of the full utilization of resources for microenterprises is financial market segmentation. There are formal financial markets for the upper 5 to 20 per cent of the population. These markets fall under the control of state credit and related financial laws and are supervised by the central bank. They comprise central, commercial, development, savings and secondary banks as well as non-banking institutions. In addition, there is a small but growing semi-formal financial market, which comprises governmental and private voluntary organizations, and so-called self-help promoting institutions which have their own savings and credit programmes. They do not fall under the state's credit law but operate with the approval of the state and its organs.

Informal financial markets comprise financial self-help groups, other self-help groups with secondary financial functions and individual financial agents, such as moneylenders, deposit collectors and trade-, crop- or land-related financial arrangements. From a policy viewpoint, financial self-help groups are of particular importance. They are found in most Asian countries and in most cultures or ethnic groups within them. Their main financial functions are usually the accumulation and depositing of savings, the granting of loans and, to some extent, the rendering of insurance services. They may be found in urban and rural areas, among traders and market-women, farmers and fishermen, craftsmen and small industrialists, wage and salary earners, and among bank employees. Despite being part of the informal financial sector and lacking legal status, most associations do possess organizational structure. Typically, they are headed by a staff of elected executives; they have written rules and regulations; they keep membership lists and they practise some form of bookkeeping. Local social control mechanisms effectively prevent defaulting or fraud, which plague so many formal credit programmes.

For more effective financial coverage of the poorer sections of the population, three different approaches have been discerned in the APRACA discussions on rural finance:

○ upgrading financial self-help groups of microentrepreneurs
○ linking existing self-help groups and banks
○ the adaptation of banks to their environment ('downgrading').

The participants decided on the linkage programme as a focal approach which may eventually comprise both upgrading and institutional adaptation.

Policies were discussed and procedures worked out for linking banks and self-help groups within the member countries. This led to baseline research and policy discussions on the national level, the results of which were fed back to the international organization. In addition to a variety of conferences, meetings and workshops, two instruments of communication deserve particular attention: one is an international training programme, the other a new journal, *Asia Pacific Rural Finance*.

Guiding principles

APRACA members have discussed the essentials of a sound policy for financial market development, and several guiding principles have emerged:

○ Working through existing formal and informal institutions rather than establishing new institutions.
○ Promoting savings mobilization by observing two prerequisites: savings should not yield negative real returns (relative to the rate of inflation); and savings mobilization must not be 'undermined' by cheap (i.e. subsidized) credit from the central banks or from donors. Thus, the interest rate on liquidity credits should equal the cost of mobilizing rural savings.
○ Promoting credit delivery at market rates. Financial institutions should be encouraged to apply market rates of interest in order to achieve a balance of the supply of, and demand for, credit in rural areas.
○ Linking savings and credit. Credit should be linked to savings: no credit without savings, no savings without credit. Participating institutions may agree upon a savings-to-credit ratio, reflecting the creditworthiness of the borrower.
○ Substituting group liability for conventional collateral. It is suggested that no other physical collateral will be requested over and above the savings deposited. For the remaining balance, the self-help group will act as a joint liability group.
○ Ensuring institutional viability. All financial intermediaries involved – self-help groups, PVOs and banks – should cover their costs of intermediation through an adequate interest margin. Over and above the costs of funds, intermediation costs include transaction costs, reserves for bad debts and the costs of extension services.
○ Covering the risk from the margin. The risk of default shall be borne by the financial intermediaries themselves. External credit guarantees, though sometimes necessary for banks as an inducement to participate in an experimental phase, are seen as contrary to programme sustainability and self-reliance.

The first APRACA countries to design pilot projects were Indonesia, Nepal, the Philippines and Thailand. In Indonesia, the pilot project started in 1988; Nepal, the Philippines and Thailand were expected to follow in 1989–90.

Pilot project in Indonesia

The Republic of Indonesia surpasses most other developing countries in terms of population size (175 million in 1988), geographical extension and ethnic or cultural diversity. The number of enterprises exceeds 30 million; more than 90 per cent are microenterprises; and most belong to the informal sector.

Until 1983, financial markets were tightly regulated. Since then, they have been gradually deregulated, and exchange rates are now allowed to fluctuate according to the market. This has led to substantially higher levels of domestic savings mobilization. Interest rate restrictions have been removed; minimum reserve requirements have been lowered to 2 per cent; and the ban on establishing new banks has been lifted. Indonesia now has the highest interest rates in the region (e.g. time deposit rates from 16 to 24 per cent), which has reduced capital flight.

For 20 years, the Government of Indonesia has experimented with financial schemes for small enterprises. Most of its credit programmes were subsidized and had no savings component; and the banks served mainly as channels for the distribution of government funds. They had little, if any, motivation to mobilize savings, to search actively for borrowers or, equipped with generous credit guarantee schemes, to scrutinize loan applications and enforce repayment. As a result, loan repayment performance was usually poor. Access to loans by the masses of the population in rural areas, and even more so by the urban informal sector, remained severely restricted – with a negative impact on productive investments and income generating activities.

In the new era of financial market deregulation, disenchantment with subsidized programmes and with their questionable effectiveness has been growing both in government and bank circles. They are now being gradually dismantled in Indonesia. The new policy environment encourages banks to embark on vigorous campaigns of domestic savings mobilization, to expand credit delivery at market rates and to experiment with innovative approaches to rural and urban finance.

The financial markets in Indonesia at present bear the marks of both old and new, regulated and free market policies. They are segmented into formal, informal and semi-formal financial markets. Banks are the core institutions of the formal financial sector. This sector also includes a number of small second-tier institutions defined as non-banks, which are supervised by primary banks, as well as registered co-operatives which fall under the co-operative law.

There are numerous informal financial institutions that operate without legal status and outside state control: moneylenders, financial self-help groups (rotating and non-rotating savings and credit associations, unregistered credit unions) and numerous other groups with secondary financial functions. In terms of origin, they may be indigenous, state- or PVO-initiated, with considerable overlaps between these three categories.

Semi-formal financial institutions include PVOs as well as governmental organizations, and act as intermediaries between domestic or foreign donors and informal self-help groups or final individual borrowers. They are extra-legal in their financial activities, but so far have obviously enjoyed the tacit tolerance of the state. In addition, officially recognized but unregistered pre-co-operatives are included in this sector.

There is a wide network of institutional resources in Indonesia: there are more than 15,000 bank and non-bank institutions; and probably more than one million which have generated their own funds from various sources and self-help groups which have built up their own savings and credit businesses. There is a small number of self-help promoting institutions which, acting as semi-formal financial institutions, have made substantial contributions to the development of a selected number of self-help groups in such fields as group formation, personal development, skills training, income generating activities and finance. For the purposes of this article they will be included with PVOs.

Both informal and semi-formal financial institutions share a number of short-comings.

○ They are not linked to the banking sector, except, in some cases, with regard to fund depositing or transfer.
○ They have no access to the refinancing facilities of the central bank: at best they depend, to a moderate extent, on external donors.
○ They are restricted in their savings and credit activities because of shortages of funds.
○ They have no access to bank training facilities; consequently they lack finan-cial skill and banking experience.

Despite substantial contributions made by the extension of the rural banking network and by special credit programmes, bureaucratic red tape, lack of collat-eral and legal requirements have effectively barred the poorer sections of the rural population from banking services. In addition, there is one obstacle which probably surpasses all others in economic importance: excessively high transac-tion costs for both banks and their clients. Private moneylenders have moved in to fill the void, charging interest rates that cover these transaction costs, but at these rates most microentrepreneurs find it difficult to use credit for the financ-ing of their business, except in some fast turnover trading activities.

An initiative has been taken by Bank Indonesia – the central bank – together with Bank Rakyat Indonesia – the largest commercial bank with a rural mandate – and Bina Swadaya – a prominent PVO – to improve the system of rural finance. After extensive consultations with APRACA, FAO and GTZ, they jointly

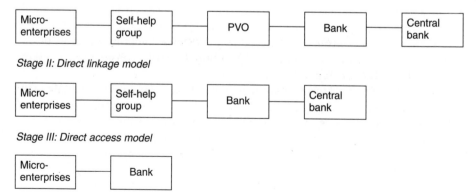

Stage I: Indirect linkage model

| Micro-enterprises | — | Self-help group | — | PVO | — | Bank | — | Central bank |

Stage II: Direct linkage model

| Micro-enterprises | — | Self-help group | — | Bank | — | Central bank |

Stage III: Direct access model

| Micro-enterprises | — | Bank |

Figure 1.1   *Evolutionary stages of institutional linkages*

formed a national task force, commissioned a study of self-help groups by Gadjah Mada University and worked out a linkage programme. This was followed by intensive national consultations with numerous organizations.

Under a pilot project, the novel approach was to be tested of linking existing financial self-help groups as grassroots intermediaries to banks for both savings mobilization and credit delivery, thus minimizing transaction costs for both banks and final borrowers. The purpose of the project was that viable financial services would be made available to self-help groups of microentrepreneurs and small farmers.

To implement the objective, the project was designed to initiate linkage processes participatively, rather than to prescribe specific models. Any specific schemes were to be the outcome of participative processes among the respective participants. There are two principal dimensions of linkage:

○ Institutional linkages between self-help groups and banks. They may either be indirect, involving PVOs as financial intermediaries or as consultants, or direct. In addition, banks may link up with the central bank for refinance. This is a novelty in Indonesia, and it is of particular interest to small rural banks which are short of funds and far from sources of refinance.
○ Financial linkages between savings and credit. In fixed ratios, the amount of credit is contingent upon the amount of savings. In dynamic ratios, the amount of credit increases with the number of successful repayment cycles, so as to ensure a gradual growth in the credit offered and the borrower's capacity to save, invest and repay.

Institutional linkages between banks and self-help groups may proceed in an evolutionary sequence of three steps, from indirect to direct linkages, with the ultimate step of making individual microentrepreneurs bankable and giving them direct access (see Figure 1.1).

Between these stages, there may be intermediate steps, with PVOs or self-help groups respectively in a consultative role. In addition, PVOs and various other agencies may supply supplementary technical and extension services.

Financial scheme

Interest rates are worked out locally by the participating institutions. The project issues guidelines and recommendations which the participants are free to modify according to local conditions. Some major recommendations are:

○ self-help groups use part of their funds for internal lending, and another part for depositing in a bank as a basis for refinance from the bank
○ savings come first: there should be no credit without savings
○ savings count as partial collateral
○ bank loans are treated as group credit, to be on-lent to members
○ interest rates on savings and credit are to be market rates, taking into consideration reductions in bank transaction costs as a result of the intermediary services of third parties

○ joint liability should be a substitute for physical collateral (on the balance not covered by the savings deposited)
○ the ratio between savings and credit should be contingent upon creditworthiness; primarily of the group and secondarily of the microenterprise
○ credit decisions for on-lending to members should be taken by the group
○ short-term credit should extend to 18 months
○ instead of penalties for arrears, banks may impose an extra incentive charge to be refunded in the event of timely repayment
○ self-help groups may levy an extra charge on the interest rate for internal fund generation (equivalent to self-imposed forced savings).

The main components of the interest rate are:

○ the cost of funds
○ a gross margin to the bank (including transaction costs, a reserve for bad debts, and profit)
○ a gross margin to the PVO (for financial intermediation and supporting services)
○ a gross margin or incentive payment to the self-help group.

Project organization

Bank Indonesia, the central bank, is the project holder and lead agency. Together with Bank Rakyat Indonesia and Bina Swadaya, it forms a national task force, which has initiated the project, functions as a policy-making body for the project and supervises its implementation. Bank Indonesia works directly with two types of participating institutions, banks and PVOs, and promotes linkages between banks and self-help groups. These linkages may be either direct, or indirect with PVOs as intermediaries. At the grassroots level, self-help groups act as intermediaries between their members and banks or PVOs.

On the national policy-making level, in Jakarta, the national task force and a technical team have been established comprising members from Bank Indonesia, Bank Rakyat Indonesia and Bina Swadaya. The general manager of the department of co-operatives and small credit, Bank Indonesia, is the head of the task force and the general manager of the project. He reports directly to the board of directors of Bank Indonesia, which is the ultimate policy-making body and has overall responsibility for the project.

A national project implementation and co-ordination centre has been set up in Yogyakarta, where the project has been established as an organizational unit of Bank Indonesia. This places the project within the organizational structure of Bank Indonesia and provides the structural basis for its sustainability.

Project implementation is managed by a national co-ordinator and his deputy in Yogyakarta. They are assisted by four professional co-ordinators: from a bank, from a PVO, for training, and for monitoring and research. There is also an advisory team, comprising Indonesian and German experts. Technical assistance is given by the Federal Republic of Germany through its technical co-operation agency, GTZ.

The project comprises four areas: Yogyakarta, Central Java, North Sumatra and Bali, including a total of 13 districts. They are managed by regional project managers in the respective Bank Indonesia branches and by PVO and training co-ordinators.

Within each district, there may be one or several participating PVOs and one or several participating banks or bank branches, plus additional village or sub-district bank units. Each participating PVO appoints a supervisor. He supervises fieldworkers who in turn work with self-help groups. Similarly, each participating bank appoints a supervisor in charge of project activities.

At district level, the PVO supervisors and the bank supervisors work closely together and jointly form a district forum. It is the task of the forum to co-ordinate implementation activities at the field level. The chairmanship is chosen by mutual consent.

During the pilot project phase, it is expected that approximately 420 self-help groups may participate in the project: 250 in Java, 150 in Bali and 20 in North Sumatra.

There are 13 participating banks with a total of more than 50 bank units involved, among them Bank Rakyat Indonesia with four regional offices, 13 branches and approximately 30 village units; three regional banks (Bank Pemerintah Daerah in Yogyakarta, Semarang and Denpasar), each with several branches; and nine unit banks, among them village and market banks. There are 12 PVOs involved in the project who work with approximately 1500 self-help groups altogether.

Under the project, the first financial transaction between a self-help group and a bank took place in May 1989. The linkage process was expected to gain momentum by the end of 1989, after an initial experimentation phase of approximately six months.

Preparations in the field started in October 1988. Almost one thousand staff members from 250 self-help groups subsequently received project-related training through participating NGOs. The first credit delivery to a self-help group was on 31 May 1989. Within the first nine months of the implementation period, 204 self-help groups deposited savings and received a total of 229 group loans with maturities usually between six and 18 months. A total of 18 banks and bank branches have been involved, among them seven private banks and 11 branches of government banks. Private banks have proved to be more dynamic than government banks and competition has made banks more responsive.

Nine NGOs have participated and have provided essential contributions in such fields as group guidance, training, financial intermediation and credit supervision. Twenty per cent of the loan volume was disbursed directly to self-help groups; 80 per cent through NGO intermediaries.

The group loans were retailed to about 3500 self-help group members, and 63 per cent of the loan recipients were women. To refinance part of their loans to self-help groups as intermediaries of microentrepreneurs, Bank Indonesia has offered a liquidity credit line to participating banks at market rates, which are defined as the average costs of loanable funds in rural areas. For some of the smaller banks, this has proven a major attraction – and at the same time a mechanism for reversing the usual rural–urban flow of funds. After the deregulation of 29 January 1990, it is expected that this refinancing function will gradually shift to large national banks which are now compelled to lend 20 per cent of their portfolio to small enterprises.

There are two major sources of internal funds in self-help groups: direct savings, including initial, regular and voluntary savings, and interest income from loans to members, which are normally on the level of market rates in rural areas. Regular savings are usually modest; the major source of funds is from interest income. No interest is paid on savings. Before co-operating with banks, self-help groups normally charged their members a flat rate (on the nominal initial loan amount) of between 2 and 3 per cent per month, which in the case of loans with 12 equal instalments amounts to annual effective rates of 44 and 66 per cent respectively.

In the framework of the project, self-help groups are required to deposit a certain amount of savings as partial collateral before they can obtain a loan. For this deposit most groups mobilize additional funds from the members instead of taking them from their internal resources. These savings deposits have grown rapidly since the beginning of the project, reaching Rp.150.4 million (US$82 547) by the end of March 1990, which is an average of Rp.737 000 ($400) per group.

In terms of volume, 89 per cent of the loans were lent, with ratios of savings to credit of between 1:4 and 1:6. The overall average ratio of savings to credit at the time of loan disbursement was 1:5; the ratio of savings to credit outstanding was 1:4. The latter figure may be used as an indicator of savings mobilized.

The total amount of loans disbursed has been Rp.751.36 million ($412 000), averaging Rp.3.68 million ($2000) per group. The average loan size per group member as final borrower was Rp.215 000 ($118). Outstanding loans as per 31 March 1990 amounted to Rp.600.6 million ($330 000).

Interest rates in Indonesia have to be interpreted within the framework of the highest rates in South-east Asia. They have soared since the beginning of deregulation in 1983, and the inflation rate in 1989 was 6 per cent. Savings accounts fetch 12 to 17 per cent, time deposit accounts in some banks as much as 24 per cent. While the prime lending rate is between 17 and 19 per cent, there are small banks which charge far more than 100 per cent p.a. for uncollateralized short-term microloans to the informal sector. Seasonal loans by moneylenders are quoted at around 240 per cent p.a.; short-term micro-loans may bear astronomical interest rates.

Project staff have been able to convince banks that self-help groups and NGOs as financial intermediaries save transaction costs and that lending rates should be close to the prime rate rather than to the rates usually charged by them to microentrepreneurs. For small rural banks, this has been a novel insight. In the framework of the project, where the staff only serve as facilitator and do not offer any subsidies, banks have lent directly to self-help groups at 24 to 29 per cent and to NGOs at 22 to 24 per cent. The latter is only slightly above the refinancing rate of large to small banks. As a basis of institutional viability, NGOs as intermediaries have added to that a margin of approximately 6–10 per cent and self-help groups another 10 per cent, from which they build their internal fund and cover credit risks deriving from joint liability. The end-user thus pays anything between 30 and 44 per cent and sometimes more, which is still usually far below the gross

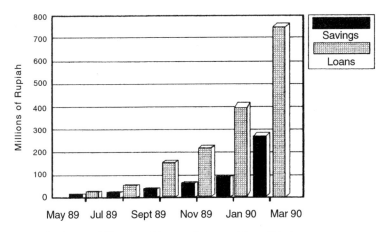

Figure 1.2   *Saving mobilized and loans disbursed to self-help groups*

profit margin of the microenterprise income generating activities.

In terms of amount, 98.6 per cent of the loans have been used for income generating microenterprise activities: 48.9 per cent for petty trade and small shops, 36.0 per cent for agriculture, livestock and fisheries and 16.2 per cent for rural crafts and industries (data for 31 January 1990).

Loan performance to date has been excellent. Eleven loans have been fully repaid to the banks. On the others, instalments, usually monthly, are being made according to schedule. The arrears ratio is 0.3 per cent. So far there has been no instance of defaulting.

Two major reasons may be cited for this: one is the quality of group guidance and credit supervision provided by participating NGOs; the other is that credit at market conditions is treated as serious financial business by both banks and self-help groups and the microentrepreneurial members.

After traumatic experiences with group loans during the days of subsidized credit channelled by banks on behalf of the government, banks are now gaining new confidence in well-organized financial self-help groups and the microenterprises of their members. As a result, only one government bank has insisted on credit guarantees by the project. To all other participating banks, credit guarantees by an outside agency have appeared irrelevant and they have not entered into credit guarantee agreements with Bank Indonesia as the project holder.

A typical self-help group

There is a wide variety of different types among the self-help groups which have been involved in financial linkages and UB Arisan Manjung in the village of Manjung, Kabupaten Klaten, Central Java, is one of the more impressive examples of self-help groups in the project.

UB Arisan Manjung has 52 members, six of them women. It originated in 1971 as a rotating savings association and, in 1975, it came under the guidance of Bina Swadaya, a private voluntary self-help promoting institution. While it retained its rotating savings business, it turned into a savings and credit association, with a permanent internal loan fund and with an emphasis on income generating activities.

It is headed by a committee of 12. There are four major sources of internal funds: initial savings (i.e. equity share), compulsory weekly savings, voluntary savings and interest income. A major part of the fund is used for loans to members; part is deposited with Bina Swadaya as solidarity savings; excess liquidity is deposited in a bank account. It has been refinanced by Bina Swadaya from donor funds, with loans increasing gradually from Rp.1.5 million in 1975 to Rp.15 million in 1988.

Sohun noodle manufacturing has been the major microenterprise activity in which at present 35 of the 52 members are involved. This has generated income and employment, and it has brought visible wealth to the village, which has also spilled over to neighbouring villages from which labourers are drawn, and to related sectors, such as trade in flour, noodle trade and transportation, the printing of labels, and so on. Indirectly it has influenced farming, goat and pig raising, tailoring and other microenterprises.

Several attempts by Bina Swadaya to promote noodle manufacturing on a group basis (UB means co-operation or joint enterprise) have failed. As a result, Bina Swadaya has accepted that the members prefer private enterprise. Bina Swadaya contributes to this with group guidance, training and finance. The group has also been innovative in the field of insurance: with a life assurance scheme for loan protection and a health insurance scheme.

Since 1971, there have been no cases of defaulting. On 21 August 1989, the group deposited Rp.4 million in savings in the bank and received a loan of Rp.14 million, which was mediated by Bina Swadaya. By March 1990, it had been fully paid back in seven equal instalments. On 21 April 1990, the group received its latest loan, Rp.30 million: Rp.25 million from the bank through Bina Swadaya and Rp.5 million from Bina Swadaya's own funds. This was the largest loan granted so far in the brief history of the project.

The balance-sheet total of UB Arisan Manjung in December 1988 before the project, was Rp.14.4 million. By December 1989, it had reached Rp.19.8 million: a 37.1 per cent increase.

Sustainability

Sustainability can be tested only after the completion of a project; yet no project can have a chance of sustained impact if certain factors are not built into the project.

○ Institutional capacity. The project is founded on the autonomy of existing organizations. In Bank Indonesia, it has a highly professional project holder with an immaculate reputation and a legitimate responsibility for the development of the financial system. The project is part of the line structure of Bank Indonesia and the participating banks. It does not depend on charismatic leaders for its success. The routine rotation of personnel is used as a means of providing training on-the-job to future project managers.

o The project does not work through public administration bureaucracies. Its partners are institutions that work in the private economy. In banks, PVOs and self-help groups, it builds on existing personnel and activities; it does not provide incentives to lure institutions into donor programmes. Through its institutional development and associated human resource development components, it contributes to the planning and financial management capacity of participating institutions.

o Motivation. To all participating institutions – banks, PVOs, and self-help groups – the linkages are expected to be profitable. This provides the basic motive for sustainability. They have all proven over time that they are able and willing to allocate personnel and financial resources to the project activities.

o Project design for sustainability. The project is systematically designed towards sustainability. It is geared towards the clearly defined single goal of giving self-help groups access to banks. It includes essential elements of sustainability, such as: domestic resource mobilization as a source of funds; market processes in the private economy; ensuring institutional viability by providing an adequate margin to all participating institutions. Participating organizations have accepted these elements on the basis of their own merits; this includes PVOs, which previously depended on external subsidies.

o Policy environment. The deregulation of financial markets in Indonesia since 1983 has provided the right policy environment for the project and its sustained impact. A deregulated financial system, a gradual dismantling of subsidies, vigorous efforts at domestic resource mobilization, credit delivery at differentiated market rates and an openness to financial innovations, are all important policy factors bearing on the sustainability of the project approach.

o Socio-cultural factors. The project builds on pre-existing socio-economic systems and grassroots organizations. In the project areas, it adjusts to local cultural conditions, types of grassroots organizations and processes of decision making. Its inbuilt flexibility to accommodating varying local conditions rests upon emphases on process rather than structure, on participation and communication rather than bureaucratic domination, on programme openness rather than dogmatism.

o International programme dialogue. Through APRACA, the national project forms part of an international programme dialogue on co-ordinated levels of policy makers, programme planners and project personnel. This provides a communication framework for policy adjustments, improvements in project design and exposure training.

In conclusion, a self-sustained impact is most likely if a project contributes to the functioning of market processes, which should actually be functioning without intervention. In this sense, the project provides an initial push towards self-supporting market processes. It removes some obstacles and establishes contact between banks and self-help groups of microentrepreneurs as business partners. It thereby creates an environment in which finance is available to the rural poor without continuous intervention.

About the authors

Dr Hans Dieter Seibel is Professor of Sociology at the University of Cologne, Germany. Dr Uben Parhusip is Adviser in agricultural economics to the Central Bank of Indonesia.

2 Savings mobilization and microenterprise programmes

MARIA OTERO

This paper was first published in March 1991.

Microenterprise programmes can be excellent vehicles to foster savings among poor populations, with considerable benefits both for those saving and for the programmes themselves. The purpose of this paper is to explore issues related to savings mobilization from the vantage point of projects that seek to reach poor people who are self-employed in productive activities. Microenterprise development projects in particular are the focus of this study.

The first section provides background for the discussion, asking why people save, and what sort of savings schemes prevail among poor populations. The second section turns to examples of savings mobilization in microenterprise programmes to identify the factors that contribute to success.

Finally, the article identifies the circumstances under which mobilizing savings makes economic sense, and provides some approaches for future microenterprise lending programmes.

DOMESTIC SAVINGS provide the assets for the economy's investment in future production. Without them, the economy cannot grow unless there are alternative sources of investment.

People's propensity to save varies considerably. Common wisdom dictates that as a person's disposable income increases, so does his or her capacity and willingness to save. Low-income groups, especially persons living at subsistence or near subsistence levels, are thought to be among those least able to contribute to an economy's savings. Most developing countries, where the poor constitute the great majority, demonstrate an overall low propensity to save. The poor, many have concluded, cannot save.

Experience has shown that many low-income people have the capacity to save and do so through informal channels which never enter the formal financial structures of a country. Informal approaches to saving involve the creation of alternative structures, such as groups or associations, through which people undertake financial activities such as lending and saving.

There is a rich body of literature, based on surveys, case studies, regional and cross-country analysis, that explores how the poor save and provides us with a better understanding of the nature of this savings capacity and the factors that propel or constrain it. Many assert that not only do the poor save, but that this fact has considerable implications for policy and resource mobilization for national economies and financial markets (Adams, 1973; Miracle et al., 1980; Maloney and Ahmed, 1988; Meyer et al., 1988).

Mobilizing savings among the poor is an interesting issue for various reasons. It has implications for the whole economy if there is a savings potential among the poor in developing countries that lacks productive outlet. Savings mobilization also raises important considerations for development programmes that are working to enhance productive income and employment among low-income groups. Finally, the process of saving regularly can be an empowering experience for people used to living at the margin, and can contribute to an improvement in the quality of their lives. Not only does saving offer a reprieve to the constant worrying that accompanies a subsistence life, but it also serves to capitalize whatever productive activity sustains the family, thereby enhancing production and income.

Factors that affect savings

Income is a key determinant of a person's capacity and propensity to save. However, there are additional factors that overall may play a more decisive role in the savings patterns that one observes. The following are identified as important.

○ The policies in the country, especially those pertaining to the real deposit rate, are determinants of how and where people save (Vogel, 1986; Meyer et al., 1988). For poor people, the interest rate offered influences the decision of whether to deposit their money in a formal commercial institution or to opt for an informal arrangement, even if the latter is riskier or ties up their money for longer.

○ In many countries, the government subsidizes lending interest rates, in order to increase access to credit among small borrowers. Subsidized lending interest rates discourage savings among possible depositors (Meyer et al., 1988; Vogel, 1986).

○ The higher the bank density, the greater the possibility of mobilizing savings. Distance and inaccessibility of a bank branch influence a person's decision on how to save, encouraging savings in kind rather than deposits with a financial institution (Meyer et al., 1988).

○ Small farmers who often save to even out their income stream over the year need a safe repository for their savings, which is convenient, accessible, and protects the value of their deposits from being eroded by inflation.

○ The perceived safety of the deposit will determine whether a person entrusts an institution with his or her savings. Financial intermediation, after all, is a unique market in that it involves the exchanges of money for the uncollateralized promise to repay at some future date. The poor, in particular, who seldom interact with formal banking institutions, understand little about investment practices and are often denied other services such as credit, so the 'trust factor' becomes even more important.

Savings schemes available to the poor

Informal savings schemes exist throughout the developing world. Most pertinent in this context are the rotating savings and credit associations

(ROSCAs), informal institutions in which groups of individuals come together to save, share risks, and borrow. Found in many countries, under a variety of names and among wealthy, middle-income and poor groups, rotating saving and credit associations are organized spontaneously among socially homogeneous groups of people, include a membership usually of between six and 50, and depend on a leader – usually the founder – who distributes and collects the resources (Miracle et al., 1980). Members contribute a fixed amount into a pot and the total assets are distributed at fixed intervals among the members in turn, agreed upon by lottery, seniority in the group, or another established arrangement.

All informal credit and savings operate on the principle of rotating access to a capital fund which is continually fed by the members' contributions. The interest rates charged to borrowers may depend on the length of the loan, where they appear in the member sequence, or other arrangements as specific situations arise. Noteworthy in these schemes is the flexible and responsive treatment given to interest rates, since early credit recipients have different concerns from late recipients who want to be assured of the safety of their deposits (Chandavarkar, 1988).

Rotating savings and credit associations provide a learning laboratory for understanding what motivates poor people to save, and under what conditions they are likely to do so. The traits of most ROSCAs – a simple but resilient savings and loan system grounded in the local culture, a flexible yet structured set of procedures agreed upon by all, high returns, easy access, trust in the mechanism, and peer pressure to meet one's obligations – recur in nearly every informal credit system, regardless of culture or country.

Some microenterprise lending programmes designed to enhance the productive activities of the poor have fashioned savings components that bear great similarities to the informal savings schemes of the poor. The inclusion of savings as a component of microenterprise programmes has received less attention. Most of the ever-growing literature on microenterprise development provides only a cursory glance at the topic, and few writers link what we have learned about savings in its informal incarnation in developing countries to the expanding informal sectors in urban areas.

The experience of several organizations – the Grameen Bank (GBB) in Bangladesh and Accion International (ACCION) in Latin America – which have mobilized savings among the poor provide interesting insights into this topic. While there are other organizations with experience in savings, such as the Badan Kredit Kecamatan (BKK) in Indonesia, the World Council on Credit Unions (WOCCU), and the Foundation for International Community Assistance (FINCA), the ones presented here serve as illustrations of the manner in which microenterprise programmes have addressed savings.

The Grameen Bank in Bangladesh

Started in 1976, the Grameen Bank assists the economically active poor who are excluded from official lending sources. The Bank's ability to mobilize savings is one of its major contributions to other organizations working with the poor (Hossain, 1988).

By March 1990, the Bank had reached 712 000 rural poor in 16 321 villages, over 18 per cent of the nation's villages. With average loans of about US$60 paid back in weekly instalments over 52 weeks, the Bank has lent over US$184 million at commercial interest rates, and has amassed over US$21.4 million in savings. Its repayment rate on loans is 98 per cent, with some branch offices reporting 100 per cent repayment. Of the 712 998 borrowers recorded in March 1990, 638 225 or 89 per cent are women (Yunus, 1990).

Savings are used as a tool to prepare the borrowers to manage credit. Potential borrowers make weekly savings deposits, and their credit eligibility is based in part on their ability to maintain self-discipline in saving. Each borrower, through his or her group, must save one taka, or US$0.04 every week. Additionally, 5 per cent of every loan amount approved is set aside at the time of disbursement. These monies go into a group fund managed by each group and designed to provide emergency and social loans to its members. Each group sets the terms for loans and decides how to allocate them.

By July 1986, the Group Fund totalled nearly US$3 million, and it had disbursed over US$1 million in loans to the borrowers. By March 1990, this Group Fund had captured US$15.4 million. The Emergency Fund, a second mechanism for savings, is capitalized by saving the equivalent of 25 per cent of the interest on all loans, and is used to provide loans in case of unexpected events such as illness or death. It currently totals US$6.03 million.

The role of savings in the Grameen Bank

The obligatory nature of savings holds one of the keys to Grameen's success in mobilizing savings. All Bank borrowers must save a specified amount if they wish to receive a loan. The Grameen Bank also provides added incentives to facilitate

Table 2.1   Summary information on the Grameen Bank (US$ in millions)

	1982	1985	1986	1987	1990 March
Total members	30 000	172 000	235 000	291 000	712 998
Number of villages	363	n.i.	n.i.	6570	16 321
Percentage women	45%	66%	74%	n.i.	89%
Amount disbursed (cumulative)	23.1	32.5	49.0	n. i.	
Amount saved	0.444	2.94	4.56	5.6	21.4

Sources: Hossain, 1988; Rippey, 1988; Yunus, 1990. (Exchange rate in 1982: Taka 21.6 = US$ 1.00; 1987: Taka 31.0 = US$ 1.00; 1990: Taka 33.5 = US$ 1.00.) (n.i. = no information)

the capturing of deposits, such as disbursing loans from the Group Fund for any purpose at terms established by the group.

The Group Fund has become an important source of capital for the Bank's lending operations, which is the primary use of the savings mobilized by the programme. The Bank has expanded its lending operations as a result of the availability of savings funds. Savings accumulated, as a percentage of loans outstanding, have increased progressively from the outset, growing from 25.1 per cent in 1984 to 45.4 per cent in 1986 (Hossain, 1988).

Because the Grameen Bank's methodology ties savings to key programme priorities, such as expansion in membership, the amount disbursed and the size of portfolio, savings have grown dramatically from the start.

Table 2.1 summarizes some of the key indicators of the Grameen Bank's growth, and places savings in the context of the overall programme. From 1986 to 1990 the Grameen Bank has more than doubled the number of members and greatly expanded the geographical coverage of the programme. The amount saved, both in the Group Fund and in the Emergency Fund, has grown nearly fourfold in the past three years, and by March 1990 totalled US$21.4 million.

ACCION International: savings mobilization among affiliated programmes

Microenterprise programmes affiliated to ACCION International (ACCION), a US private non-profit development organization, reach the smallest producers and vendors in 12 countries in Latin America. These programmes provide small loans at commercial or higher interest rates, as well as training and varying levels of technical assistance to programme participants. The programmes currently reach about 50 000 men and women in 70 large and small cities, and they disburse approximately US$2.3 million a month or about US$25 million a year in loans averaging around US$370 in size. The repayment rate among these programmes is good to excellent, with some programmes recording less than 1 per cent defaults and less than 5 per cent late repayments. On average, between 50 and 55 per cent of the programmes' clients are women, many of them working in textile processing, food processing and commerce (ACCION, 1989).

Several ACCION-affiliated organizations have experimented with capturing savings. These organizations have found that the legal structure and regulations in each country constitute the most important factor that enables or prevents the mobilization of savings. In fact, in most Latin American countries, private non-profit institutions are prohibited by law from accepting savings deposits. A survey of ACCION-affiliated institutions in Bolivia, Paraguay and Costa Rica in 1987 revealed that these organizations were interested in mobilizing savings but each country's banking laws restricted their participation in this activity (ACCION, 1987).

Savings schemes in ACCION programmes currently exist in Colombia, Honduras, the Dominican Republic and Bolivia. In the case of Colombia, the programmes are permitted to capture savings but cannot use savings for lending activities. Asesores Para el Desarrollo (ASEPADE) in Honduras is able to capture savings directly, which it has been doing for the past five years (Gomez, 1988). The Foundation for the Promotion and Development of Microenterprises (PRODEM) in Bolivia cannot capture savings and instead has devised another mechanism to enable its borrowers to set money aside.

Four reasons exist for promoting savings in ACCION programmes, two of which relate to the benefits that the potential depositor draws from savings, and two to the benefits the programme experiences. Depending on overall programme philosophy and needs, each programme gives a varying degree of priority to each.

Saving carries an educational function which instills regularity of habit, and contributes to a borrower's shift in perception regarding his or her situation – from a day-to-day struggle to survive, to a longer-term view based on planning with a growing cushion of savings.

Saving among borrowers is a means of capitalizing their business and of decreasing dependency on the moneylenders to whom even programme borrowers must turn in case of an emergency. Savings are an alternative source when responding to an immediate need for cash, without diverting funds from the business. Saving also presents an opportunity to introduce the borrower to the formal banking sector. This contact constitutes an important first step towards accessing other bank services, especially credit. If the savings are deposited in a bank, they can help dispel the myths regarding the poor's incapacity to save in a disciplined and regular manner. In Colombia, some banks will provide credit to microenterprises and use their savings as collateral for the loan.

Programmes that capture savings directly, use them as a guarantee or risk absorber against bad loans. From this perspective, savings become another way of protecting the programme and maintaining the real value of its portfolio. The relationship between savings and the overall portfolio becomes a factor that is analysed as part of portfolio monitoring.

Programmes use savings to expand their lending activity. Some programmes allocate a certain percentage of the savings to the credit fund, maintaining a reserve much as financial banking institutions do. This mechanism allows them to respond to the growing need for credit among borrowers, without requiring long waits. Other programmes turn to savings only when they encounter an unexpected liquidity problem, most often caused not only by an increase in demand, but also by delays in grant or loan disbursements to the programme. Microenterprise programmes do not, however, make use of deposits to cover administrative and other operating costs, since in efficient programmes these are covered partly through interest income earned by the programme.

ACCION's method for capturing savings

Each programme establishes a certain amount, usually proportionate to the size of the loan, that the individual or group must save. The amount varies considerably from programme to programme, as does the interest paid by the borrowers, which is usually the established commercial rate. The borrower then deposits the savings either as part of each payment on the loan or in a lump sum at the time he or she receives the loan.

ACCION-affiliated programmes in Colombia, Honduras and Bolivia have mobilized the equivalent of over US$700 000 in savings. While this figure is insignificant in relation to overall savings, or to the experience of the Asian programmes, it is nevertheless indicative of the potential for savings mobilization if microenterprise programmes faced no legal or structural constraints in this area. Using Colombia and Bolivia as guides, ACCION-affiliated programmes together could mobilize a significant amount, over US$1 million in the first year, and larger amounts in subsequent years. The challenge for them is to address the legal and policy requirements which currently do not permit these institutions to operate in this area.

Women and savings

The issue of gender as a determinant of behaviour is of paramount interest in all microenterprise programmes, in part because women are predominant in the informal sector, and in part because researchers and practitioners have to recognize and learn more about the productive activities of this significant sector of the labour force. The Grameen Bank has registered a consistent increase in the percentage of women it reaches to its current level of 89 per cent. ACCION programmes also reach women, who comprise at least 50 per cent of its clients. In Bolivia's PRODEM, 71 per cent of its 11 700 clients are women. By understanding how women's productive activities and their access to resources are determined in part by their gender, one can begin to formulate more appropriate and responsive programmes that enhance their economic activities.

Blumberg suggests that when the income resulting from production is controlled by the woman, and where her production is not restricted, the consequences are generally positive for the woman and the well-being of her family (Blumberg, 1989). Further, data presented from various countries demonstrate that women who receive credit in microenterprise programmes prove to be good borrowers in part because they have so little access to credit that they make the most of an opportunity to borrow. The programmes examined here show that provision of credit to women is also an opportunity to enable them to save.

While much has been written on women and credit, the existing knowledge of poor women's propensity to save remains scant (Maloney and Ahmed, 1988). Women participate actively in informal savings groups, at times limiting participation in the group to women only. However, there are few empirical data regarding their performance in this area. Following the Grameen Bank, the ACCION programme and other microenterprise lending programmes have introduced compulsory savings schemes in their credit programmes.

One can conclude in very general terms that since the level of savings in the microenterprise programmes analysed here has increased at the same time as the percentage of women reached by these programmes has grown, women demonstrate a significant propensity to save. This potential appears to be tied to the structure of the savings component, however, and not only to the gender of the depositor. Considerable work is needed to understand the constraints and the opportunities for saving that exist among low-income women. Hence, this topic remains as a gap in our understanding of the savings mobilization component in microenterprise programmes.

Issues for savings mobilization in microenterprise programmes

Developing countries experience a low level of domestic savings. Data show that the propensity to save among rural and urban poor households remains outside national efforts to mobilize domestic savings (Holst, 1987). Financial institutions in general are ill-equipped to stimulate savings among this population, in part because of the structural bottlenecks discussed above, and in part because of existing national policies that discourage savings. Organizations that implement well-structured and sustainable microenterprise assistance programmes help to fill this institutional gap.

For the implementing institutions, a savings component holds substantial benefits:

○ it can contribute to an improved repayment rate
○ it increases resources for lending and reduces dependency on external sources
○ when savings serve as a type of guarantee, the level of risk assumed by the programme is decreased and shared with the borrowers
○ the savings component serves as a mechanism for establishing a closer relationship with a bank, and increases confidence in the organization.

From the borrower's point of view, the obligatory nature of savings schemes assures that each person develops a capital base, regardless of how small. The interaction with a bank, the process of earning interest, the discipline of saving, and the decision of how to use savings, all constitute part of a capacity-building process which equips each participant with tools he or she needs to continue engaging in productive activities. By blending these areas of new learning with familiar features – an emphasis on group savings, a recognition of the importance of character references, and a reliance on kinship relationships as the basis for economic transactions – the savings component provides not only a capital base but also a human development dimension.

Important lessons emerge pertinent to a discussion of methodology:

○ It is not just people's marginal propensity to save that determines the savings mobilization capacity of a programme. The experience documented here strongly suggests that it is the structure of the savings component that influences how much people save.
○ Successful methodologies for savings mobilization by microenterprise programmes resemble the traditional savings schemes that have been successfully operated by the poor for generations.

o The only way that a programme will have measurable impact is if it establishes from the outset a capacity for gradual but constant expansion (Otero, 1988). All other methodological facets of the programme flow from this consideration.

o Programmes are successful at mobilizing savings when these are tied directly to the credit operation. Every time a person receives a loan, he or she must deposit a specified amount in savings. As the credit portfolio grows, so does the mobilization of savings among programme beneficiaries.

o The programme must have appropriate internal systems. While there is no one way to formulate a savings component, several factors should appear in all systems, including small regular deposits, computerized monitoring, a savings record for each borrower, and the option of supplementing savings that are required for the credit operation.

o The rate of return is a powerful determinant to savings mobilization in both formal and informal systems. The same applies to microenterprise programmes. In cases where the institution captures savings, the interest it pays on deposits should be comparable to the market rate. In cases where the participants make deposits direct to a designated bank, the microenterprise development organization should ascertain that the interest rates the bank offers are competitive.

o Whether savings should be obligatory or voluntary remains an open question. Evidence indicates that when saving is obligatory the level of savings mobilized grows appreciably. If savings deposits are secure, accessible, and yield a good return, programme participants seldom express dissatisfaction with this approach.

o There are important arguments against forced savings schemes, which should not be ignored. Could forced savings contribute to a decrease in the family's standard of living, especially for those living at a subsistence level, by diverting funds otherwise used for basic needs? Does the obligatory nature of savings enhance a poor person's understanding of its importance and create a different attitude towards it, or does it merely increase dependence on the programme?

Grappling with the legal framework

Each country's regulations on savings are based on important justifications which allow credible, well-constituted institutions with sound financial and operational guidelines to participate in this activity. Regulating those institutions taking deposits, reserve requirements, and other regulations are ways of protecting depositors from dealing with questionable institutions that could endanger their assets.

While these considerations are certainly valuable, private non-profit organizations with sound financial and operational records have not been studied as a category that could fit into this legal scheme. Most of the microenterprise development programmes are conducted by private, non-profit institutions. Of the 87 programmes that USAID studied under its stocktaking exercise of micro-enterprise development programmes in 1989, 58 were implemented by non-profit organizations.

Private, non-profit institutions in most countries face restrictions regarding savings. Some are considering alternative institutional structures as a possibility for savings mobilization. This approach requires that each institution studies the variety of possible ways it could create a new institution to capture savings, and then determines which is most suitable for its own institutional and program-matic needs. Some examples are the creation of a credit union or a savings-and-loan co-operative which is adjacent to the non-profit institution. In each case the institution would have to devise the institutional nature of this arrangement, the relationship with the borrowers, and the mechanisms needed to access these savings for lending purposes.

The gist of these suggestions is not to promote the creation of additional structures in settings where there may be a glut of development institutions. Rather, it is to expand the framework of qualified, private non-profit organizations that reach microenterprises and which resemble financial institutions. As donors and governments tend to encourage formal financial structures to work with microenterprises, private non-profit organizations will have to consider ways of advancing their own institutional capacity so as not to be bypassed in their work. The interest in finding ways to capture savings also fits into this broader concern.

Conclusion

The review presented in this paper, the conclusions it draws regarding the sav-ings capacity among the poor and the suggestions it makes about mechanisms that can respond most appropriately to mobilize savings, highlight the impor-tance of focusing on this component of the overall economic equation in developing countries.

Clearly, the relationship between savings mobilization and microenterprise pro-grammes is just beginning. The experiences of the Grameen Bank in Bangladesh, ACCION International in Latin America, and other organizations such as Self-Employed Women's Associations (SEWA) in India and the Badan Kredit Kecamatan (BKK) in Indonesia provide the groundwork and also point to the questions we must address next (Sebstad, 1982; Goldmark and Rosengard, 1983).

This review suggests that the current challenge for microenterprise assistance organizations is to design savings schemes that:

○ operate within the confines of existing banking laws or develop structural mechanisms that permit deposits
○ overcome the tendency among microenterprise programmes to circumvent the issue of savings
○ take into account the interests of both the organization and the programme participant, and
○ do not lose sight of broader policy goals.

Credit and savings relations will continue to undergo alterations as they respond to changes of the environment, demands upon them, and incentives. The informal sector holds promise for mobilizing domestic savings, which we are only now beginning to take seriously. The experience of the past few years suggests that microenterprise development programmes may be an effective way of tapping into this savings potential.

References

ACCION International/AITEC, (1989), 'Program statistics for 1989', mimeo, Cambridge.

ACCION International/AITEC, (1987), 'Savings policies for microenterprise assistance programs affiliated with ACCION International: a survey', photocopy, Cambridge.

Adams, Dale W., (1973), 'The case for voluntary savings mobilization: why capital markets flounder', in *Small Farmer Credit: Analytical Papers*, AID Spring Review of Small Farmer Credit, Vol. XIX, Washington, DC.

Blumberg, Rae Lesser, (1989), 'Making the case for the gender variable: Women and the wealth and well-being of nations', Technical Reports on Gender and Development, No. 1, Women in Development Office, USAID, Washington, DC.

Chandavarkar, Anand G., (1988), 'The role of informal credit markets in support of micro-business in developing countries', paper presented at the World Conference on Support for Microenterprises, Washington, DC.

Goldmark, Susan and Jay Rosengard, (1983), 'Credit to Indonesian entrepreneurs: An assessment of the Badan Kredit Kecamatan Program', Development Alternatives, Inc., Washington, DC.

Gomez, Eduardo, (1988), 'Políticas de ahorro para los programas de microempresas afiliados con ACCION International', draft, Cambridge, Mass., ACCION.

Holst, Juergen, (1987), 'Savings and credit for development: The UN Secretariat's International Integrated Programme', paper presented at Programme for International Economic Co-operation for Nigerian Government Officials, Nigeria.

Hossain, Mahabub, (1988), 'Credit for alleviation of rural poverty: The Grameen Bank in Bangladesh', International Food Policy Research Institute, Research Report 65.

Maloney, Clarence and A.B. Sharfuddin Ahmed, (1988), *Rural Savings and Credit in Bangladesh*, Bangladesh, The University Press Limited.

Meyer, Richard, L. M.A. Baqui Khalily and Leroy J. Hushak, (1988), 'Bank branches and rural deposits: Evidence from Bangladesh', *Economy and Sociology*, Occasional paper No. 1462, Ohio State University.

Miracle, Marvin P., Diane S. Miracle and Laurie Cohen, (1980), 'Informal savings mobilization in Africa', *Economic Development and Cultural Change*, Vol. 28, No. 4, pp. 701–721.

Otero, Maria, (1988), 'Micro-enterprise assistance programs: their benefits, costs, and sustainability', paper presented at the World Conference on Support for Microenterprises, Washington, DC.

Rippey, Paul, (1988), 'On bringing village banks to Africa: observations after visiting the Grameen Bank', Council for International Development, Washington, DC.

Sebstad, Jennefer, (1982), *Struggle and Development Among Self-Employed Women*, AID Washington, DC.

Vogel, Robert C., (1986), 'Savings mobilization: the forgotten half of rural finances', in D.W. Adams, C. Gonzalez Vega and J.D. Von Pischke, *Agricultural Credit and Rural Development*, Ohio, Ohio State University.
Yunus, Muhammed (ed.), (1990), *Grameen Dialogue*, Vol. 1, No. 3, May 1990.

About the author

Maria Otero is now the President and CEO of ACCION International, based in Boston, Massachusetts. She wrote this paper while she was ACCION's Representative to Washington, DC.

3 Raising the curtain on the 'microfinancial services era'

STUART RUTHERFORD

This paper was first published in March 2000.

Unlike the previous two eras, when financial services for the poor were clearly characterized first by agricultural loans, then by microloans to business women, the new microfinancial services era promises a diversity of financial products, and with it confusion about how these products will benefit the poor. This paper attempts to clarify the situation by defining all financial services for poor people as means of turning their savings into usefully large lump sums – sums that are then used to meet needs arising from life-cycle events and from emergencies, and from opportunities to invest in land, in productive and household assets, and in businesses.

Savings can be turned into usefully large lump sums by means of three basic patterns – 'saving up', 'saving down' and 'saving through' – and the various informal financial services employing these devices which are used by poor people worldwide are described.

Good financial services for poor people are therefore ones that make it convenient to store the savings and convenient to take out the lump sums, in any range of values, over any time span, and using any or all of the three basic 'swap' types. The best financial services for poor people do this in an affordable and reliable (sustainable) way.

Debates about finance and poverty reduction have been shaped by changing conceptualizations of who the poor are and the nature of poverty. During the subsidized agricultural credit era (1950s to 1970s), the poor were seen as small or marginal farmers, usually male, whose poverty could be overcome by credit-induced increases in productivity. From 1980 to 1995 they were seen as mostly female microentrepreneurs with no assets to pledge – but a world to conquer with microcredit-financed investment that would raise their incomes. Recently, they have become a diverse group of vulnerable households with complex livelihoods and varied needs... We are now entering the 'microfinancial services era'. (Matin et al., 1999)

THE INSTITUTIONAL ARRANGEMENTS and product designs that characterized financial services for poor people during the first two eras depicted in Imran Matin's vivid historical simplification are well known. The small and marginal farmers of the 'agricultural credit era' were generally offered seasonal loans tied to specific crops and recovered in balloon repayments made after the harvest was gathered. Sometimes the credit was delivered in kind, especially where the authorities wanted to promote some specific agricultural regime, such as 'green revolution' crops needing ample treatments of fertilizer and pesticides. Where loans were in cash their values were linked to farming input prices. In either case, loan values varied between borrowers on the basis of the acreage devoted to the crop, and rose only in line with inflation. The credit was delivered by institutions that were newly and specially set up, a task usually done by governments using their own resources along with foreign grants and soft loans. The institutions took the form of specialized agricultural banks or agricultural credit co-operatives: in some countries both were widespread.

In the succeeding 'microenterprise era', private institutions, often originating in the voluntary sector, played a much larger role, fetching cash from both private and public sources at home and abroad and retailing it to 'women entrepreneurs' organized in groups at village or neighbourhood level. In most models, including the two most widespread – the 'Bangladesh' model originated by Grameen Bank and BRAC and the 'Village Banking' system that had its roots in Latin America – borrowers remain continuously in debt for long periods ranging up to several years. During this time, the values of successive yearly or half-yearly loans steadily rise, reflecting a supposed growth of the microenterprise being financed. Loans are repaid by tapping into regular enterprise cash flows on a frequent basis – often weekly, sometimes monthly. Group members are asked to accept 'joint liability' for each other's loans, meaning that the flow of loans to all members in the group can be restricted if any one member fails to repay on time. This is intended to encourage members to monitor each other's businesses and to advise the institution against lending to unsuitable colleagues.

Whatever the strengths and weaknesses of these approaches – and experience has taught us many lessons – the arguments which supported them were clear, even though they may now appear simplistic. Farmers need crop loans. Poor businesswomen need a steady supply of easily-repaid loans which grow with their businesses.

Complexity and variety

As we move into Matin's 'microfinancial services era', however, and begin to deal with 'vulnerable households with complex livelihoods and varied needs', do we have a similarly clear idea about the kinds of financial products that will be required, or of the institutions that are going to deliver them? Do we have even a real sense of what 'financial services' mean for poor households? 'Complexity' and 'variety' are words that threaten to lead away from, rather than towards, conceptual clarity.

We can already appreciate that savings and insurance services, as well as credit, will feature in the new complexity. So it looks as if 'agricultural credit' and 'microenterprise credit' are certain to lose their old monopoly on our imagination. Variety implies that not every poor person is doing the same kind of thing with the same needs all the time. So simple uniform products like a 'hybrid wheat package' or the Grameen's one-year business loan look as if they're about to be dethroned.

But in their place…? How are we to get our minds around the myriad uses for financial services that millions of different users will seek to satisfy? How can we come up with products that are easy to understand and deliver, and with institutions that can keep tabs on these products and recover their costs from the margin? How can we be sure that all this will really help poor people? This article begins to answer the first of these questions about product design. More detail about this and the subsequent questions is given in my book *The Poor and their Money*.

Functions and uses

The questions in the previous paragraph have been phrased deliberately to lead to a trap. They invite us to think about financial services for the poor exclusively in terms of the *uses* to which loans (and other pay-outs) are put. They obscure the equally valid approach of thinking about the *function* of financial services.

It is the function of financial services – seen from the point of view of the user – to help manage money. This is their primary task, and this is how people actually use them. Forgetting that simple fact – believing instead that the main task of financial services is to improve agriculture, or to grow women-owned businesses, or for that matter to pull people out of poverty or to make women's voices more powerful – has led to many of our past misunderstandings. In the eras of agricultural and enterprise credit it led us to overlook the fact that borrowers have many other money management needs besides financing their crops or businesses. We now know, for example, that many 'enterprise loans' are used for non-enterprise purposes, and most field workers I talk to (most recently in East Africa but more intensively in south and south-east Asia) now turn a sensibly blind eye to rules that insist on verification procedures to demonstrate that loans have indeed been invested in borrower-owned businesses.

Managing money

So exactly how do financial services help to manage money? Textbooks will list a formidable range of tasks performed for the economy by financial services and the markets in which they are offered. They include easing transactions through cheque-clearing systems, payment cards, or foreign exchange facilities, for example. Then there is the financial intermediation that banks and insurance companies provide – above all the pooling of savings to make them available for investment and to protect against risks. As well as acting as channels for investment, financial service markets accumulate and communicate information about borrowers and firms, thus reducing the costs and risks of investment. Finally, from the individual user's point of view, such textbooks may observe that financial services allow people to 'reallocate consumption across time' (*The Economist*, 23 October 1999, pp. 101–102).

This observation may seem rather dry and obscurely expressed, but it is worth careful examination, for it is the key to understanding the function of financial services for poor as well as not-so-poor people, and the conceptual foundation on which we can build a sound approach to microfinance in the twenty-first century.

Reallocating expenditure across time

We need to rephrase the textbook's observation, and to start with we must get rid of the contentious word 'consumption', since in this context it means expenditure of *all* kinds, including even business investments, and not just consumable items like food and festivals. Being able to reallocate expenditure across time is simply the ability to pay *now* for things you need (or think you might need) in the future, and to pay *in the future* for things you need now.

Because our income does not arrive in exact rhythm with our outflow of expenditure, we all need this facility. The poor need it no less than other groups of people. Indeed, they may need it more. This is not just because their incomes are uncertain and irregular (which is often true), but because the absolute amounts of cash they deal with are very small. As a result, anything more than the tiniest expenditures will require sums of money greater than they have about them at the time – in their pocket, purse or home. Expenditure of almost any kind can require them to look for a way of financing the expenditure, or part of it, out of yesterday's or tomorrow's income.

Expenditure *of any kind*, note, and not just for farming inputs or microenterprises. Life-cycle events, such as birth, schooling, marriage, home-making, retirement and death; and emergencies, including personal ones like illnesses and accidents and impersonal ones like cyclones, fires, floods and droughts, all require the expenditure of sums bigger than those available on an everyday basis. Besides needs, there are opportunities: opportunities to invest in land, business, buildings and comforts like fans and TVs. These too involve spending sums that force the poor to look for ways of using past and future as well as presently available income.

How do poor people tap into past and present income to finance this wide and constantly pressing range of expenditures? They do it in many ways, but it helps if we group them into three main strategies, which I call 'saving up', 'saving down' and 'saving through'. They are illustrated in Figure 3.1. 'Saving up' involves financing an expenditure out of income already earned. 'Saving down' is the converse: financing present expenditure from tomorrow's income. 'Saving through' is a hybrid – it means financing expenditure made now out of a mix of income earned both yesterday and tomorrow. Let us consider each in turn, from the point of view of a poor household in the developing world.

Saving up

Saving up – keeping back cash now so that it can be spent in the future – is hard for poor people. Strange as it may seem, this is *not* primarily because they have little or nothing to save (though that may also be true). As we shall see, saving is an inescapably essential task for the poor – without it life simply cannot be managed. The difficulty comes not so much with finding the resources from which to save, as with the practical problems of saving *up*. It is very hard to find a safe place to store cash. Formal opportunities to do so at banks and the like are rarely accessible. Cash kept at an insecure slum or village home can be stolen, lost,

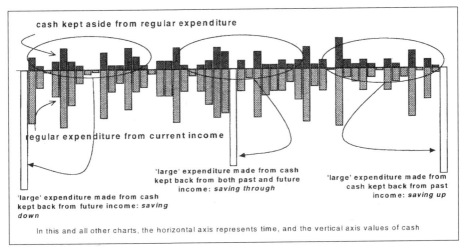

Figure 3.1   *Saving down, saving through and saving up*

burnt, blown or washed away. It can be captured by mothers-in-law with hard voices, visiting relatives with hard-luck stories, and alcoholic husbands with hard · knuckles. How do you keep even a few cents back when the children are hungry?

Because holding cash is so hard, savings created by not spending all of yesterday's income are often kept in kind – in livestock, tin roofing sheets, and even trees. Such methods of saving have some advantages: the piglets may produce young, the tree may mature into something worth many times its original value as a sapling. But there are disadvantages, too. The piglet may die. The tin sheets rot. Above all, when you need to realize the value of these 'in kind' savings, it is bothersome. You can sell a piglet in order to have cash to buy some medicine, but it may be a bad time of the year for piglet prices, and what are you going to do with the $10 left over when you've bought the medicine? Spend it, perhaps, if you do not have a good place to save cash. There is also the problem of how you keep the rain out if you sell the tin sheets. Finally and crucially, how and where did you save up the cash to buy the tin sheets in the first place? These disadvantages force the poor to pay a high price – very much higher than you and I pay – to save cash. This high price is expressed in two ways: high levels of risk and low or even negative interest rates. All round the world the poor entrust their savings to people and institutions that are less than fully reliable. 'Money guards', such as relatives, employers and shopkeepers, hold vast sums of the poor's cash – and sometimes cheat them. Tens of thousands of informal savings clubs of all kinds spring up daily round the world, and too many of them are inefficiently or fraudulently run. Yet poor people persevere with these high-risk methods, for lack of better alternatives. Most vulnerable are the poorest, those most likely to be illiterate and powerless.

A good safe place to save money can be expensive. Deposit collectors – people whose job it is to collect and store savings from their poor clients – do the same job as a savings bank, but most make a charge for the service, rather than pay interest (see Figure 3.2). In West Africa it is common for deposit collectors

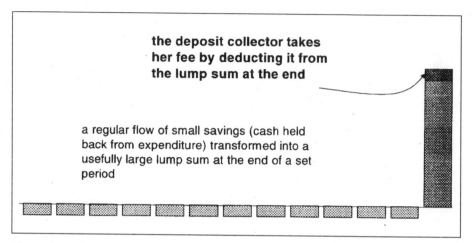

the deposit collector takes her fee by deducting it from the lump sum at the end

a regular flow of small savings (cash held back from expenditure) transformed into a usefully large lump sum at the end of a set period

Figure 3.2   *Saving up with a deposit collector*

to collect savings on a daily basis, and to charge one day's savings per month. Often, the charge is levied even if the client does not save every day, producing a neat incentive to save regularly. (Note that we can measure this charge in two ways. Either the charge is measured as a percentage of the amount saved, in which case the West African collectors charge about 4 per cent, assuming they collect savings 25 days a month. Or we can work it out as a negative 'interest rate' on the savings. In that case, the one dollar charged on the $25 saved in the month is levied on an average savings balance during the month of $12.50, making the interest 8 per cent a month).

In southern India, a slum-based woman deposit collector I studied collected equal daily savings for 220 days, and then gave back 200 days' worth to her client, keeping the remainder as her charge. Her clients were happy with the service, and were envied by women in neighbouring slums who have no reliable deposit collector. As one client told me, 'without this system, how else could I be sure to have a thousand rupees ready at the beginning of the next school year to pay for fees, books and clothes for my children?' Like many women, she saves a little of the household's income each time she goes to the market – saving money while it is on its way out, so to speak. Like many poor income earners, her husband, a labourer, is hopelessly bad at saving income as he earns it (saving it while it is on its way in).

Saving down

Not surprisingly, when a marriage contract for a daughter is suddenly proposed, or illness strikes, or the opportunity to buy a cheap rickshaw unexpectedly occurs, few poor households have got enough cash *saved up* to manage the required outlay. They may then try to tap future income – by *saving down*. To do that, they need to find someone or some institution willing to give them a cash advance against part of their future income. They often start with friends or neighbours who may be in a position (by having some funds saved *up*) to make them a loan.

Such loans may be offered without interest if there is an assumption that the borrowing household will reciprocate the favour on some other occasion.

With or without interest, the loans will be repaid by withholding a part of future income. Some lenders will be happy to get their money back in small instalments, and in that case the borrower can repay as and when they can keep cash back from everyday expenditure. Many loans in the informal world, however, are repaid in a single 'balloon' repayment (there are interesting reasons for this which are outlined in Rutherford, 2000). In that case the borrower has got to find a way to save up the full amount of the loan – by definition difficult for households that resorted to saving *down* precisely because saving *up* was so hard in the first place.

There are informal moneylenders, especially common in Asian towns and cities, who advance cash against future income, and are willing to take it back in small frequent instalments. Normally, they take their payment for this service up front, by deducting it from the sum they advance (see Figure 3.3). What they do is the 'opposite' of what deposit collectors do – and as is often the case with opposites, there is a good deal of similarity between the two services. Deposit collectors and urban moneylenders neatly illustrate the mirror-images of saving 'up' and saving 'down' that we saw so clearly in the first chart. The deposit collector takes the savings first, over an extended period of time, then returns them at one go in a lump sum, deducting a charge. The moneylender provides the lump sum 'up front', deducting a charge, then collects the savings in small frequent amounts over an extended period of time.

The costs of using a moneylender are usually greater than a deposit collector, but it is not hard to see why. The moneylender, unlike the deposit collector, has to provide the capital for the lump sum in the first place. He also bears the risk of the contract not being honoured, whereas in the case of the deposit collector it is the client who takes that risk. Finally, the moneylender has to acquire the

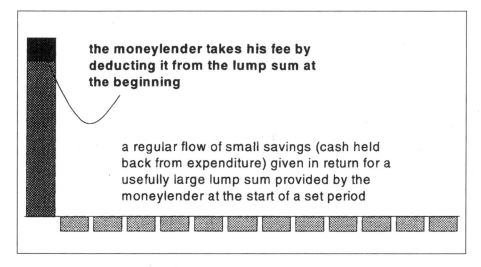

the moneylender takes his fee by deducting it from the lump sum at the beginning

a regular flow of small savings (cash held back from expenditure) given in return for a usefully large lump sum provided by the moneylender at the start of a set period

Figure 3.3   *Saving down with an urban moneylender*

information that will enable him to decide how much he can risk advancing to his client, while the deposit collector simply returns whatever the client managed to save, and it is the client who has to try to find out whether the deposit collector has a safe pair of hands. This problem of 'information' is a crucial one for all lenders, which has been famously discussed in the microfinance literature, above all in relation to the 'joint liability' contracts which are a feature of most group-based microfinance schemes.

Savings as the basis of all financial services

The fact that deposit collectors and urban moneylenders offer fundamentally similar, though mirror-imaged, services, is not just a matter of aesthetic interest. It drives home the point that the money deposited with the deposit collector and the money repaid to the moneylender come from exactly the same source – cash held back from regular day-to-day expenditure by an act of will. 'Cash held back from regular day-to-day expenditure by an act of will' is a pretty good definition of savings, and savings is exactly what these deposits and repayments are.

Deposit taking and lending are alternative ways of managing savings. Both transform a series of savings into a lump sum large enough to pay for the daughter's wedding, or bury grandfather or buy a rickshaw. A good definition of financial services for the poor is that they are 'money management services that help the poor turn their savings into usefully large lump sums'. This definition puts saving at the centre of financial services, rather than seeing it as a rather overlooked alternative to loans.

Saving through

This may become clearer as we investigate 'saving through'. To illustrate saving through, we turn away from services that the poor buy (such as those of deposit collectors and moneylenders) to those they can and often do set up for themselves – savings clubs (see Figure 3.4). One particular kind of savings club is known as the ROSCA, or rotating savings and credit association. In such a club, members agree to meet on a periodic basis, say weekly, for as many times as there are members – say 12, as in Figure 3.4. At every meeting everyone brings along a fixed sum of money, say $1. On each occasion one of the 12 members walks away with all $12 contributed on that occasion. After 12 meetings everyone has put in 12 lots of $1 and come away with one usefully large lump sum of $12. The order in which the lump sum is taken can be decided by agreement, by chance (drawing lots), or by an auction (Rutherford, 2000). Auction ROSCAs have an in-built pricing mechanism by which those who take the lump sum earliest contribute more than others. ROSCAs can also be run commercially, as they are, for example, in southern India's 'chit funds' on a huge scale.

Because there are no charges involved, the simple function of this device stands out clearly: all it does is turn a series of savings into a lump sum – and some of the savings are made before the lump sum arrives, and some after (unless you are the first or last taker). That millions of poor (and not so poor) people around the world

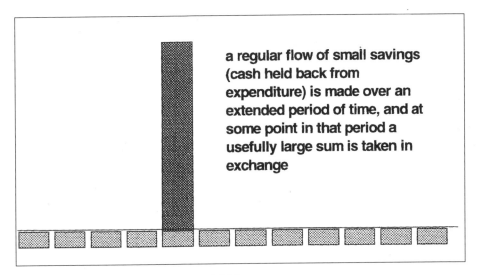

a regular flow of small savings (cash held back from expenditure) is made over an extended period of time, and at some point in that period a usefully large sum is taken in exchange

Figure 3.4   *Saving through with a ROSCA*

are today using such devices demonstrates the need to manage savings in this way.

There are other devices that follow this 'saving through' strategy. Most savings clubs use it, even if they are not of the strict 'ROSCA' type. A commercial service available in many countries, pawnbroking, uses it. The gold necklace you take along to the pawnbroker is a store of cash saved from past income, and this act of past saving allows you to use the pawnbroker's service. He then gives you a cash advance, which you repay out of savings made from future income. When you have made the repayment in full (including a service charge), you get your original store of past savings back. This feature – enabling past savings to be used as a 'passport' to an advance on future income – is so convenient that it will ensure that pawnbroking will remain popular with the poor, even if misguided governments drive it underground by trying to ban it.

Perhaps more importantly, 'saving through' features in some kinds of insurance, such as health and property insurance. We can see this in the simple case of vehicle insurance. When you insure your car, you make a series of regular small savings – perhaps annually or monthly – in the form of 'premium' payments. When you crash your car into a lamp post the insurance company pays out a usefully large amount – large enough to repair the car, with luck – after which you go on paying your premiums until the next need for such a sum arises. (Of course, unlike the other examples described here, the lump sum bears no relation to the value of the small contributions, not in the individual case, anyway. Insurance is dealt with more fully in Rutherford, 2000).

An accident of birth

Although each can be found on every continent, informal 'saving up', 'saving down' and 'saving through' devices are not evenly distributed round the world. For example, in South Asia you will find a large number of saving-through

ROSCAs and a large number of moneylenders (for saving down), but far fewer deposit collectors (for saving up). Move to West Africa and the situation is quite different: in many states saving up through deposit collectors is very common indeed, and ROSCAs are also widespread, but there are relatively few opportunities to save down through moneylenders. In East Africa it is different again: there you find one of the densest areas of saving-through ROSCAs but very few deposit collectors and very few moneylenders (at least, moneylenders willing to lend to the poor).

No one knows why this is so, and there is a PhD thesis waiting to be done on the micro-economic effects of these differences. But one thing is clear – the poor everywhere need to turn their savings into usefully large lump sums, and whether they do it through saving up, saving down or saving through is to a great extent a matter of where they happen to live.

The cycle

The fundamental similarity in the function of these three different-seeming strategies – saving up, down and through – is even more striking when we notice that many users of such devices start a new 'cycle' as soon as one has finished. One woman told me she'd been in her 'merry-go-round' (as she calls a ROSCA) with the same members for nearly 50 15-day cycles over a two-and-a-half year period. West African deposit collectors often run on a repeating monthly cycle. Many urban moneylenders offer a new loan as soon as the previous one is paid off, as do Grameen Bank, BRAC and the Village Banks. If you are in such a cyclical regime, then you have simply got into a habit of making regular frequent small pay-ins matched by regular occasional large pay-outs. It may hardly matter which came first, further blurring the distinctions between saving up, down and through. The user may not even remember. This is the essence of 'basic personal financial intermediation', as I have called the process of swapping savings for usefully large lump sums.

Financial fractals

The basic pattern of 'many small savings equals usefully large lump sum' has fractal-like qualities, i.e. it is 'self-similar', exhibiting the same pattern if it is inverted and if it is done at any scale. Our examples have already shown how the 'savings-leading-to-a-lump-sum' pattern of 'saving-up' is essentially the same as its inverse, the 'lump-sum-repaid-through-savings' pattern of 'saving-down', or borrowing. The same is true for matters of scale (the amounts of money involved) and of term (the period over which the savings/lump-sum swap takes place). Saving up for a week to buy a sack of rice is essentially the same process as saving over a lifetime for a pension. We can see this by looking at devices like the South Indian 'marriage funds' that are so popular among poor and not-so-poor people in that part of the world (see Figure 3.5).

The marriage fund offers short-term low-value opportunities to borrow (to 'save down') nestled within a long-term, high-value 'savings up' opportunity to

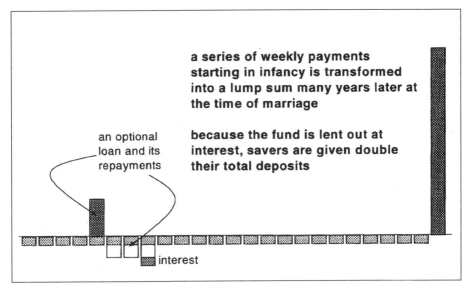

Figure 3.5   *The South Indian marriage fund*

provide for a major expenditure – the marriage of a child. Users open an account in their child's name and pay a small weekly deposit – often at church on Sundays or at the weekly social evening at the local trade association. When the child marries, he or she gets double the total accumulated deposits (providing not less than three years have elapsed). This doubling of the deposits is made possible by lending the fund out short-term to registered users at an interest rate of (usually) 4 per cent a month.

Good microfinancial services

Financial services for the poor help them turn savings into usefully large lump sums. This definition merely rephrases a conventional definition of financial services, but it also provides us with the conceptual clarity that seemed elusive in the opening paragraphs of this paper. The observations that the paper has used to support that definition do more than that. They allow us to go on to define what we mean by *good* microfinancial service products. We end, therefore, with some notes on key characteristics of good microfinancial products. Once these have been established, it will become possible to define more exactly the kind of institution that will be required to deliver such products, and the kind of legal, regulatory and economic environment that will best promote the healthy growth of such institutions.

Turning savings into usefully large lump sums is what financial services do: for no matter what use, over no matter what timescale, in no matter what value, and by any one or any mix of three major strategies for effecting the swap – saving up, saving down and saving through. The first requirement of a good financial service product, then, is that it *makes it easy to deposit the pay-ins* and thus maximizes the user's opportunity and propensity to pay-in. This is true no matter whether the pay-ins take the form of savings deposits, loan repayments or insurance premium payments. Easy pay-in systems are those that are close at hand, regular, frequent, quick, safe, flexible and affordable.

The second requirement is to *offer a disciplined regime for making the pay-ins.* Making pay-ins – essentially saving – is like taking exercise. Everyone knows they should do it and in their heart wants to do it. They are popular subjects for New Year resolutions. But in practice it is hard to save or to exercise without some disciplined regime to help you. This is why fixed-period, fixed-sum regular pay-ins feature so often in the devices we have illustrated in this paper. One ideal is an automatic deduction from the payroll, but very few really poor people have the regular salaries or the kind of employers that are needed to make that work. So a good alternative is to insist on fixed sums at fixed intervals, as in a marriage fund or annual savings club, or as in the standard Grameen Bank, BRAC or Village Bank product. Moreover, such regularity is helpful to the institution offering the service, since it makes bookkeeping easier and more predictable, and helps to identify cases where clients are in difficulties or junior staff are being dishonest. An alternative discipline is that of the frequent regular opportunity to pay in, as being field tested by organizations such as *Safe*Save in Bangladesh, where a local collector calls every day without fail and can accept deposits on the spot with a minimum of paperwork but with complete assurance that the deposit will be properly credited to the client's account.

The third requirement of a good financial service product is that it *makes it easy to take out the lump sum* (again remembering that the lump sum may take the form of a savings withdrawal, or a loan, or an insurance pay-out, depending on the strategy being employed). Such a system would have unambiguously clear rules, so that accessing the lump sum would be as mechanical as extracting cash from an ATM (cashpoint) with a debit card. It should also be close at hand, available at convenient hours, and unencumbered with complex paperwork or waiting time.

The fourth requirement is to accept a wide range of values of deposits. Since poor people have fluctuating amounts of cash available to save, it makes sense to accept, wherever possible, any value of deposit (including zero, as in the *Safe*Save example mentioned above). But as we have seen, there are some circumstances in which fixed-value deposits make sense, both from the point of view of the user and the institution, because they promote discipline. In that case, the deposits should be small (so that very poor people can reach them) but capable of being deposited in multiples, so that those able to afford more than the minimum can do so. For example, in the marriage funds of South India, users pay a fixed sum each week, which must be a multiple of ten rupees (about 20 cents US). Similarly, in many good ROSCAs, better-off members can have several 'names' in the scheme, enabling them to deposit and take out larger sums.

The fifth requirement is to offer a wide range of *timescales* for the savings-to-lump-sum swap. Like anyone else, poor people need to be able to finance tomorrow's groceries as well as next year's school fees and next century's retirement costs. On the longer-term swaps, some users may express a preference for illiquidity: that is, they may prefer to protect the savings from the temptation to withdraw and use them until a certain period of time has elapsed or until a certain event has occurred. This preference needs to be recognized and accommodated.

The sixth requirement is to offer a full range of *swap strategies*. People need to be able to draw on both previous and future savings, so they need to save up, save down and save through. Without this, they are unlikely to be able to maximize their savings potential. For example, if they are offered only loans (savings-down facilities) they may be unable to exploit their capacity to make occasional low-value savings, especially if the loan has a fixed or infrequent repayment schedule.

The pre-eminence of product design

The six key requirements listed here are all matters of product design. Other requirements – those that have to do with the institutions that are to deliver the products, and with the legal, regulatory and economic environment in which institutions can flourish – will be important to the microfinancial era of the twenty-first century. Suitable institutions may take many forms, from user-owned co-operatives to not-for-profit foundations (such as NGOs) to for-profit fully commercialized businesses. But all will be strongly committed to serving the poor, strongly committed to low costs, and equipped with management systems and governance regimes that allow them to ensure that the costs of their operations can be fully met from charges made for the services they offer. They will also be committed to remaining in operation long enough to complete in full all the swaps they offer. Note that there is a wide variety here. Some ROSCAs need last only as long as the cycle requires – basically one meeting per active member, maybe a matter of a few days. Conversely, an institution committed to long-term contractual savings devices such as pension schemes needs to be around for the long haul. Thus there is a natural gradient from the local, user-owned and unregulated device through to the supra-local, professionally owned and managed, and regulated institution.

Key environmental characteristics will include stable economic management (including sound anti-inflationary policies), reliable and enabling legal and regulatory regimes (including provisions to permit the safe mobilization of savings) and public awareness of the benefits to both the poor and to the economy in general that flow from a fully operational system of financial services for the poor.

2010

What sort of financial services will be available to the poor in the future? Luckily, I came across this short extract from an autobiography written in the year 2010 by a Bangladeshi family who, driven by poverty, migrated from the countryside to Dhaka in the late 1990s. They told their ghost-writer:

In the 1990s in our village most poor people looked after their money at home, or stored it with relatives, or used unreliable clubs or went to moneylenders. It's true there were experimental microfinance schemes for the poor, but for typical poor villagers like us the only formal schemes were run by the NGOs, and most of them offered only one kind of service – an annual loan repayable in weekly or monthly instalments. They weren't so easy to join, either. They mostly took only women, and you had to satisfy some formal and informal conditions before you could get included in the groups they formed. You had to be running some kind of business – or at least pretend you were – to get a loan. The bigger NGOs were quite reliable but were inclined to boss us around at the endless weekly meetings, while the smaller local ones were more friendly but less reliable.

Things are quite different now in our village. The bigger NGOs are registered as financial services companies, and are regulated partly by the government, and partly by their own self-regulatory schemes. They dominate the market for savings accounts and for domestic and business loans, and they have a wide range of products on sale. They have become more like regular banks in terms of the products on offer, but they continue to offer on-the-spot services, coming to the villages on a regular weekly schedule to meet and deal with the customers. Advances in computerized management have helped enormously to improve efficiency and reliability. Most customers – men and children, now, as well as women! – have individual accounts. But there are still some group-based schemes. For example, most of these companies act as agents for insurance companies, and are able to offer very cheap life and accident policies by using groups.

The smaller non-profit NGOs have mostly left the financial services business, though there is no lack of competition, because there are some large regional companies that grew out of bigger local NGOs. However, NGOs are still allowed under the law to offer management services, and many of the better ones provide such services, for a fee, to village-based ROSCAs and other kinds of savings clubs. As a result, these kinds of clubs have become much more reliable than they were, and are much more varied in terms of the kind and numbers of people that join, the savings amounts and frequencies, and so on. Probably, more people than ever use them, despite the success of the companies!

Of course, we've been in the big city for over 12 years now and, as you might expect, things are even more advanced here. In the older areas with better infrastructure, cash machines – which accept as well as dispense cash – are common, and many slum dwellers use them to store and retrieve cash for the short to medium term for a small fee. In other areas daily collection services have become the norm, though here again computerization and regulation have largely eliminated the fraud and inefficiency that used to go on.

The savings options have become much broader in the city than in the villages. Some companies even offer access to the international money, bond and stock markets and to dollar and euro-denominated accounts. Their skill – as it always was – is in taking products which are familiar to better-off people, and finding new ways to package them which are *attractive* and *useful* to the poor.

References

Imran Matin, David Hulme and Stuart Rutherford, (1999), *Financial Services for the Poor and Poorest: Deepening understanding to improve provision*, Institute of Development Policy and Management (IDPM), University of Manchester, Finance and Development Working Paper 9. Available on the IDPM website: www.idpm.man.ac.uk

Rutherford, Stuart, (2000), *The Poor and their Money*, Oxford University Press, Delhi.

About the author

Stuart Rutherford wrote this paper while he was a Visiting Fellow at the Institute of Development Policy and Management, University of Manchester, UK. He is currently with The *Safe*Save Co-operative Ltd in Dhaka, Bangladesh.

4 Towards a more market-oriented approach to credit and savings for the poor

HENRY R. JACKELEN and ELISABETH RHYNE

This paper was first published in December 1991.

Over the past decade a number of similar initiatives to provide credit and savings to the poor have been evolving which treat the poor as commercial clients rather than 'beneficiaries'. These initiatives are proving in a variety of cultural settings that the poor are able to save and to repay loans made at unsubsidized rates of interest.

This paper argues that if credit and savings services for the poor are provided on a scale appropriate to the market (loans and savings services in the range of $15–$1000) on a sustainable basis (high recoveries, high mobilization of savings on a break-even or profitable basis), then the clients themselves have proven that the service is justified. A distinctive and universal characteristic of these programmes, however, is that it may take some years of operation before these programmes achieve a critical mass of operations which allows them to be self-sustaining financial entities. This is where donor and government support can play a critical promotional role. Finally, this paper suggests that if the early indications of success throughout the world continue, with appropriate support from donors and governments, it is conceivable that hundreds of millions of clients could be benefiting from these services by the end of the decade.

THE PARIS DECLARATION of September 1990 from the Second United Nations Conference on the least developed countries (LDCs) concluded that the deterioration in the economic, social and ecological situation in most LDCs during the 1980s required a new and substantive plan of action to reverse this trend.

The tragic by-product of the inability to create real, sustained economic growth is that in all societies in the developing world large portions of the population continue to rely on non-formal sector sources of income. The phenomenon of the increased growth of poor populations in LDCs has led to a considerable body of research and thought concerning how the poor survive. What has emerged from these efforts is a greater attention to and a more developed concept of the 'informal sector'. While the 'informal sector' is a broad concept encompassing all economic activities which are essentially outside the formal sector in terms of government taxation and regulation, the largest component of this sector, in terms of population and economic activity, is the economic activities carried out by the poor. In developing economies as different as Brazil and Bangladesh a majority of the population subsists on employment from informal sector sources. In fact it has become an almost universal trait of developing societies that a vast market of goods and services are produced in what is known as the informal sector.

For over a decade, many attempts by donors (both governmental and non-governmental) have been made to reach this substantial market, with limited success. Concepts of 'entrepreneurship' have been developed to define the phenomenon of self-employment in the informal sector, and projects to provide technical assistance, training and credit have proliferated throughout the world. In most cases these projects, even when deemed successful, have had limited impact, have not proven to be sustainable, and have been seriously questioned in terms of cost-effectiveness.

However, within this generally disappointing environment of both development in general and assistance to the informal sector in particular, a number of similar initiatives to provide credit and savings services to the poor have been evolving over the past decade, showing great promise for the future. An underlying characteristic of these programmes is that they treat the poor as commercial clients rather than 'beneficiaries'.

A more commercial approach

A commercial approach argues for the delivery of services at a scale and cost commensurate with the needs and ability of the market for which they are intended. Simply stated, the services grant small loans ranging from $15 to $1000 and they provide savings services for similar amounts. A commercial approach explicitly strives to provide the services intended, charging the real costs of providing these services, including a margin to cover loan losses.

In development terms a 'more commercial approach' could be equated with 'self-evaluating'. Unlike most development efforts which require cost/benefit analysis and impact evaluations to justify the use of resources, a strong case can be made that projects which provide credit and savings services for the poor can be evaluated on the basis of readily available financial data. If a programme provides financial services in the amounts appropriate to the needs of the poor, has excellent recoveries, mobilizes savings and demonstrates the ability to break even or be profitable using unsubsidized sources of funds, a prima facie case exists for the effort being justified. Moreover, extensive financial services to the bottom sectors of society result in greater mobilization of resources and financial intermediation for socially valuable purposes.

We would also argue that if institutions are successfully providing services at the scale envisioned, a self-evident case can be made that the poor are benefiting in two distinct fashions: users of services at the lower range ($15–$200 loans) are in all likelihood in the bottom range of income in their societies; in addition, wealthier segments of the society gaining access to institutional services are creating employment for the poor. This second argument is in fact a more credible version of the infamous 'trickle down' theory often used to justify massive development projects. We would argue that 'trickle down' in this instance is far more likely to occur as the distance of the 'trickle' is minute compared to most large-scale development efforts.

Financial institutions in LDCs

The role of the institutional financial sector in LDCs has been severely circum-scribed by a number of factors, chief among them:

○ Interest rate policies: governments throughout the LDCs have normally opted for rigid interest rate policies which have often remunerated savings and charged interest on loans at a rate well below the annual inflation in the country.
○ Directed credit: governments in LDCs have more often than not made con-trol over finance an important tool of their development strategies, resulting in financial institutions being required to lend not according to normal bank-ing considerations but to government edicts. These have proven to be less than efficient in allocating scarce resources.

A combination of the above factors, in addition to predominantly government ownership of these institutions and a lack of competition and management con-straints, has resulted in a system of banking better understood as 'bureaucratic banking' which is inefficient, largely insolvent and a growing problem to be resolved, as amply documented in World Bank and other publications. In many, if not most, of the LDCs, it is common to find that the institutional financial sec-tor has contracted rather than expanded in its ability to provide financial services, to the point that only a very small number of potentially bankable enterprises are receiving financial services.

This inability to capture savings and provide credit services to a majority of their economically active populations severely hampers the ability of LDCs to mobilize domestic resources. All substantial reviews of the effects of economic development efforts in LDCs have consistently pointed to the inability of these societies to mobilize savings, resulting in a high dependence on external aid and debt. For sustained growth to be achieved in these economies, it is clear that this barrier must be overcome. A major step towards achieving these goals is the introduction of realistic interest and exchange rate policies which many LDCs have been pursuing. These policy reforms, while vital are, however, only a first step. An additional constraint, however, to resource mobilization and the provi-sion of financial services to the informal sector is operational.

In essence, the present banking systems in LDCs are at a point of develop-ment where they are unable to reach a large segment of formal sector borrowers requiring loans of $10 000 or more who can provide guarantees. To reach infor-mal sector borrowers and savers requires the ability to provide lending and savings services capable of making far smaller loans on a largely unsecured basis and capturing savings of similar amounts. In other words, a bulk of the services require a scale of operation and lending conditions which are impossible for the present banking systems to contemplate.

While substantial policy reforms have begun to occur in many LDCs, it will take decades perhaps before a vibrant and rational financial sector emerges in these countries capable of reaching the large majority of economic activity represented in the informal sector. An alternative to awaiting the rebuilding of existing banks in LDCs may be the conversion of existing banks or the creation of new and specialized financial institutions designed to reach the informal sector.

Credit and savings in the informal sector

While extremely difficult to measure on an empirical basis, it is clear that there is a wide array of credit and savings services available in the informal sector. Moreover, the means of delivery of these services are often of ancient origin and occur in two distinct forms: first, 'agents' such as the ubiquitous moneylenders, traders, suppliers and extended family sources, and second, traditional group-based practices. While these two basic forms of informal sector credit and savings are very common, they have serious limitations in efficiently mobilizing and rationally allocating financial resources in a society. While agents play an important role in their local economies, they most often operate on a very localized basis, cannot diversify their risks, often have quasi-monopolistic rights over micro-regions and consequently charge extremely high effective rates of interest. Traditional practices such as rotating savings and credit associations (ROSCAs) include numerous variations, ranging from burial societies to groups purchasing consumer items. The capital available in these mechanisms, however, is limited to the resources of the participants.

The basic differences between institutional credit and the various types of credit and savings operations conducted in the informal sector are that the latter rely on: character-based assessment; pragmatic and flexible concepts of collateral (including non-collateralized lending); extremely simplified documentary requirements; small amounts of credit or savings per transaction; extremely rapid and decentralized approvals; and above all, easy accessibility to the client, since all forms of informal sector credit and savings must occur in relative proximity to the clients.

Formal financial institutions have generally assumed that they would be unable to imitate the practices of the informal financiers on a large scale. This is particularly true given the poor quality of the financial sector in most countries. This paper will argue that major breakthroughs have occurred in a variety of cultural settings which clearly demonstrate that institutional credit and savings services can imitate the main characteristics of informal sector practices in a cost-effective manner and at a scale commensurate with the vast needs of the informal sector in LDCs. Moreover, these initiatives can coexist within an otherwise ineffective and even insolvent financial sector, as separate and specialized financial institutions.

Past attempts to provide financial services to the poor

The history of credit programmes funded by donors and governments and targeted at the poor have largely been based on what we would categorize as the erroneous premisses that the poor cannot pay the real cost of credit and that the

m these flawed premises flowed a series of additional
ed the development of a commercial or even cost-effective
elivery. To summarize, these errors consisted of:

osidized rates of interest instead of market or above-market rates,
r   n a rapid depletion of the value of loan funds
o creat.. , solely credit programmes instead of offering a means of accumulating savings as well, thereby making these programmes exclusively dependent
   on outside sources of funds
o a heavy orientation towards social welfare in terms of staff skills and attitudes, resulting in a lack of financial skills to manage loans properly, and a
   lack of will to enforce strict discipline resulting in poor borrower response
o interventions scaled to a small number of borrowers
o overly ambitious attempts to provide multiple services in training, technical
   assistance, and group formation as well as credit, resulting in very costly programmes where overheads were often equal to, or even exceeded, the amount
   of loans disbursed.

Three cases have been selected to demonstrate an alternative approach. While
only one of these, Grameen Bank, is in an officially designated LDC, we are of
the firm opinion that the experiences and principles demonstrated by the other
cases are equally applicable to LDCs, particularly in urban or densely populated
rural areas.

Grameen Bank, Bangladesh

Begun as a project in 1976 by an individual with a few hundred dollars, Grameen
is the most famous example of 'banking for the poor' and has had a substantial
impact throughout the world on the role of credit in providing assistance to the
poor. Grameen Bank has expanded at a rapid rate from a total of close to 60 000
borrowers in 1983 (its first year as a registered bank) to over 800 000 borrowers.
At present, Grameen disburses close to $100 million a year and has generated
over $25 million in member savings and shareholdings. Borrowers pay the max-
imum allowed interest rate in rural Bangladesh (16 per cent). The effective cost
to borrowers under Grameen's methodology is, however, significantly higher.
Because of a forced savings programme (through loan deductions) as well as
weekly savings obligations, the effective annual interest rate is 24 per cent.
Grameen lends on an unsecured basis using five-person group guarantees,
whereby each individual is responsible for the others, and future access to credit
is determined by all members repaying loans. The range of loan size is between
$10 and $160, with an average loan size of $70.

Table 4.1 Comparison of three credit and savings programmes[1]

Programme	BRI Unit Desa	Grameen Bank	PRODEM[2]
First year operation	1984	1976	1987
No. of borrowers	1 800 000	800 000	20 000
No. of savers	6 600 000	800 000	20 000
Percentage of women borrowers	25%	85%	78%
Range of loan size	$15–$13 500	$10–$160	$50–$1000
Average loan size	$252	$70	$227
Interest rate	10–12% above market rate	market rate	10–12% above market rate
Cumulative disbursements	$2 745 000 000 (1984–March 90)	$278 000 000 (1976–90)	$13 000 000 (1987–90)
Credit disbursed annually	$606 000 000	$100 000 000 (1991 est.)	$7 724 000 (1990)
Savings	$460 000 000 (Dec 89)	$26 000 000 (Oct 90)	$551,000
Profitability	$21 000 000 (89)	loss	marginal loss
Overheads as percentage of loans outstanding	11–15%	14%	14–17%
Repayment rate	86.7%	97%	99.7%
No. of employees	13 000 (Jun 90)	10 000	150
No. borrowers per staff member	139	80	133
No. savers per staff member	508	80	133

1. All figures in US dollars. The figures are taken from various reports prepared by the projects concerned.
2. Figures for PRODEM are estimates.

Because of government-imposed interest rate limits, Grameen is not a profitable bank. The current interest rate is insufficient to pay for the cost of funds available in Bangladesh (6–10 per cent) plus the overheads (14 per cent per annum) and a margin for loan losses or profit. Moreover, owing to its social orientation, it is probable that Grameen would not adjust its interest rates if no ceilings existed, as the large flows of donor resources to Bangladesh allow for easily accessible, subsidized funds. Donors provide subsidies to Grameen by advancing funds prior to loan disbursement (allowing it to earn substantial interest on deposits) and by charging a low rate of 2–3 per cent per annum on loans to the Bank. While Grameen is a subsidized effort and therefore not 'commercial', it needs to be understood within the context of Bangladesh, where institutional credit (granted only on a secured basis) achieves only a 30 per cent recovery rate in rural areas and less than 10 per cent in urban areas. Grameen, lending smaller amounts on an unsecured basis, has consistently maintained recovery rates of 97 per cent. Thus, Grameen may be considered the least subsidized (as there is no subsidy greater than the failure to collect loans) and therefore the most commercial bank within the distorted banking environment of Bangladesh.

Bank Rakyat Indonesia (BRI) Unit Desa system, Indonesia

The government-initiated and owned BRI Unit Desa system of Indonesia is far less well-known than Grameen but is a far larger example of a successful institution capable of lending small amounts of credit and capturing small amounts of savings, while also being remarkably profitable. There are over 1 800 000 borrowers in the Unit Desa system and the range of loan sizes varies from $15 to $13 500. While this range covers the needs of a wide range of enterprises, the average loan size in 1989 was only $360 and estimates based on a representative sample of loans concluded that 80 per cent of all loans granted were in the $100–$500 range. More important than its lending success, Unit Desa is also the pre-eminent example of a successful case for the mobilization of voluntary savings. From a total of $38 million in 1984, a concerted effort was made to mobilize savings which grew to $460 million in 1989, representing over 6 600 000 savers with average deposits of $70.

The BRI Unit Desa system is a result of the conversion of a failed subsidized agricultural credit programme for rice farmers which was initiated in the early 1970s and grew to service 3.7 million farmers. In 1983 the government decided to curtail this programme severely and reorient the sizeable staff (13 000) and servicing locations (3600 units) to a radically different type of lending. Instead of lending at subsidized rates to farmers, the BRI Unit Desa system began to lend to small off-farm productive activities at higher than commercial rates of interest. This was made possible by wide-ranging reforms of financial sector policies promulgated by the government in 1983, which essentially eradicated subsidized interest rates and artificial ceilings on lending and savings interest rates.

The investment of the government in this system was sizeable, starting with a grant of some $60 million and an additional $190 million in loans at a market rate of 12 per cent per annum. In addition, the system made a loss of some $25 million in 1984–5, but subsequently became increasingly profitable and in 1990 made $21 million in profits. From being heavily dependent on loans, the Unit Desa system has evolved into a self-financing system through its profitability and successful savings mobilization.

PRODEM, Bolivia

Of the three cases examined, PRODEM is by far the smallest, with some 20 000 borrowers. It was initiated only in 1987, however, and has developed a sufficient track record that local investors as well as the Inter-American Investment Corporation (a subsidiary of the Inter-American Development Bank) and the Calmeadow Foundation are raising over $5 million to capitalize its conversion into a private sector commercial bank. PRODEM is also the best example of a large number of programmes sponsored by ACCION International, a US NGO, in 12 Latin American countries reaching over 80 000 clients in the informal sector. PRODEM charges a rate of interest of between 10 and 12 per cent per annum above the commercial rates in Bolivia, has generated savings equivalent to one-third of its loan portfolio solely through a forced deduction on loans, and has disbursed some $13 million in lending since its inception, with an audited 99.88 per cent recovery rate. The programme operates predominantly with five-person groups, but lends to larger businesses (loans of up to $1000) on an individual basis.

These three programmes, although situated in radically different contexts, all focus on low-income populations and have refuted much of the traditional thinking on credit for the poor. While not all of them are profit-making financial institutions, they have given irrefutable evidence of the following:

The poor can afford unsubsidized credit. The misconception that the poor need to be subsidized has been perhaps the greatest barrier to the creation of effective programmes. All three cases demonstrate that borrowers can pay the real cost of credit. In the case of Grameen, a substantial subsidy exists, but there is evidence that borrowers could pay a rate that would make the bank profitable (the current effective rate assuming forced savings as fee income). Equally important, these cases and many others prove that the poor can be trusted with credit.

Why the poor can pay. Successful lending experiences have opened a window of understanding on the economic activities of the poor. It is becoming clear that many borrowers do not focus on one activity but may have a myriad of activities carried out by various members of the household. As capital is fungible, it is impossible to trace accurately where these small amounts of capital are used. In practice, this type of lending may be used as general working capital support to the family unit which is extremely efficient in managing these activities.

The poor can save. The experience gained in Bangladesh, Indonesia, several countries in Latin America and, much more recently, in Africa has shown that substantial savings (at least one-third of loans outstanding) can be generated from the poor. The BRI case clearly demonstrates that a vast market of small savers can be reached. The cases of Grameen and PRODEM (neither of which have attempted the mobilization of voluntary savings) prove that a 'forced' savings mechanism through deductions on loans is also a viable strategy. It should be noted that both Grameen and PRODEM report that the forced savings are extremely popular with their clients. The reason for this popularity is that deductions on loans allow informal sector clients to build up some form of security, almost an insurance policy, through equal loan payments which, at the end of the repayment period, yields a tangible asset.

Small loans reach the poor. Of the three examples, only Grameen makes it explicit that the scheme is targeted at the poor. It defines this target by a ceiling of landholding for first-time borrowers of up to 0.5 acres of arable land. The other two cases do not have ceilings. BRI Unit Desa is insistent that it does not focus on the 'poor', but only on clients that can pay. In the case of Unit Desa, however, an impact evaluation found that 75 per cent of the clients owned 0.5 acres or less of cultivable land. This finding from Unit Desa underscores the contention of the writers of this paper that the most effective means of reaching the poor is to ensure that small loans (and savings services) can be granted efficiently.

Financial institutions imitating informal sector practices

The three cases chosen imitate informal sector practices in the following manner:

Proximity to the client. All three cases have at their core a locational strategy which is the base from which informal sector practices can be imitated. The BRI Unit Desa system has the simplest strategy, using the 3600 service locations where clients come to transact business. Each unit has a four-member staff that can handle over 2000 clients (borrowers and savers). Grameen has a more complex strategy based on a network of over 800 branches. Grameen brings the service directly to the villagers through bank workers who carry money to and from the villages and are based at the branch. Each bank worker is capable of servicing 250 borrowers (who meet on a weekly basis). A Grameen branch is capable of servicing 2500 clients. PRODEM is a very different model as its market is densely populated urban areas. PRODEM has only four branches, though each branch is projected to reach some 10 000 borrowers.

Character-based assessment and pragmatic concepts of collateral. Character assessment is fundamental in any type of banking. In 'normal' banking, however, this is usually accompanied by the financial analysis of a loan request and guarantees. For informal sector lending, character assessment is most often the only means by which borrowers are analysed. Grameen and PRODEM, in the radically different contexts of rural Bangladesh and urban Bolivia, use the identical system of five-person group guarantees as a means of character assessment. These groups are self-selected individuals who are informed that, if they agree to be 'jointly and severally' liable for each other's debt, they will have access to credit. Normally these groups form for the express purpose of obtaining credit. In addition, a guarantee savings fund is established through a 5 per cent deduction on all loans made for the group. This is considered as a partial guarantee. The BRI Unit Desa system is distinctly different, as all clients are treated as individuals and, technically speaking, all loans are collateralized. In BRI, the collateral obtained for loans of $15–$500 is most often a land title or tax receipt, usually on the small plot of land where the borrower's home is located. These titles are more symbolic than real and in the history of the BRI system no action has ever been taken to cash in on this collateral (even though loans have been written off). It should also be noted that land titles are commonly available in Indonesia and do not *per se* restrict borrower access.

Extremely simple documentary requirements. A common feature of all these programmes is that documentation is designed for the maximum ease and utility of the borrower. In addition, both BRI and PRODEM have devised analytic cash-flow tools for the approval of larger loans.

Small amounts of credit or savings per transaction. As amply noted earlier, all programmes operate within a range of lending which clearly targets microenterprise levels of activity. In addition, two of the programmes, PRODEM and BRI, work with larger-scale clients. In the case of BRI, in practice few loans for less than $50 are made, while in the case of Grameen, it is rare to find loans of over $200.

Simplified repayment terms. The three cases described all use the same principle of equal instalments to repay loans. This imitates the informal sector practice with one vital difference: principal repayment is included in the instalments. Most informal sector repayment arrangements charge a 'rental' on capital employed which translates into equal interest payments, with the principal due at the end of the lending arrangement.

Extremely rapid and decentralized approvals. While the three cases have varying times between the first request and approval of loans, all three cases use an automatic, graduated system of repeat loans, which translates into rapid approvals. This feature has been found to be one of the key elements of success of these programmes as borrowers find it in their interest to repay loans in order to obtain additional credit.

The three cases chosen are excellent examples of how formal sector financial institutions can imitate the age-old practices of informal sector sources of credit and savings services.

It is fascinating to note that in all three cases representing different environments, sizes of programmes, methodologies and levels of economic development, the overhead costs compared to average loans outstanding is in the vicinity of 15 per cent per annum. This level of overhead can be considered to be two to three times what a 'normal' bank making much larger loans would incur in operational costs. The level of overheads of these very different cases implies that one of the important elements of making institutional credit and savings available in small amounts is the ability to charge interest rates substantially above the commercial rate of interest. This is what both PRODEM and BRI have been doing at a level of 10–12 per cent above normal commercial rates, with no detriment either to the demand for services or the quality of recovery.

Credit and savings for the poor in perspective

While we are optimistic about the prospects for similar micro-credit and savings services for densely populated areas of LDCs, we would wish to emphasize that credit is a means and not an end in itself. The efficient provision of financial services to the poor will not resolve constraints originating from a lack of skills or access to markets. Credit and savings will only assist the clients served by allowing them a greater range of choices to survive in the informal sector based on their abilities and hard work. As such, this type of intervention should not be construed as a panacea for the poor. It is a useful and fundamental complement to the existing abilities of the poor as well as to development efforts which seek to remove more basic constraints. We would argue, however, that to enhance prospects for financial viability, financial services should be promoted as a separate area of support and project activity and not 'integrated' into more ambitious schemes.

On a more national or 'macro' level, we would point out that the expansion of financial services into the informal sector is desirable in itself, if these services are sustained by the clients with no subsidy required. This is particularly true in

LDCs where a large part of economic activity resides in the informal sector.

An additional cause for optimism in promoting micro-credit and savings services is that the means to manage and staff these programmes and institutions is available throughout LDCs. In terms of staffing, individuals with basic skills who can be trained to perform the complex tasks required are abundant in most LDCs, as witnessed by the substantial number of educated, un- or under-employed individuals and the contraction of government bureaucracies. The basic 'technology' in financial services is the means accurately to record and manage disbursements, recoveries and balances in savings or checking accounts. The revolution in information technology has made computers available throughout LDCs and, as important, 'user friendly' software has been developed, minimizing the amount of training and specialization required to utilize this technology. For programmes with ambitions to become viable institutions, this technology can be vital in tracking the many thousands (and hundreds of thousands) of transactions that micro-credit and savings services require to become self-sufficient.

The optimism expressed in this paper stems not only from the growing success of a number of individual initiatives but also from the changing policy environment which has long been one of the principal barriers to the evolution of viable financial institutions specializing in micro-savings and credit services. Chief among these changes is a diminishing use of subsidized credit and artificial interest rate ceilings and a consequent return to a more rational (and not directed) allocation of scarce financial resources. In addition, the growing acceptance of private sector initiatives by LDC governments can pave the way for a wide range of non-governmental organizations (and even private entrepreneurs eventually) to initiate (often with government support) micro-credit and savings programmes.

Credit and savings services as an infant industry

Credit and savings services for the informal sector should be viewed as a worldwide infant industry that requires special support during the research and development stage. To extend the analogy to product development in private industry, the product has been conceptualized, designed, and pre-tested in a number of settings (such as BRI, Grameen and PRODEM). The industry is moving into the latter part of the research and development stage, and is entering the preliminary stages of commercialization. At this stage, the product needs to be tested in and customized for a wide variety of markets in many different countries, and the institutional capacity to produce and deliver the product must be created.

In a number of years, if these tasks are carried out successfully, the product will become fully commercial, though it is never likely to be a great moneymaker. At the end of the current research and development stage it is hoped that institutions will be able to increase the number of customers served exponentially, to a level commensurate with the potential market. At that point, if profitability has been proven, private institutions will begin to enter the market on their own.

Until then, the pioneers in the industry will have to be non-profit-making organizations and governments or private institutions receiving special support.

There is a great precedent and economic justification for donors, governments and non-profit-making organizations to sponsor financial market research and development. By their very nature, financial innovations quickly become public knowledge, rapidly available to the competition. Therefore, a single private institution, whose survival depends on its profits, cannot afford to invest in perfecting a product when the chances of keeping the market to itself are small and development costs are high. When the product is expected to be only marginally profitable, the incentive is virtually nil. Because of such externalities, governments have often played demonstration roles in financial markets, sometimes quite successfully. In this case, the externalities cross international boundaries, as techniques developed in one country can be applied in others. When one adds the benefits to developing countries of increasing the participation of the poor majority in the economy, the argument in favour of donor, government and non-profit support for credit and savings services becomes quite strong.

A strong justification for involvement, however, is not an excuse for unrestrained subsidization. The analogies of product development and business start-up provide more than a hopeful scenario. Expectations of viability must be kept clearly in mind, especially during the initial years when subsidies are large and results small.

This paper outlines a possible three-stage process for moving towards the commercialization of institutions. The first step is to develop a cost-covering operation focusing primarily on lending; the second step begins with the expansion of savings mobilization; and the third step is to move to full independence, in which concessional sources of finance are no longer used and the institution becomes a genuine financial institution.

Stage One: achieving break-even lending operations

Lending operations will be the major source of income for the financial institutions serving the informal sector. Therefore, the single most important challenge at the operating level is creating and sustaining break-even or profit-making lending. Once institutions can demonstrate their solid control of lending operations they become worthy of seeking voluntary savings, or borrowing commercially, and of being treated as genuine financial institutions.

Not everyone would agree that this level of financial performance is necessary or possible. We contend, however, that financial self-sufficiency is the only standard compatible with reaching the vast majority of people in the informal sector for two simple and compelling reasons: scale and sustainability. Continued reliance on heavy subsidies dooms operations to be small and vulnerable, because subsidized sources of funds are in short supply relative to potential demand. In most cases, only operations that require little or no external subsidy will be in a position to grow to nationwide coverage, and only such operations will continue to exist into the future after the initial demonstration stage is passed and external support is withdrawn.

Many people oppose a focus on self-sufficiency, not because they fail to see the link between profitability and scale, but from scepticism that profits can be achieved in lending operations for the informal sector. Profitability remains to be tested in many countries, but stunning examples have been set by lending operations that break even or better (such as BRI). Many other of the best-known programmes still depend on some form of subsidy (including Grameen and PRODEM), albeit far less than the previous generation of credit programmes. We can, however, be optimistic that break-even operations can be achieved in many or most least-developed countries, on the basis of what has been learned about the techniques that work with the informal sector; the institutional structures that support those techniques; and the ability of the customers to pay for the cost of services.

A lending operation can be considered self-sufficient when it is able to cover the costs of administration, loan losses, and funds raised through receipts from interest charges and other fees. The costs it faces, particularly the cost of funds, must be at the non-subsidized, commercial level. Achieving self-sufficiency requires mastery of four tasks:

○ *Developing an effective client methodology.* Virtually all the programmes that come close to breaking even use the special lending techniques adapted from the informal sector, as described earlier.
○ *Streamlining administration to control costs.* For very small loans, administrative techniques must be extremely simple, so that paperwork is minimized, and volume per staff member maximized. Despite streamlined procedures, administrative costs will still be high relative to loan sizes, requiring high interest rates.
○ *Full-cost pricing.* From the start, institutions should charge a rate that will ultimately support a viable lending operation. Loans to the informal sector will require interest rates at least 10 per cent higher than standard commercial rates. The informal sector can afford such rates.
○ *Accountability.* Managers and staff must be held accountable for results and rewarded for good performance. Good management is essential, but more important is the requirement for accountability that comes from operating as a business, where survival depends on good performance.

To summarize, self-sufficiency in lending operations is an essential prerequisite for reaching large numbers and for becoming a permanent, independent institution. An institution that has achieved this should be ready to seek the confidence of others, such as savers, who can provide funds for lending. Evidence is clear that self-sufficiency is surprisingly within grasp, provided it is clearly sought.

Stage Two: mobilizing savings

We place savings mobilization in the second stage not because it is less important than lending, but because it brings with it greater responsibilities. Any institution that accepts savings, particularly from relatively poor people, must be able to safeguard the funds it accepts. As those funds must be lent out in order to earn income, an institution accepting savings ought first to become a competent lender.

Savings can be introduced slowly from the very start, through compulsory savings features incorporated into loan formulae. Borrowers are asked to save a set proportion of their loan amount during the time when the loan is outstanding or as long as they are members of the institution. These features can play an important role for the lending institutions in providing liquidity and increasing the effective interest rate. Because they are so closely tied to individual loans, they may actually enhance security. Customers reportedly like these features, which allow them to set aside funds for longer-run purposes or for insurance against emergencies. PRODEM and the Grameen Bank have successful compulsory savings features that supply up to one-third of their loan capital.

As programmes mature, they can consider offering voluntary savings programmes – passbook savings accounts or savings certificates. These services respond to the fact that many more people are prepared to become savers than borrowers. BRI, the model of successful voluntary savings, now has 6.6 million savers, providing credit to 1.8 million borrowers, and is fully financed by savings. The key to BRI's success has been a customer-oriented design, which recognizes that many of the lessons of informal sector credit also apply to savings: an emphasis on the convenience of location, timely access, and simple procedures (as well as a positive real return). If other institutions begin to offer such market-oriented savings instruments, the amount raised may greatly exceed their expectations regarding the potential of the informal sector to be a source of funds. In creating a microenterprise bank in Bolivia, BancoSol, PRODEM is about to take this step.

Institutions that are able to build strong savings programmes have several advantages. They can take advantage of economies of scale in providing both credit and savings services to the same communities. The physical and human infrastructure needed to provide both services is likely to be much the same. At the same time, their source of funds is less vulnerable to changes in the financial markets than are institutions dependent for funds on formal financial institutions. Moreover, institutions built around savings may become better integrated into their communities. Clients tend to develop loyalty to the institution and make demands for accountability.

Moving into savings raises the stakes considerably, however, because it shifts the consequences of failure from the original funding source (donors or governments) on to the savers – the very people the institutions intend to serve. The failure of a savings-based institution has repercussions throughout the country that last much longer than those resulting from a failed credit programme. Such failures can sour public and government attitudes towards the financial system for many years afterwards, and prevent the success of new efforts. The first line of protection against failure must be strong institutions with proven capability to manage loan assets and built-in features of accountability. Whenever savings are involved, however, there must also be some external source of scrutiny that can represent the interests of the savers, guarding against imprudent management or purposeful abuse. Thus, countries with institutions moving into the second stage must make sure provisions for supervision are adequate.

Stage Three: becoming independent

Once an institution has created a financially viable lending operation and has established its capacity to accept and secure savings deposits, it is ready to become independent of the supports that have helped establish it. In product development terms, the institution is ready for full commercialization. Institutions in this third stage will no longer receive financial support from soft sources, such as donors or governments. Funding sources must ultimately be found from private sources within the nation itself, through a combination of deposits and commercial borrowing. If one takes a large-scale and long-run perspective, this movement to private sources should be the ultimate goal.

The key test for the third stage is whether an institution is able to operate in the financial system as a player on equal footing with other financial institutions. In more practical terms, institutions in the third stage should be creditworthy, that is, able to earn the trust of suppliers of funds. The main requirements of creditworthiness are clear legal status and a proven ability to run financially sound operations.

When funds are borrowed from commercial lenders, requirements may be particularly difficult to satisfy. Normally, banks require collateral that fully covers the amount they are lending. For institutions lending to the informal sector using character-based techniques, this requirement can be virtually impossible to satisfy. The main assets of the credit and savings institution – unsecured loans – do not meet the banks' criteria, and programmes that are structured as non-profit organizations have no equity capital to bolster bank confidence. Creative solutions are needed. In fact, well-functioning operations that lend to the poor should be good credit risks as long as they cover costs and show low delinquency. Both sides need to change, however, before borrowing can go forward. The lending operations need to be configured not as non-profit programmes, but as well-capitalized financial institutions. At the same time, banks need to be willing to lend on the basis of proven experience – demonstrated portfolio quality and good cash flow – not on tangible collateral.

A key issue at this third stage is the process for transforming institutions from their initial forms into more legally independent entities, with owners and equity capital. Grameen Bank was transformed from a programme to a financial institution in 1983, at the time when it was just set to expand, and the transformation helped pave the way for the expansion. PRODEM is now in the process of creating a microenterprise bank to which it will turn over its loan portfolio and main operations. Again, this transformation should lay the foundation for significant expansion. The BRI Unit Desa system, as a programme of an existing bank, had a secure institutional home from the start, and this proved to be an important advantage.

Origins of successful credit and savings institutions

At present, most of the least developed countries lack credit and savings institutions with healthy financial viability and national coverage. In searching the current institutional landscape, policy makers should pursue the avenues most likely to lead to successful credit and savings institutions. We now look at three sources from which such institutions may grow.

Both Grameen Bank and PRODEM offer examples of a model in which a programme begins small and, after achieving a critical size and level of viability, grows dramatically. At the start, the programme operates in one location, perfecting its lending methodology. As its portfolio grows, the programme perfects its management structure and procedures, possibly opening a handful of outlets. At some point, the programme reaches a critical mass of size and experience from which it can move into a phase of rapid expansion, multiplying the number of clients and outlets. In Grameen's case, the early experimentation lasted from the mid-1970s until about 1983. PRODEM, which now appears to be into the expansion stage, was able to move more quickly, as it was in a position to draw on the previous decade of ACCION International's experience. Given the learning that has taken place in this field during the past decade, organizations starting from scratch may enjoy clear advantages – they can anticipate the path they will follow. If the lending techniques, organizational visions, management structure, and legal status of the anticipated mature organization appear in the initial phase, some painful transitions can be avoided.

While the creation of new organizations that can grow exponentially is perhaps the ideal, the situation found much more frequently in least developed countries is that of a multitude of small organizations, each providing services in a limited area. Typically, few of these organizations will take a commercial approach to their lending operations, and few will have achieved any substantial measure of financial viability. For a variety of reasons, it may be effective to help improve and expand these organizations so that, taken together, they form a system of nationwide coverage. This strategy requires a central entity that can perform a training and upgrading function, often called a second-level institution. This organization must take on many of the management tasks that are internal when a single organization is growing. As an external entity, however, it is not in a strong position to enforce its direction on the lending organizations, particularly regarding so difficult a subject as moving towards financial viability. The external position of the second-level institution constitutes the chief disadvantage of an approach that links smaller organizations together.

Prior to its present successful credit and savings programme, the BRI Unit Desa system was a bankrupt network of lending outlets purveying government-funded lines of agricultural credit at subsidized rates. Unprofitable government-owned financial institutions can be found throughout the developing world. Given the existing resources in these institutions, in the form of physical plant, management, and staff, it is tempting to think that these institutions could undergo the type of transition that BRI engineered, and that this would offer a quick route to the expansion of services. BRI's experience shows that such a transition is possible. However, the commitment to effect this kind of transformation should not be underestimated. BRI's success resulted from a great deal of financial support for staff training, technical advice, and loan capital; the full commitment of its leadership to operating on a businesslike basis, with the Unit Desas required to be profitable; and excellent management. If all these elements can be brought to bear in another country – and only if they can be – another success of BRI's magnitude may emerge.

The government's role in supporting credit and savings services

Whether credit and savings institutions for the informal sector emerge from private initiatives or from the transformation of government banks, governments will have to be involved, if national coverage is ever to be achieved. Governments in LDCs, as elsewhere, have three basic functions vis-à-vis financial markets, and these functions are just as crucial for credit and savings institutions as they are for commercial banks. These functions are: to ensure that general financial market and economic conditions are supportive, as part of the macro-economic policy; to set out the ground rules for institutions that allow for them to pursue financial viability; and to ensure that financial resources entrusted to them are well managed. The government's role in these areas changes somewhat as institutions move through the three stages to full independence.

At each stage, benign financial market conditions are essential. Governments must do their best to ensure low or moderate inflation, reasonable prevailing interest rates, and a monetary policy that allows for reasonably liquid financial markets. Credit and savings institutions do not require a special set of macro-economic policies; rather, they need the same kind of policies that make for healthy financial institutions in general. Without these, institutional development efforts will be severely handicapped.

The government's role during stage one

During the time when an institution is perfecting its lending operations, a government's most important task is simply both to allow and to require that those operations are set up on a businesslike basis. This entails, in addition to charging full-cost interest rates, the adoption of good accounting and portfolio management practices. A major failing in all types of institutions in the developing world has been a reluctance to manage defaults and arrears in a transparent manner, and particularly to write off uncollectable loans. Such lax practices make it very difficult for insiders and outsiders alike to assess the financial condition of a lending operation, hindering both judgements about readiness for expansion, and internal abilities to correct problems at early stages. Accountability must be built during this stage, to provide the confidence needed before the acceptance of savings is permitted.

From this early stage, governments need to recognize that the techniques of lending to the informal sector differ from those of standard commercial banks.

In particular, they must understand the unconventional techniques of motivating repayment, and they must be willing to allow for those techniques to substitute for formal collateral requirements.

Governments may also provide financial support during the early stages, in the form of initial capitalization, subsidies for start-up operations, or special technical assistance. Such support and subsidy is appropriate, provided that it is done in the manner of a business start-up, with the clear expectation – set out in a definite timetable – that subsidies are temporary.

Supervising the introduction of savings during stage two

When an institution has proved itself to be a responsible lender, the government should allow it to begin to accept savings deposits. Many institutions, particularly those begun by NGOs, never begin to accept savings because of legal and regulatory thresholds that come into play at this point. Savings mobilization from the general public is restricted to specified types of financial institutions, conforming to specified regulation. The fledgling credit and savings institutions do not resemble the established categories of commercial banks or other institutions empowered to accept savings. They may be far smaller; they may have too little equity – or, as the children of non-profit organizations, none at all – and they have a very different mix of services.

In most cases, it is not feasible at stage two for these institutions to shape themselves into formal financial institutions. (PRODEM is doing so, by establishing a commercial bank, in large part because no other regulations allowed for it to accept savings.) Rather, governments need to allow such institutions to accept savings by exception to general regulations. In return, governments will need to be assured from the beginning, and on a continuing basis, that the institutions it accepts are accountable and competent in their lending operations and stewardship of funds. It is not appropriate for the government simply to open the doors to any institution wishing to accept the savings of the informal sector. Only proven institutions under strict control should be given permission.

During this second stage, if governments have provided financial support to an institution, it should now begin to diminish, or to move quickly on to nearly commercial terms, leaving little subsidy. As institutions expand, they need increasing amounts of loan capital. Some of this will come from the introduction of savings. Whatever additional amount is needed may not yet be forthcoming from private sources, so governments may still wish to provide loan capital. At this stage, however, institutions should be able to pay non-subsidized interest rates for that capital.

Supporting full independence during stage three

As institutions reach the final stage, and prepare for full independence, ownership issues become paramount. A permanent ownership structure, with adequate equity capital, and accountable owners is needed to ensure that the institution will have what it needs to continue operation into the future. There must be people who have both a clear stake in the performance of the institution and the ability to monitor and manage that performance. Governments need not be actively involved in the creation of ownership structures. They should continue to be flexible enough, however, to allow experimental forms of ownership to develop, building on the experience gained during the second phase.

After financial assistance to credit and savings institutions has fully ended, there will be a continuing need for supervision. At present, as the first few institutions begin to reach full independence, supervision can be done on a case-by-case basis, with an eye toward the eventual formalization of the process as the number of institutions grows. Institutions should be held to high standards of financial soundness, in the areas of capital adequacy, asset quality (management of arrears), liquidity, and return on portfolio. The exact standards of financial soundness for such institutions in each of these areas may not be the same as those for mainstream financial institutions, because the nature of the operations is different.

The role of donors

We recommend that donors adopt a pragmatic and commercial approach to supporting projects and programmes which provide credit and savings services for the poor. Whether motivated by social considerations, economic development grounds, or a mix of both, donors should recognize the importance of financial discipline and the need to achieve self-sufficiency in costs and funding for this type of endeavour. Donor support should function as an incentive to creating viable financial institutions rather than as an ongoing subsidy which creates long-term dependence.

Specifically, we would recommend that donors address policy issues by providing technical assistance in the following areas:

Interest rate reform. First and foremost, donors should support the current trends towards market-determined interest rates. In relation to services for the poor, this should encompass support for higher than commercial rates for small loans, given the cost considerations involved with providing these services.

Entry of new financial institutions. Often successful credit programmes are inhibited from mobilizing savings because of legal requirements concerning financial institutions. Donors should support flexibility in legal requirements and appropriate regulatory supervision to allow successful credit programmes for the poor to evolve into credit and savings institutions.

We suggest that the characteristics of donor financial support should be:

Flexible funding. Donors should adopt a more commercial approach in identifying and funding these initiatives. First of all, donors should give priority to programmes committed to 'full-cost pricing' that have the ambition and drive needed to achieve the critical mass of clients required for viability. The funding of loan capital and operating cost support should be kept separate from each other and tied to performance indicators. Strict concepts of performance based on realistic targets should also be established between recipient and donor. A realistic timeframe based on the experience of similar programmes should be established. Audited annual statements should determine the indicators and level of funding (or possibly discontinuation) to be granted for the following period. In this manner, donors could make a five-year or more commitment, which would allow for institutional stability on the part of recipients and which would be tied to standards of performance.

Replication, cross-fertilization, and networking. Donors have the unique ability to invest in a wide variety of programmes providing credit and savings services for the poor. If there is a commitment to learn from these experiences, donors can play an important role in disseminating 'lessons learned' and bringing them to the attention of governments. Donors can also assist in the development of technical expertise available to emerging programmes and projects.

In closing, we restate our conviction that the cases described, representing close to three million borrowers and over $3 billion in disbursement of credit, as well as $500 million in savings mobilization, are indicative of the vast potential market for financial services for the poor in developing countries. If donors and governments opt to enter these markets on pragmatic and commercial terms, it is more than possible that hundreds of millions of clients could eventually have access to financial services that will improve their economic well-being.

About the authors

Henry R. Jackelen is a Senior Technical Adviser at UNCDF (United Nations Capital Development Fund) in the area of credit and enterprise promotion. When she contributed to this paper, Elisabeth Rhyne was Project Co-ordinator for the GEMINI Project, USAID's worldwide resource to assist microenterprise development. She is now Senior Vice-President, African Operations and Research, Development and Policy at ACCION International. This paper does not represent the positions of USAID or UNCDF, but the views of the authors.

5 Microinsurance – the risks, perils and opportunities

WARREN BROWN

This paper was first published in March 2001.

Donors and microfinance institutions (MFIs) have recently begun experimenting with the development of insurance schemes to protect clients against the risks that can lead them further into poverty. This paper attempts to inject a strong note of caution into the discussions surrounding these activities. It argues that vulnerability does not translate directly into 'demand' for microinsurance and, moreover, even where markets for microinsurance do exist, MFIs lack the skills and resources to develop or manage all but the most basic microinsurance products. As an alternative to microinsurance provided and managed directly by MFIs, this paper recommends that MFIs develop partnerships with established insurers in order to provide the benefits of insurance to their clients, without taking on the insurance risk.

Recognizing that not all MFIs will accept these arguments, the final section of the paper lays out a series of prerequisites which MFIs that insist on developing their own insurance products ought to consider, both to ensure they are providing good value to clients and to increase their prospects for financial sustainability.

THERE IS A RISING TIDE of microfinance institutions wanting to develop insurance products for the low-income market. The rationales they give for this interest include: protecting poor clients from risks, reducing an MFI's loan defaults and earning additional income for an MFI's loan portfolio. While there is no question that the poor are highly vulnerable to a wide variety of risks, this vulnerability cannot necessarily be translated into a demand or need for insurance. Moreover, the mere existence of vulnerability says nothing about the question of whether MFIs are suitably equipped to provide insurance. In fact, most are not.

Insurance is a risky business that, in many developed markets, commercial lenders are prohibited from entering. Though potentially complementary, banking and insurance products can also be mutually destructive. Just as loan losses can erode the reserves required to meet insurance claims, losses in insurance operations can deplete depositor assets and an MFI's loan capital in a single catastrophic event.

Before launching insurance initiatives, MFIs and the donors who support them should understand the risks and be certain that the required resources and skills are in place to manage them. This assessment should be frank. Few MFIs have reached financial sustainability and even fewer have successfully integrated a savings component into their product line. Most continue to rely on compulsory savings, and these are often managed irresponsibly or illegally. Some MFIs forthrightly admit their use of savings products to fund doubtful loan books; many more do the same but attribute their actions to rationales that donors find more attractive.

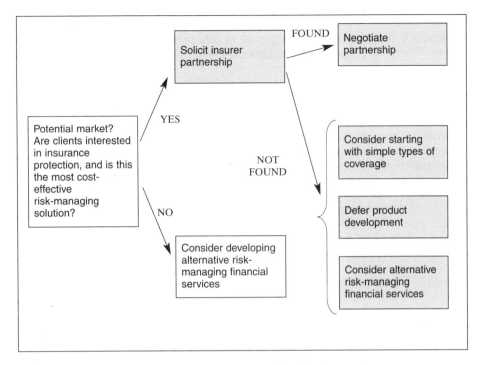

Figure 5.1   *Decision tree for microinsurance product development*

This paper attempts to assist organizations in assessing (1) whether there is a potential market for microinsurance; (2) how that market can be served through strategic partnerships; and (3) the resource requirements that dictate why most insurance products are more than most MFIs can reasonably manage on their own. Figure 5.1 lays out these sets of questions in decision-tree format.

Defining microinsurance

The term 'microinsurance' is growing increasingly familiar in the microfinance industry. There are two parts to the definition of 'microinsurance' used in this paper. First, 'insurance' refers to a financial service that uses *risk pooling* to provide compensation to individuals or groups that are adversely affected by a specified risk or event. Risk pooling involves collecting large groups, or pools, of individuals or groups to share the losses resulting from the occurrence of a risky event. Persons harmed by such an event benefit from the contributions of those who are not affected and, as a result, they receive compensation that is greater than the amount they have invested in the insurance policy. Thus, products that allow an affected individual to receive only up to the amount they have contributed are considered savings products, not insurance. 'Micro' indicates that we are discussing insurance products designed to be beneficial to, and affordable by, low-income individuals or groups.

Box 5.1 Assessing client interest in different types of insurance in Cambodia

The Groupe de Recherche et d'Echanges Technologiques (GRET) has operated a micro-credit programme in Cambodia for many years. In the process of pilot testing a health insurance scheme, GRET conducted market research to test households' satisfaction with the plan. The results of this research confirmed that clients appreciated the benefits provided by the insurance and that even those who had not become ill were satisfied in knowing that the protection was available and that they had helped others in the community.

This same market research uncovered that, in addition to health care costs, losses resulting from the untimely death of livestock were a significant threat to many households. However, when asked if they would be interested in property insurance on their livestock, the majority of the respondents said 'no'. While they were satisfied with participating in a health insurance scheme, they preferred to manage losses relating to livestock death on their own, stating that 'in the case of the animal's death, the meat is still edible' and 'the animal's death is the sole responsibility of the owner'.

Part I. Verifying the potential market for microinsurance

Before jumping on the insurance bandwagon, MFIs and donors should consider three basic questions regarding the potential market for microinsurance:

o Do clients want assistance in reducing vulnerability to risks through insurance?
o Is insurance the most appropriate financial service for providing this protection?
o Are clients willing and able to pay a price at which the insurance can be delivered profitably?

Is there client interest in reducing vulnerability to risk?

One can easily create a compelling story about how an insurance product will protect the poor against devastating losses or smooth households' volatile incomes. However, this scenario can overshadow the more fundamental question of whether an MFI's clients actually *want* insurance to reduce their vulnerability against certain risks. If a household does not want the kind of protection that a specific type of insurance provides, no matter how compelling the rationale to MFI managers and funders, there is no justification for developing the product. As Box 5.1 illustrates, poor households are not interested in insurance protection against *all* risks.

It is the responsibility of the MFI to ensure that a proposed product is of interest to clients, particularly if the insurance is to be made mandatory for all borrowers or savers.

To be sure that they have addressed this question, MFIs can use tools like MicroSave-Africa's PRA methodology (for details, visit the web site http://www.uncdf.org/sum/msa) to test clients' level of interest in insurance. If their response is positive, the MFI should go on to consider the remaining questions in this paper. If it is negative, the MFI should consider other ways it might assist its clients in managing risk.

Is insurance a potential solution?

The second question in establishing whether a potential market exists for microinsurance has two parts. The first asks whether insurance can, from a technical perspective, be feasibly offered against the proposed risks. The second considers whether other financial services, particularly savings, might be a more effective alternative.

What can and cannot be insured? MFIs should verify that their proposed coverage meets the following basic insurance principles:

○ *Large numbers:* Insurance works by sharing risk across a large population. If the pool of policyholders is too small, volatility in the number of claims can quickly exceed the plan's reserves, leading to bankruptcy. Although no precise minimum number of policyholders can be established, less than 1000–2000 is likely to create undue risk for the provider.

○ *Specified risks only:* Insurance can be designed to protect only against specific risks for which the chance of loss can be calculated. Despite the attractive 'development benefits' of blanket insurance coverage against all or an unspecified set of potential causes of loss (e.g. building insurance against all causes of damage), coverage of this type provided by MFIs and governments has consistently failed when unexpected claims overwhelm premium income and the insurer is faced with the difficult and unpopular choice of folding the plan or arbitrarily reducing the benefits paid out in order to keep claims expenses within the plan's means.

○ *Not covariant:* Risks covered by insurance should be able to affect only a relatively small portion of the total insured population at any given time. Covariant risks, such as a flood or HIV/AIDS, are likely to cause similar damage to a large portion of an MFI's clients at the same time. If a client base is concentrated in a single community, an epidemic or disaster can quickly bankrupt the insurance plan.

○ *Controls on moral hazard:* Policyholders' ability to influence whether the risk actually occurs must be limited or controlled. If a policyholder can control the timing or likelihood of loss, claims can quickly increase beyond expectations, leading to bankruptcy. These risks are especially high in the provision of health and property insurance.

○ *Balance of risk/controls against adverse selection:* The pool of insured households should include both high- and low-risk cases so that the average risk occurrence within the pool is similar to the average in the population at large. Adverse selection occurs when low-risk policyholders opt out of purchasing the coverage, or high-risk policyholders opt in in greater numbers than expected. Controls need to be in place to ensure that high-risk policyholders do not overwhelm the pool.

A good example of the potential consequences of insuring against risks that do not meet the above criteria is outlined in Box 5.2 (adapted from Hazell, 1992).

What should and should not be insured? In addition to risks that simply cannot be insured against, there are some risks where insurance is technically possible, but may not be the most appropriate tool for clients to manage risk. For example, dowries and school fees – events that cause financial stress, but which occur with greater certainty – can often be more effectively covered through access to savings rather than insurance. In developed markets, people tend to use savings or credit before insurance against most risks. Why should poor households be any different? If an MFI's clients don't yet have access to flexible savings and credit, MFIs and donors should consider that providing insurance may be premature, particularly in the light of recent evidence showcasing the success of innovative savings products and collection systems (Rutherford, 1999; Wright, 1998). Moreover, MFIs are more likely to have the expertise and resources to offer savings products. Insurance, as Part III of this paper describes, is another matter altogether.

Box 5.2 The dismal history of crop insurance

To improve the ability of rural farmers to repay loans from agricultural development banks (ADBs), many governments developed crop insurance programmes in the 1970s and 1980s. These programmes typically provided loan repayment and occasionally income supplements to farmers suffering crop yields below an established minimum. Similar programmes were developed in countries as diverse as Brazil, India, the Philippines and the USA. In each country the results were disastrous, with expenses (administrative and claims) totalling 2 to 5 times revenues in any given year. The failure of these programmes was, in large measure, the result of trying to provide insurance in uninsurable conditions:

o *Unspecific coverage*: By guaranteeing a minimum crop yield, these programmes were essentially insuring against all possible causes of poor crop yield, a virtually endless list of risks.
o *Covariant losses:* Many of the programmes were bankrupted when a drought or other natural calamity hit the region in which the programme operated, affecting most of the insured members at the same time.
o *Moral hazard:* Farmers were less likely to follow sound husbandry practices because all severe yield losses were protected, leading to an increase in claims.
o *Balance of risks*: Coverage was often focused in specific geographic regions and provided only for poor farmers, essentially covering only the highest risks.

Can coverage be provided that is both affordable and financially viable?

Even in situations where these first two criteria have been met (clients are interested in reducing their vulnerability, and the cause of the vulnerability is insurable), MFIs may experience challenges in designing coverage that is both affordable for clients and financially viable for the institution. Confirming affordability can be difficult, as clients will often say that they 'cannot' afford the full cost of a product when it is described to them in general, but are willing to pay when they are presented with a product that meets their needs and demonstrates clear value to them.

If an MFI can confidently answer the preceding three questions in the affirmative, there probably is a potential market among their clients for a certain type of insurance. It does not necessarily follow, however, that the MFI should meet these needs on its own. For most MFIs and most types of insurance, there is a strong logic to form a partnership with an established insurer to deliver insurance benefits to their clients. This is the focus of Part II, which describes the rationale for these partnerships and identifies how an MFI can negotiate with potential partners to obtain the best coverage possible.

Part II: Responding to client demand through partnerships

If demand for insurance has been established, the challenge is to determine the most effective strategy to create, deliver, and manage the product for long-term profitability and client satisfaction.

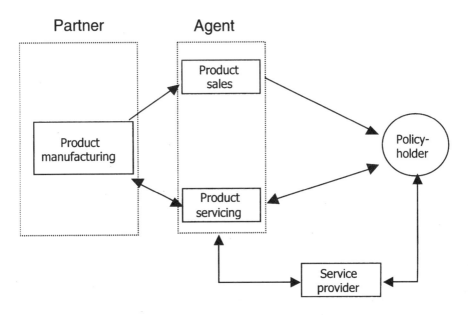

Figure 5.2   *The partner–agent model of insurance delivery*

The most common mechanism used by formal insurers to get insurance products into the hands of consumers is through agents. Agents act as an intermediary between an insurance company – mutually owned, private or public sector – and its market. They perform the sales and servicing activities of the insurer to improve efficiency for both the consumer and the company. This model has proven effective in developed insurance markets with the entire range of products, including life, health, disability and property insurance. More recently, several MFIs have successfully used this model to provide insurance benefits to their clients.

In an MFI–insurer partnership, the MFI acts as the *agent,* marketing and selling the product to its existing clientele through the distribution network it has already established for its other financial services. The insurance provider acts as the *partner*, providing the actuarial, financial and claims-processing expertise, as well as the capital required for initial investments and reserves as required by law. The partner also generally manages the relationship with external service providers involved in claims provision (e.g. health care provider, funeral home). Figure 5.2 illustrates a partnership arrangement.

The experiences of a number of MFIs suggest that partnering can be beneficial not only to the MFI, but to their partners and clients as well.

MFI benefits. For the MFI, the potential benefits of partnering include:

○ limited initial capital investment and low variable costs
○ rapid product launch and scaling-up
○ compliance with legal and regulatory requirements
○ potential for stable revenue stream from commissions, and
○ opportunities to learn the business without taking on the risk.

Partner benefits. For insurance companies that partner with MFIs, there can also be a variety of benefits:

○ access to new markets
○ access to clientele with verifiable financial records
○ reduced transaction costs in serving a new market
○ improved political or public image, and
○ compliance with licensing requirements in some countries (e.g. in India), which stipulate that an insurer maintains a certain portion of its portfolio in low-income areas.

Client benefits. Low-income clients who traditionally have not had access to insurance protection may be the greatest beneficiaries of the partner–agent model. Preliminary evidence suggests that this model allows greater insurance coverage at a lower cost than if an MFI designs and provides the coverage on its own. For example, of the insurance schemes studied by the author, most of the MFI-designed programmes that provide their own life assurance tied to their loans limited the coverage to just the outstanding loan balance, occasionally offering small additional benefits (US$25–100). The cost of this coverage ranged from 0.5–2 per cent of the loan value. In contrast, the products offered through an insurer–MFI partnership provided larger additional benefits (US$800–1000), often against a greater number of risks, for premiums of 0.35–0.5 per cent.

Challenges of the partner–agent model

The partner–agent model is not, however, without its challenges. Several factors may limit or prevent an MFI from partnering with an established insurer to provide coverage to its clients.

Limited availability of potential partners. In some markets, there may be few or no insurers available or interested in partnering with an MFI, although an increasing number of formal insurers are becoming interested in the area. The challenge for MFIs is to understand how to communicate the opportunity to potential partners in a way that will be meaningful and understood by organizations unfamiliar with the development sector.

Coverage of more complex risks. Most existing partner–agent relationships tend to provide the least complex form of insurance: basic life coverage. Until they have more experience with the low-income market, potential partner insurers may be reluctant to provide coverage against more complex risks.

Difficulties ensuring rapid repayment of claims. Given the relative size of the claims, partner insurers may place little importance on processing claims requests, unless a specific process is established for processing microinsurance claims.

Difficulties in negotiating an equal partnership. Because most MFIs know little about what they should attempt to negotiate in establishing a partnership with a formal insurer, the MFIs often end up with less-than-ideal partnerships. MFIs should, at a minimum, carefully consider the commissions to be paid to the MFI, the exclusions from the policy and the information requirements for submitting a claim to ensure that a formal insurer's offer is congruous with the realities of low-income policyholders and beneficial to the MFI. Box 5.3 provides a brief set of guidelines to assist MFIs in selecting a partner.

Equally important to the development of productive partnerships is for MFIs to improve their abilities to market their services to potential insurer partners. MFIs are more likely to attract established insurers and to negotiate a rewarding partnership if they are:

o conversant with the details of insurance operations
o confident in their understanding of clients' needs and preferences for insurance coverage (other publications that will assist MFIs in conducting market research and understanding the insurance business include Brand, 2000, and Brown and Churchill, 2000), and
o convincing in demonstrating their capacity to sell and service insurance policies professionally.

> ## Box 5.3 Due diligence checklist for selecting a partner
>
> Before selecting a partner insurance provider, an MFI should consider the follow-
> ing list of questions. While they are not 'hard and fast' requirements for selection,
> they do provide good talking points with which to begin a conversation with a poten-
> tial insurance provider.
>
> o What is the national reputation of the insurance provider?
> o How is the insurer currently financed? Does it have a stable, conservative asset
>   portfolio?
> o What is the claims experience of the insurer and their history of claims payouts?
>   Are they willing to guarantee a fast turnaround on claims from MFI clients?
> o How interested is the insurer in serving the low-income market?
> o Will the insurer adjust their products so that they are responsive to the needs
>   and preferences of low-income households?
> o Are they willing to make a medium- or long-term commitment to the MFI?
> o Are they willing to pay a commission to the MFI for performing the agent role?
> o Are there issues related to regulatory compliance?
> o Will the insurer give the MFI responsibility for verifying claims?
> o What can the insurer do to minimize the number of exclusions, without jeop-
>   ardizing the sustainability of the plan?

Part III: An insurer's capabilities

In spite of the arguments against doing so, we recognize that, driven by a lack of suitable partners or the desire for greater premium revenues, some MFIs will elect to develop and manage insurance products on their own. Consequently, Part III summarizes the prerequisites for the provision of insurance in seven areas, highlighting common problems for MFI-run insurance schemes. These can be thought of as pre-conditions that MFIs ought to satisfy before developing a self-managed insurance product. It is important to note that the level of complexity and required resources and skills for the following activities are much greater for health and property insurance than for life assurance.

(1) Actuarial analysis (pricing)

For an insurance scheme to be viable, premiums must be high enough to cover future claims and, consequently, managers need to be able to predict, with a reasonable degree of accuracy, what future claims will be. If these predictions prove to be inaccurate, unexpectedly high insurance claims can decapitalize an institution. MFI-designed and managed programmes tend to encounter difficulties in three areas:

Estimating future losses. Although experience can often provide a reasonable estimate of potential future losses, few MFIs use this information to set prices. Where reasonable historical information is not available or where historical averages are not likely to reflect future losses – in many countries HIV/AIDS, for example, is radically changing the average death rates – pricing should incorporate a sufficient margin of error to reflect the uncertainty in future claims behaviour.

Establishing reserves. In addition to covering claims and administrative expenses, insurance premiums need to establish reserves. Reserves are funds set aside each year to protect the insurer against unexpectedly high claims. If claims expenses exceed annual premium revenues, claims are paid out of the reserves and the scheme remains solvent. For this reason, insurance regulations typically require a new insurer to provide a minimum initial amount of capital before starting operations. MFIs, however, typically have limited liquid reserves, leaving them exposed to unexpectedly high losses, particularly during the early years.

Reinsurance. Reinsurance is the shifting of part or all of the insurance risk originally written by one insurer to another insurer. Formal insurers use reinsurance to limit this risk in both new and established lines of business. To date, no such reinsurance is available to MFIs that offer insurance on their own (except for an experiment being conducted by the ILO's Social Finance Unit, supported by the World Bank, in creating a reinsurance scheme for community-based health insurance schemes). This leaves them highly exposed to small fluctuations in claims expenses.

(2) Marketing

Marketing of microinsurance involves more than just selling policies. Experience indicates that for a programme to be successful, the MFI must also educate prospective clients about the potential benefits and cost of the product and ensure that consumers know how to 'use' it (e.g. how to make claims). Marketing of insurance is also less straightforward than credit or savings because clients must be willing to continue to pay premiums even when they are not receiving any direct benefits. With this in mind, MFIs should consider the following marketing-related questions:

o *Do the staff that will be marketing the product have the training, materials, knowledge and time required to sell, educate and train clients?* Marketing insurance can be a multi-stage process (see Box 5.4). Even if the insurance is to be mandatory, training is needed to ensure that loan officers feel comfortable marketing the product and can answer clients' questions and guide them through the claims process.

o *How will the MFI ensure that clients are not being coerced or unduly pressured to purchase the proposed product, particularly if the product is to be mandatory for all borrowers or savers?* Several private insurers, particularly in different parts of Africa, have become profitable by selling a good volume of policies to poor households. However, in many cases these new policyholders did not understand what they were purchasing or how to make a claim. Without mechanisms to monitor client satisfaction, MFI-offered insurance policies that are mandatory for borrowers or savers run the risk of exploiting MFIs' existing relationships with clients, and potentially damaging the MFIs' loan or savings portfolios.

Box 5.4 Multistage marketing at GRET

In order to market its health insurance, GRET designed a multistage information session approach. Before making insurance available in a village, GRET uses two 'promoters' to generate interest in the insurance and answer questions. These promoters, in agreement with the commune head, organize a group meeting for all commune members (usually about 2000 members) to explain the basics of the insurance. Using a graphics-intensive presentation, the promoters explain what insurance is, how GRET's system works, and how benefits will be provided.

A week after this initial meeting, the promoters return to the village to have conversations with individual families. At the end of these conversations, the families are informed that the insurance agent – who is responsible for selling policies and collecting premiums – will return the following week to ask if they want to purchase a policy.

---

(3) Underwriting

Underwriting is the process of verifying whether insurance coverage should be provided to a particular potential policyholder. Typically this involves confirming that the potential policyholder meets the eligibility criteria determined by the MFI. For example, if a life assurance policy excludes death due to pre-existing illnesses, the underwriting process needs to document all illnesses existing when a policy is purchased. MFIs need to consider the following questions:

○ *Can the MFI check or confirm the accuracy of the information provided by the prospective client?* If prospective policyholders can misrepresent their age, health status or other relevant information, an MFI may unknowingly change the risk profile of its portfolio. In a small programme, the inclusion of even a handful of high-risk policyholders may lead to serious unexpected losses.
○ *Can the MFI monitor changes in the characteristics of the market and its portfolio, which may change the nature of the risk it has assumed?* If the characteristics of the market and the insured portfolio change over time, this may change the nature of the risk that has been insured. For example, if the average age of policyholders in a life insurance portfolio increases from 35 to 40 over time, the probability of claims will also increase.
○ *To avoid adverse selection, will a large percentage of the market be insured?* If the insured population is only a small percentage of the potential market (as would be the case for most MFIs, given their small size), stronger underwriting procedures are needed to avoid adverse selection.

(4) Investment management

While the majority of premium income is needed to cover administrative and claims expenses, the difference in time and value between receipt of premiums and payment of claims and expenses gives an insurance plan the opportunity to earn investment income. The investment manager must balance the desire to earn greater investment returns and the need to maintain sufficient liquidity to meet claims and expenses. With this in mind, MFIs should ask the following two questions:

o *Are any of the insurance premiums or reserves intended to be invested in the MFI's capital fund?* Many MFIs are tempted to use insurance premiums as an additional source of capital to fund their loan portfolio. Initially, this may seem like a wise decision: funds invested in an MFI's loan portfolio may bring in more revenue than funds invested in a savings account or similarly liquid instrument. However, unless an MFI is fully operationally sustainable, funds invested in its loan portfolio will actually shrink rather than grow over time. In addition, if an MFI needs to use its insurance reserves to pay unexpected claims, it cannot quickly call in the illiquid loans it has made with the policyholders' premiums. Furthermore, in many cases, using insurance reserves for on-lending is illegal.

o *How will the insurance plan deal with inflationary cost increases, particularly in high-inflation environments?* This is a particularly thorny issue for health and property insurance that promise to provide certain services or replacement assets in the future in exchange for taking a premium today. If the premiums received today are not earning a real rate of return, they will probably be insufficient to cover the higher cost of claims in the future.

(5) Claims management

The systems and staff responsible for verifying whether a claim should be paid out, and for ensuring that claims are processed quickly, are key. Verification ensures that fraudulent claims are not made, while processing time is a key factor in policyholders' satisfaction with the product. Key questions to consider in assessing an MFI's capability to manage claims include:

o *Have processes been developed to verify that only claims covered by the insurance are paid out?* Do the staff responsible for verification have the knowledge and information needed to assess the validity of claims with accuracy and consistency? For life assurance claims, the MFI must have procedures to handle situations in which the body is not available and to ensure that local staff cannot collude with clients to 'verify' fraudulent claims. For health and property insurance, the difficulties in verifying claims are greater. For health insurance, claims verification involves a whole range of checks, including, for example, photo ID verification to confirm that a patient is indeed insured and detailed tracking information to ensure that certain doctors or patients are not making an unusually high numbers of claims. Verification of property insurance claims can also be problematic because the cause of the loss is not always readily apparent. For example, it is difficult for an MFI to determine whether a fire that destroys an insured asset was an accident or deliberate.

○ *Can the MFI reasonably ensure that claims will be processed in a timely fashion?* Based on current experience, a turnaround time of two weeks or less for life insurance claims is reasonable. The fastest performers pay out claims the same day. For health insurance, payments are often made monthly between the health care provider and the insurance plan. If clients are reimbursed by the insurance plan for medical expenses incurred, claims processing times need to be less than a few days if the coverage is to be truly valuable to clients. Standard claims processing times for property microinsurance have yet to be established, however standards of 1–3 weeks should be a reasonable objective.

(6) Product management and administration

Co-ordination and communication among all of the activities mentioned thus far is crucial to the smooth operation of an insurance product. Without effective management and administration of this communication and information sharing, insurance plans can quickly run into financial difficulties. Two areas where many MFI's lack the capability to manage the full range of activities involved in offering an insurance product include management information systems and management time/expertise:

○ *Does the MFI have the IT and management systems required to collect and generate the information needed to manage an insurance plan effectively?* Access to up-to-date, accurate information is crucial to the success of an insurance plan. Particularly for health and property insurance, even a one- to two-month lag in access to claims information can hide potential problems long enough for them to become serious. Manual accounting systems and processes, while simple and cost-effective, are probably inappropriate for all but the most basic forms of insurance.
○ *Does MFI management have the additional time and knowledge necessary to manage effectively a new insurance product?* In addition to the time and effort needed to develop a product, MFI management will need to dedicate time to manage the product once it has been launched. If an MFI is currently having difficulties with its credit portfolio, for example, management's time may be better spent focused on that issue rather than on a new product.

(7) Regulatory compliance

Can an MFI provide insurance legally? Insurance regulations mandate that providers maintain substantial reserves, report regular financial results and have trained underwriting and sales staff. Given the small size of microinsurance policies, these regulations can unintentionally restrict an MFI's ability to provide insurance profitably to the low-income market. Therefore, many MFIs offer their insurance products at the margins of the law. While there are differing perspectives on this activity, all MFIs thinking about offering insurance should consider the following questions:

○ *Does the plan for the proposed insurance product at least comply with the 'spirit' of the insurance regulations, if not the actual regulations themselves?* Minimum capital requirements and other regulations may be inappropriately high for an organization serving a low-income market, but an MFI should still be able to demonstrate that it has sufficient capital and reserves to cover any reasonable, unexpected losses. Insurance regulations also typically require that insurers provide regular reports on their financial status to the relevant body; there is no reason why MFIs should not be able to do the same. In addition, MFIs should be able to demonstrate that policies are being sold in an open and fair manner and that clients are not being misled in the sales process.

○ *If an MFI does plan to operate an unregulated insurance product, is it reasonable to assume that local regulators will allow this to happen? For how long?* Some MFIs may be able to avoid regulations if they are offering only basic life assurance tied to their loans, but will this ability continue indefinitely? What will happen if they want to offer more coverage? The deregulation of the insurance industry in India has recently forced SEWA to decide whether to formalize their insurance offerings or find an alternative way to provide this coverage.

Conclusion: a future for microinsurance

There is little doubt that many of the risks faced by the low-income clients served by MFIs are insurable, and, in these cases, well-designed microinsurance products can have an important development impact. The challenge is to ensure that the product being developed (1) is appropriate for the needs and preferences of the households, (2) is financially viable and (3) is provided through institutions that have the resources and expertise to manage the finances and the risk inherent in the product.

MFIs possess some, but not all, of the resources required to get the job done. With the possible exception of life assurance, most MFIs lack the key expertise and resources needed to provide these microinsurance products sustainably and profitably. Fortunately for MFIs interested in entering the microinsurance market, the most likely source for these resources and expertise – established insurers – lack the client knowledge and distribution network in the micro market that MFIs possess, creating the opportunity for win-win partnerships.

Experience suggests that if an MFI is to develop an insurance product, it is best to start with a very limited product, developed and managed in partnership with an established insurer. Over time, as the MFI develops experience in handling insurance products and collects information on utilization, it may consider taking the product in-house. In general, however, complex health and property products should be avoided by individual MFIs unless a suitable partner is available.

The questions in this paper should encourage donors to assess frankly the ability of an MFI to manage a proposed insurance product, particularly if the MFI has no partner with whom the risk can be shared. Donors should also question the opportunity cost of an MFI's focus on insurance product development, particularly if there are existing problems with the institution's portfolio quality or operational efficiency.

References

Brand, Monica, (2000), 'The MBP guide to new product development', prepared for the USAID Microenterprise Best Practices Project, Development Alternatives, Inc., Bethesda, Maryland.

Brown, Warren and Craig Churchill, (1999), 'Providing insurance to low-income households: Part I – a primer on insurance principles and products', Microenterprise Best Practices Project, Development Alternatives Inc. Bethesda, Maryland (http://www.mip.org/pubs/mbp-def.htm).

Brown, Warren and Craig Churchill, (2000), 'Providing insurance to low-income households: Parts I and II', Microenterprise Best Practices Project, Development Alternatives Inc. Bethesda, Maryland (http://www.mip.org/pubs/mbp-def.htm).

Brown, Warren, Colleen Green and Gordon Lindquist, (2001), 'Cautionary note for MFIs and donors considering developing microinsurance products', USAID's Microenterprise Best Practices (MBP) research facility.

Cohen, Monique, and Jennifer Sebstad, (2000), 'Microfinance and risk management: A client perspective', AIMS Paper, USAID, Washington, DC.

Hazell, (1992), 'The appropriate role of agricultural insurance in developing countries', *Journal of International Development*, Vol. 4 , No. 6, pp. 567–82.

Rutherford, Stuart, (1999), *The poor and their money: an essay about financial services for poor people,* Department for International Development (DFID), New Delhi, India.

Wright, Graham, (1998), *Beyond basic credit and savings: developing new financial services products for the poor,* MicroSave-Africa.

About the author

Warren Brown is Director of ACCION International's Research and Development Department. Much of the work incorporated in this paper took place while Warren was with Calmeadow as a Microfinance Research Specialist. The author is indebted to many people for their assistance, including: Colleen Green; Gordon Lindquist; Monique Cohen; Peg Birk; Michael McCord; Zan Northrip; Craig Churchill and USAID's Microenterprise Best Practices Project for their support to produce the longer paper on which this is based: Brown and Churchill (2000). This paper also summarizes a more detailed report by Brown, Green and Lindquist.

6 Regulating microfinance – the options

ROBERT PECK CHRISTEN and RICHARD ROSENBERG

This paper was first published in December 2000.

The regulation of microfinance is being discussed all over the world. The incentive for many MFIs is the legal right to accept deposits for on-lending, and thereby to expand the scope of their programmes. Other actors may have different motivations that may not be beneficial to microfinance, such as the desire on the part of many governments to impose interest rate ceilings.

This paper cautions against the 'rush to regulate'. It first outlines the practical problems faced by bank supervisors who are asked to take responsibility for MFIs, and points to the costs of supervising MFIs. The various options for regulation are discussed, and the recommendations include the following:

○ *Credit-only MFIs should generally not be subject to prudential regulation in which the government supervisory agency is expected to monitor the financial soundness of the licensed institution.*
○ *Small community-based MFIs should not be prohibited from deposit taking just because they are too small or remote to be regulated effectively.*
○ *The push to create special regulatory windows for MFIs may make sense in a few developing countries, but in most it is probably premature at present, running too far ahead of the organic development of the local microfinance industry.*
○ *Self-regulation by MFI-controlled federations is highly unlikely to be effective.*

FORMAL CREDIT AND SAVINGS for the poor are not recent inventions: for decades some customers neglected by commercial banks have been served by credit co-operatives and development finance institutions. These organizations have legal charters that govern their financial operations and allow them access to savings or other public funding. But the past two decades have seen the emergence of powerful new methodologies for delivering microfinance services, especially microcredit. Much of this innovation has been pioneered by NGOs, who typically do not have a legal charter authorizing them to engage in financial intermediation. Governments, donors, and practitioners are now talking about new legal structures for microfinance in dozens of countries. Much of the attention is focused on NGO microfinance (though it is worth noting that, even today, most of the world's microfinance clients are served by banks, credit unions, and other licensed institutions).

Regulation of microfinance is being discussed in one country after another. But the people doing the discussing are often motivated by differing objectives, which tends to confuse the dialogue:

○ Looking to fund themselves, NGOs with microcredit operations often want to be licensed (and thus regulated) in order to access deposits from the public, or credit lines from donors or governments.

○ Sometimes NGOs believe that regulation will promote their business and improve their operations.

○ Some NGOs and governments want financial licences to be more widely available in order to expand savings services for the poor.

○ Donors and governments may expect that setting up a special regulatory window for microfinance will speed the emergence of sustainable MFIs.

○ Occasionally, where unlicensed MFIs are already taking deposits, the central bank's motivation in pushing to license them is to protect depositors.

○ Many MFIs charge surprisingly high interest rates. Government may view these rates as exploitative and want to protect small borrowers.

○ Occasionally governments look to regulation as a means of clamping down on bothersome foreign-funded NGOs or other groups that it would like to control more tightly.

○ In some countries there is simply no legal structure under which a group can lawfully provide loans to poor clients. Unless such a structure is developed, loans may be legally uncollectable.

For all these reasons, microfinance today seems to find itself in the midst of a rush to regulate. There is no shortage of people willing to offer views on when and how to do it. Experimentation with supervision is so recent, however, that we can't rely much on its historical results to guide us. So readers looking for one-size-fits-all advice may be frustrated here.

We should like to start by stating our belief that the future of microfinance lies in a licensed setting, because it is the only setting that will permit massive, sustainable delivery of financial services to the poor. Thus, the cautionary overall message of this paper is not meant to question the importance of microfinance regulation and supervision, which are essential to any licensed framework. Rather, we are raising questions about timing, and about certain expectations that may turn out to be inflated. In focusing heavily on certain problems, we don't want to imply that they have no solutions – only that they are problems that need to be dealt with realistically.

The supervisor's challenges

The problems of bank supervisors (meaning, the government official responsible for prudential oversight of financial institutions) in poor countries may not sound like a 'visionary' place to start our reflections. But unless we give this subject its due, our planning of frameworks can lead us into an alluring dreamland of elegant structures that cannot be implemented. The most carefully conceived regulations will be useless, or worse, if they can't be enforced by effective supervision.

For bank supervisors in many developing countries (though certainly not all), the central fact of life is responsibility for supervising a commercial banking system with severe structural problems, often including some sizable banks teetering dangerously close to the edge of safety. The collapse of one – or a half-dozen – of these banks could threaten the country's financial system with implosion. In trying to manage bank risk, the supervisor may have to work in a political minefield,

---

**Box 6.1   Rural banks in the Philippines: the burden of supervising
small intermediaries**

In the Philippines, the smallest licensed intermediaries are 'rural banks'.
Supervised by the central bank, they are integrated into the payments system. Their
operations include credit and deposit services for relatively poor clients. As of
September 1997, 824 rural banks were serving half a million clients. These banks
had only about 2 per cent of the banking system's assets and deposits, but they
made up 83 per cent of the institutions the central bank had to supervise. Branches
of the 52 commercial banks outnumbered offices of the 824 rural banks by more
than 2 to 1.

Supervising the rural banks has severely stretched the resources of the
Philippine central bank's supervision department, tying up as much as one-half of
its total staff and budgetary resources at times. In the early 1990s one in every five
rural banks had to be shut down, and many others had to be merged or otherwise
restructured. A 1996 report estimated that 200 inspectors were assigned to the
rural banks. Even this level of resources was viewed as inadequate.

Minimum capitalization of $100 000 to $1 000 000 in equity is now required to
constitute a rural bank, depending on the size of the municipality where the bank is
located. According to the 1996 report, the experience with the Philippine rural
banks showed that minimum capital for such institutions should be set higher rather
than lower, in order to provide more stability and to rationalize the demands on the
financial authorities.

---

because the owners of banks are seldom under-represented in the political
process. Monitoring healthy banks is challenging enough, but the real problems
come when it is time to deal with institutions in trouble. When a sick bank finally
crumbles, its president can start sleeping again (though perhaps in a different
country), while the supervisor has to stay awake at night worrying. The minister
of finance may be pacing the floor with her, since in many countries a govern-
ment-issued financial licence carries with it a guarantee, implicit or explicit, that
the government will bail out depositors if a licensed institution collapses.

If a bank supervisor displays resistance to adding MFIs – mostly small, mostly
new, mostly weak on profitability – to her basket of responsibilities, we should
recognize that her reasons might be better than narrow-mindedness or a lack of
concern for the poor.

Ownership issues

Even the supervisor who is willing to oversee MFIs faces serious challenges, not
all of which are obvious. The most basic problem stems from ownership structure. The ownership of a commercial bank typically includes persons with large
amounts from their own private pockets at risk in the bank. Such owners want a
financial return from the bank, and can get it only after all others' claims are paid
off. They have a strong incentive to watch the performance of the bank's

---

Box 6.2 Finansol (Colombia): non-profit governance problems

Corposol, a leading Latin American microcredit NGO, acquired a licensed finance company and renamed it Finansol. Corposol held a controlling share in the licensed company. The same was true for PRODEM and BancoSol in Bolivia. But, unlike PRODEM, Corposol from the beginning subordinated Finansol to its broader agenda, treating it simply as an instrument to capture commercial funding. Initially, Finansol was given only the staff necessary to run a back office for the loan port-folio. Corposol and loan officers on its payroll continued to manage all loans. Yet Finansol was accountable to the authorities for the quality of the loan portfolio – a fact that introduced a constant tension in the Corposol–Finansol relationship.

This dual structure was justified as a means to avoid the interest-rate cap placed on Finansol by Colombia's usury law. With the tacit consent of the authorities, the NGO Corposol was able to charge a 'training fee' that was not included in calculat-ing the finance company's effective interest rate for purposes of the usury limit. The training fee was far higher than actual training costs, generating about 40 per cent of Corposol/Finansol's total income, and covering almost all administrative expenses of the two entities.

Later on, Corposol used this dual structure to deflect another regulation. To con-trol inflation, in 1995 the central bank restricted loan portfolio growth in banks to 2 per cent annually. Corposol/Finansol evaded this limit by simply moving loans into the NGO, making the true portfolio situation even less transparent. Corposol man-agement could move the portfolio back and forth between the companies at will, with little concern for arm's-length pricing.

The board of directors included respected and successful Colombian business people. None of them had substantial amounts of their own money at risk, and it turned out that they did not have enough incentive to scrutinize management's per-formance seriously. The board did not require of management the basic reports necessary to evaluate the performance of Corposol's diverse activities; nor did they act decisively when the failures finally became apparent. It took external reviews – ACCION'S CAMEL exercise, and later the bank superintendency's inspection – to reveal the depth of mismanagement. By then it was too late. Corposol folded com-pletely, huge loan losses were incurred, and Finansol survived only by the skin of its teeth.

---

manager closely to make sure that this performance is consistent with the health of their investment. This kind of owner is a very important line of defence for the safety of the bank. The supervisor cares about capital adequacy ratios, not just to provide a cushion in time of problems, but also to ensure that the owners con-tinue to have enough incentive to watch management closely.

Most of today's MFIs do not have this kind of ownership: money from private, profit-seeking pockets seldom accounts for much of their equity base. Almost all MFIs have a governing board that is supposed to provide independent oversight of management. But where members serve on that board for altruistic reasons and do not have serious amounts of their own money at risk, with a few heroic exceptions they tend not to look over management's shoulder the same way business investors do. The problem derives not from the personal quality of MFI board members, but rather from the organic structure of their incentives. This ownership problem is not solved just by getting a banking licence (see Box 6.2).

Supervisory tools

One of the supervisor's most powerful tools when a financial institution gets into trouble is the capital call: she tells the owners, 'Put more capital into your bank to shore it up, or else I'll close you down.' If the supervisor has caught the problem early enough, the owners are likely to comply, in order to avoid losing the capital they have already committed to the bank. (Note that commercial bank owners tend to be people who can come up with additional money at short notice; many countries make this a condition of getting a licence.) Capital calls lose much of their power, however, when applied to a typical MFI, as the Colombian bank supervisor discovered in the case of Finansol (see Box 6.3).

Another common supervisor's tool is to order a temporary halt to new lending until a problem is cleared up. A commercial bank can often stop new loans without jeopardizing the collectability of its existing loans. MFIs cannot. The main reason their clients repay is their expectation of reliable and responsive

---

Box 6.3 The collapse of Finansol: a bank supervisor's limited options

In February of 1996 the Colombian bank superintendency halted new lending by Finansol, a licensed MFI, because of escalating repayment problems. Three months later, the superintendent declared Finansol to be technically insolvent – loan losses had wiped out over half of its equity during the year. (The lending freeze had worsened Finansol's repayment problem: when the word got out that clients couldn't get new loans, many stopped repaying their old ones.) The superintendency issued a capital call, requiring the finance company's owners to recapitalize it within 60 days.

Donor agencies proved either unwilling or unable to help with the recapitalization. The initial private bailout plan, backed by the prestige of both ACCION International and Citibank, failed. Uncertainty about the recoverability of Finansol loans scared private investors away.

Given the tattered state of the Finansol portfolio, and the fact that it was largely unsecured, the superintendent had little chance of finding a merger partner for the failing finance company. There was little choice but to extend the recapitalization deadline: the only alternative was to close Finansol down and watch its unsecured portfolio become completely uncollectable. ACCION, Profund, Citibank and others participated with good faith money, but their contributions fell far short of the investment required. Ultimately Finansol could be saved only because a government apex, Finansol's principal creditor, was forced to surrender most of its debt in return for shares of equity as the only hope of recovering anything substantial from the disaster.

future services. If the MFI denies prompt follow-up loans to clients who have punctually repaid prior loans, the MFI is breaching an implicit contract with its customers, many of whom will stop repaying their *existing* loans the minute the word gets out. Thus, a stop lending order to an MFI will wipe out the institution's loan portfolio if kept in place for very long (see Box 6.3 for an example of this).

A related problem is that an MFI's principal asset consists of micro-loans that have little value once they are out of the hands of the team that originated the loan. When a bank is in trouble, the supervisor's first choice will often be to 'encourage' acquisition by, or merger with, a stronger bank. Many of the sick bank's loans are backed by collateral or guarantees, so the borrowers' incentive to repay is not tied to their relationship with the sick bank. But if the sick organization's only assets are unsecured microloans, the picture is less encouraging. Once clients' confidence in the MFI as a going concern is shaken, they tend to stop paying their loans, and collection of these loans can cost more than the amounts recovered. A healthy MFI will seldom be interested in taking over such a contaminated portfolio.

While on the subject of supervisors' tools, there are also problems with monitoring microcredit loan portfolio quality, the main locus of risk for most MFIs. Some of the traditional inspection and audit tools that bank supervisors use turn out not to work very well in evaluating microloan portfolio risk. Formal procedures don't work well with tiny unsecured loans to informal borrowers – for instance, reviewing amount and registration of collateral, or mailing letters to clients to confirm account balances. Wholesale renegotiation of troubled loans is a common problem in MFIs; detecting it is a burdensome process requiring extensive review of individual loan records and on-site visits to a large proportion of branches.

Supervisors can't place meaningful reliance on independent external audits of MFIs; at least as such audits are practised now. The authors have yet to encounter an audit of an MFI that included procedures sufficient to warrant real confidence about the state of its portfolio. (The problems with MFIs' external audits are discussed in CGAP, 1998).

Better portfolio-monitoring techniques can be transferred to supervisory agencies through technical assistance. We must recognize, though, that the road is often rockier than expected. In Bolivia, the bank superintendency has received lavish support for training and technical assistance from at least three different donors to build new systems and skills to handle non-bank financial institutions. Seven years into the process, it is still far from complete. In this institution, stronger staff have repeatedly been pulled off – no doubt for good reasons – to deal with commercial banks in trouble.

The point of this daunting catalogue of obstacles is not that supervision of microfinance is impossible – only that it involves serious challenges that are not always taken into account when discussing legal frameworks.

In Peru and Bolivia the supervisory agencies appear so far to be doing a creditable job of supervising MFIs. But it is important to note that both of these countries had greatly improved their capacity to supervise commercial banks *before* specialized MFIs were added to the supervisor's responsibilities. Unlike MFIs, commercial banks pose systemic risk, because the failure of one or more of them can imperil the country's financial structure. Thus, it could be argued that supervisory attention and resources, including donor assistance, should not be diverted away from bank supervision until that difficult task is being managed effectively.

The costs of supervision

The costs of the supervisory agency itself tend to be relatively low in the case of banks – for instance, $1 per $1000 of assets supervised – and can usually be passed on to the banks and their customers. Supervision of MFIs is likely to be much more expensive, given the MFIs' generally smaller asset base, their much larger number of accounts, their high degree of decentralization, and finally the more labour-intensive nature of inspecting their portfolio. For a decentralized MFI of 10 000 clients, we could easily imagine supervision costs from 1 to 5 per cent of assets, which may have to be passed on to the MFI and its clients. The MFI might be able to absorb these costs, but these are just the supervisor's costs. What about the costs to the supervised institution?

BancoSol's chief financial officer estimated that complying with the bank superintendency's reporting requirements cost an amount equal to about 5 per cent of portfolio in the bank's first year of operations, declining to an estimated 1 per cent by the last year, over and above what BancoSol would be spending for its own information needs.

There are substantial non-financial costs as well. Regulation can cramp competition and stifle innovation. The act of writing a set of rules for microfinance involves the rulemaker in a certain amount of 'model building' – making decisions as to what kinds of institutions are the best to do microfinance, and sometimes even what kind of loan methodologies are best. If Latin American NGOs had not been allowed to experiment with microcredit products that were inconsistent with the legal provisions of the regulated financial system, it is hard to imagine how microfinance in the region could have flowered as it did.

Regulation and interest rates

There is one potential 'cost of regulation' that deserves separate treatment. Pushing governments to develop legal frameworks for microfinance may result in the imposition of interest rate controls. These controls can make sustainable microcredit impossible, or at least discourage outreach to poorer customers.

Even the most efficient MFIs have found it impossible to reduce their administrative costs much below about 10 to 25 per cent of their portfolio, depending on methodology, loan size, and location. By contrast, comparable costs in an efficient developing country commercial bank are usually below 5 per cent, often well below. A sustainable MFI – that is, one that could pay commercial cost for its funding without losing money – must therefore charge an interest rate that could sound obscene in the normal commercial bank market or in the arena of political discussion. The lower the usury limit, the more borrowers there are at the low end of the spectrum who cannot be served sustainably.

When modern microcredit emerged in Latin America, almost all of the countries had legal limits on interest rates. These limits were set far too low for sustainable microcredit. Most of the microcredit pioneers practised regulatory avoidance by mounting their operations in NGOs. The authorities were unconcerned with their existence. Innovation flourished, minor disasters abounded, and out of the ferment emerged a critical mass of successful MFIs that were strong enough to justify a formal financial licence. In the meantime, government policy and public attitudes about interest rates had changed (in part because the authorities saw the tremendous demonstrated demand for these high-interest-rate loans), so that by the time strong MFIs were ready for licensing, interest rate repression was no longer an issue in most of the countries. All this happened because the governments involved were not prematurely forced to take a public position on microcredit interest rates.

In West Africa, a framework for microfinance had been promulgated long before the MFIs had reached this stage of maturity, and has included extending usury limits to cover credit-only programmes previously free to make their own pricing decisions (Box 6.4). In Bangladesh, where donors have supported an active dialogue with the central bank on regulation, the central bank president said at a recent conference that one of the main objectives of regulation ought to be to restrain the 'exploitative' interest rates charged by some MFIs.

When groups push to get the regulation train rolling, they need to recognize that the people who end up driving the train may be pursuing objectives quite different from their own.

Who should be regulated?

This is a contentious issue. Should credit-only MFIs be regulated? What about 'member-owned' institutions? What about small ones? Before we discuss each case, some terms should be defined.

Prudential and non-prudential supervision

It is important to distinguish between these: we refer to some requirements as non-prudential, not because they are insubstantial, but because they do not involve the financial authority in vouching for or assuming any responsibility for the soundness of the 'regulated' institution. Examples of such requirements include: registration and legal chartering of licensed entities; disclosure of ownership or control; reporting or publication of financial statements; transparent disclosure of interest rates to consumers; and submission of names of borrowers and status of their loans (on time? late? by how much?) to a central credit information bureau (databases to which all participating lenders provide the names of defaulting clients, or names of all clients along with an indication of their repayment behaviour).

Depending on the combination of elements, a package of non-prudential regulation could be painless, or burdensome in the extreme. But these requirements don't entail the government taking a position on the financial soundness of an

---

Box 6.4 The PARMEC law (West Africa): interest rate restrictions

The West African Monetary Union has long had interest rate controls on the books, but as a practical matter these controls were generally not enforced in the case of credit-only MFIs. In the late 1980s the central bank, with donor assistance, embarked on a major effort to regulate the non-bank financial sector. The new PARMEC law, promulgated in 1993 and ratified by the member countries during 1998, underscored the universal applicability of the usury limits, and made their enforcement much more likely. Many MFI operators are caught in a bind: they can't cover the costs of their programmes without a higher interest rate, but they feel themselves at serious legal risk if they charge sustainable rates.

---

institution. They don't embroil the government in any accountability, explicit or implicit, as an insurer of depositors' losses in the event of failure.

Once we step over this threshold of vouching for soundness, the character of regulation changes dramatically. Prudential regulation and supervision of financial intermediaries involves definition of detailed standards for financial structure, accounting policies, and other important dimensions of an institution's business. Enforcing these standards and otherwise monitoring institutional soundness require much more intensive reporting, as well as on-site inspection that goes beyond the scope of normal financial statement audits.

When we refer to 'regulation' in this paper, we are generally discussing prudential, not non-prudential, regulation and supervision.

'Illegal' microcredit

It is illegal in some countries for NGOs to offer credit, because this activity is not specifically authorized in the laws under which NGOs function. In many countries the financial laws, if interpreted strictly, would prohibit anyone without a financial licence from intermediating money (borrowing from one party while lending to another), or from carrying on a business of lending money, regardless of the source of funds. Sometimes the laws don't permit a non-profit organization to generate interest income that exceeds its expenses.

The first question to ask about these laws is whether they are enforced. Many microcredit NGOs operate where such laws are on the books but are unenforced. This kind of benign neglect, a sort of regulation by winking, is a practical alternative that ought to be considered when weighing up regulatory options.

Clearly, there are some countries where existing financial institutions have no interest in microfinance, for the present at least, and where the only near-term alternative for microcredit experimentation and diffusion lies in NGOs and other socially oriented organizations. If the legal framework makes this alternative very difficult *in practice*, then trying to change that framework should be a priority. But this problem can usually be addressed without building a whole structure of prudential regulation for specialized microfinance institutions. One simple option might be to amend the law authorizing NGOs to include credit in their activities.

Credit-only MFIs

When discussing 'credit-only MFIs', we include those that require clients to make savings deposits in order to get loans, as long as they don't mobilize substantial amounts of voluntary deposits. Neither of the classical justifications for prudential regulation apply with much force to such obligatory deposits. (1) Most of the MFI's clients are in a net debtor position most of the time, so the risk to them in the case of the MFI's failure is relatively low. (2) Compulsory deposits pose no significant risk to the country's financial system, not only because their amount is small but also because the restrictions on withdrawal of these deposits greatly reduces the risk of a run on them.

In some situations there may be a reasonable case for *non-prudential* regulation of credit-only MFIs, even though they do not put depositors' money at risk. We would not argue in principle against requiring such MFIs to register and identify the parties that control them; to give clients transparent interest rate information; to produce financial statements in a meaningful format; or even to participate in a credit bureau. Even this regulation, however, can entail risks. In some countries each additional governmental requirement represents an opportunity for corruption. And it may be hard in some countries to do non-prudential regulation without bringing interest rate controls into effect.

When we move up from non-prudential level to prudential regulation and supervision, where the supervisor is responsible for the soundness of the licensed institutions, the balance tips decisively against regulation of credit-only MFIs by a government supervisor. As we have discussed already, the costs of such regulation tend to be higher than is generally recognized, and given the serious challenges confronting supervisors in developing countries, there may be a low likelihood that the regulation of these marginal players is going to be effective.

An often-invoked rationale is: 'Most MFIs in this country are weak and do not perform well. We need prudential regulation in order to improve these organizations.' The problem is that bank supervisors aren't usually very good at *improving* bad organizations. They are better at *excluding* bad organizations, or shutting them down.

Small community-based MFIs

The reach of prudential regulation should have some explicit 'lower boundary' that excludes certain classes of smaller intermediaries. To begin with, most countries have many completely informal financial service providers such as moneylenders and ROSCAs (rotating savings and credit associations); prudential regulation of these is practically impossible. But moving up the scale, one finds a grey area of somewhat more formalized organizations – for instance financial co-operatives, community-based building societies, South African *stokvels*, and so on – where the decision about prudential regulation has to balance competing factors. On the one hand, one would like to protect their depositors. But the small size and large numbers of such organizations may make effective oversight difficult or prohibitively costly, and anyway they seldom pose any real risk to the country's financial system.

Because the issues involved are so country specific, it is hard to offer general suggestions about where to set the lower boundary of prudential regulation. Countries use different benchmarks, including:

○ asset size
○ number of members
○ ownership and control by members, which is thought to provide some substitute for external supervision, and
○ the existence of a common bond among members that limits expansion and perhaps makes effective oversight by members more likely.

Sometimes these factors are used in combination. For instance, an exemption notice issued in 1995 under South Africa's banking law limits the scope of regulation under that law by excluding member-owned organizations with a common bond (e.g. all members work in the same business district), but only if their assets are less than about $1 500 000. Organizations with assets below that limit but above $150 000 are subject to limited non-prudential regulation, including requirements of an annual audit and membership of a 'self-regulatory' federation.

The Bolivian bank superintendent has chosen to limit the reach of supervision to the larger credit unions. However, at one point he was considering a more drastic step: prohibiting deposit collection by credit unions that are too small to be supervised cost-effectively. His final decision seems to be to allow such credit unions to continue taking deposits from their members, as long as there is adequate disclosure of the fact that they are not backed by official supervision. We think this decision is a wise one.

Especially in rural areas, 'unsupervisable' deposit takers may be the only ones willing to operate in a given locality. Clients are often well aware that such organizations are risky, but continue to use them because the other available savings options – cash livestock and so on – are even riskier. We do savers a great disservice if we remove unsupervised community-based depositories because of our paternalistic judgement that they are not safe enough (this point is compellingly illustrated in Wright, 2000).

The principle behind this 'lenient' recommendation needs to be applied carefully. One would not, for instance, argue that an unsound bank should be allowed to keep its licence on the grounds that it is the only formal deposit option in the area. The difference is the licence to intermediate, which puts the financial authorities in the position of (1) vouching for the institution's soundness, and, in most countries, (2) standing behind deposits as an insurer, whether explicitly or implicitly.

Opening separate prudential regulatory windows for specialized microfinance institutions

In many countries the core argument for licensing MFIs runs along the following lines: 'The commercial banks won't serve poor customers. Most of the institutions reaching a poor clientele right now are NGOs. Since these institutions do not have financial licences, they cannot leverage their resources by capturing deposits, and they cannot provide a savings service to their clients. The requirements for a regular banking licence are too high for the institutions interested in poor clients. Thus we need a separate window for MFIs, with lower barriers to entry and standards better suited to microfinance. The existence of such a window will improve the performance of the NGOs trying to qualify for it, and will draw forth solid new entrants not yet on the microfinance scene.'

This argument has a certain logic, and may be the best policy line in a limited number of countries. But we want to suggest that in most countries it is probably premature right now.

The fundamental question, which seldom seems to get enough attention, is whether the country has MFIs that are suitable for licensing but cannot use an existing window. A financial 'licence' is the government's representation that the institution is strong enough to be a safe intermediator of commercial-source funding, whether it be from retail depositors, institutional investors, or central bank credit lines. To qualify as a safe depository for such commercial-cost money, an MFI should be profitable enough not only to cover its costs today, but also to pay the full commercial costs of the money its licence will allow it to leverage, in addition to generating a surplus to fund growth and perhaps give a return sufficient to attract high-quality investors.

We believe that it is irresponsible to license MFIs that have not demonstrated their ability to operate at this level of sustainability. How can a supervisor vouch for the soundness of an institution unless she is reasonably sure it can operate profitably with the new sources of money it wants access to? Unprofitable institutions that eat up their equity capital will inevitably put depositors at risk.

The vast majority of NGO MFIs do not yet meet this test. In many countries, there is not a single NGO MFI that has achieved this level. Sometimes even profitable MFIs have accounts and information systems that are by any reasonable standard unauditable. In most countries, we have to recognize that shortage of licensable MFIs is the binding constraint to the growth of microfinance, rather than the absence of a tailor-made regulatory regime.

Regulation as promotion?

Some agree with the picture painted above, but argue that a new regulatory window for microfinance will be a powerful lever to improve the existing MFIs, or to attract competent new actors into microfinance. The discussion of this issue can be broken into two parts.

First, is a new window likely to be an effective spur to improvements in existing MFIs? There has not yet been enough experience to justify a conclusion on this point, but our initial tendency is to be sceptical. Where special windows have been opened in South America, the NGOs getting the licences and providing most of the service are mainly NGOs that were already profitable when the new window became available to them. More generally, our experience with hundreds of NGO MFIs leaves us with the impression that a relatively small percentage of their managers have the ingredients needed to reach sustainability: a not-so-common combination of talent, drive, and willingness to pay the heavy prices associated with sustainability (including the price of spending one's day the way bankers spend their days.)

A second issue is whether a new regulatory window will attract new high-quality actors into microfinance. In Indonesia and the Philippines, the availability of a special legal charter with low capital requirements brought forth large numbers of private rural banks. These banks certainly 'extended the frontier', reaching many customers who did not formerly have bank access. In Indonesia, the banks were not effectively supervised, and the majority of them are now insolvent (see Box 6.5). In the Philippines, the financial authorities had to carry out a massive restructuring of the rural banks in the early 1990s, as noted in Box 6.1: 20 per cent of them had to be shut down, and a large number of the others had to be merged to rescue them. Monitoring the Philippine rural banks ties up a major portion of the supervisory resources of the central bank and the deposit insurance agency.

We should also review the experience with the licensing of financial co-operatives. In most poor countries, legislation was passed decades ago chartering member-owned financial co-operatives such as credit unions, *mutuelles d'épargne et de crédit, cooperativas de ahorro y crédito*, etc. In response, many new institutions emerged: by 1997, there were 18 000 credit unions affiliated with

---

Box 6.5 The BPRs and Bank Rakyat Indonesia: the impact of local risk on small MFIs

The 1992 Indonesian banking act authorized two different bank types: commercial banks (Bank Umum) and people's credit banks (Bank Perkreditan Rakyat–BPR). BPRs are very small secondary banks whose assets average about $160 000. In 1998 the 2420 BPRs had around 4 million clients, but accounted for only 0.5 cent of the country's bank assets.

BPRs are supposed to be supervised through the central bank's regional offices. Regulation, reporting, and supervision of BPRs are basically similar to those for primary banks, raising the question of whether the regime is appropriate for very small banks. In any event, supervision has not been effective: at present an estimated 60 per cent of the BPRs are in trouble, largely due to loan losses.

It is worth noting that during the same crisis BRI's massive Unit Desa system fared much better. The number of Unit Desa depositors grew from 17 million before the crisis to 23 million in July 1999 – a 'flight to safety' motivated by BRI's government guarantee. Somewhat more surprisingly, there was virtually no sustained increase in the historical loan delinquency level of around 3 per cent portfolio at risk. The Unit Desa system continued to generate adjusted returns of over 4 per cent on assets.

Part of the Unit Desas' success during the crisis stemmed from the fact that borrowers tended to repay their loans even in the face of a cash flow crunch, in order to preserve their highly valued relationship with the bank. But there seems to have been another factor: in a large commercial bank like BRI, local risk is diversified throughout the system and administered internally. A large bank will find it easier to move cash to branches with liquidity problems, to bring in crisis teams when local performance deteriorates, and to replace weak local managers.

the World Council of Credit Unions in poor countries around the world. These credit unions have made some important contributions, but for present purposes three results after decades of experience seem particularly relevant.

Although WOCCU-affiliated credit unions in poor countries held about $6 billion in member savings in 1997, it is hard to find any cases where there has been sustained, effective prudential supervision of credit unions by the government (defining prudential supervision as 'effective' when at least 80 per cent of the licensed institutions are in fact solvent, and this situation stays stable over decades), or by the credit unions themselves. More recent efforts to put credit unions under bank supervisors in South America have so far had mixed results.

In addition to all this, developing-country credit unions have shown a strong tendency toward disruptive boom-and-bust instability. In more than a few poor countries, the majority of credit unions are insolvent – that is, unable to pay off all depositors.

The experience with credit unions and Asian rural banks may suggest that setting up a new legal charter can bring new players on to the scene, but this does not guarantee that these new entrants will be effectively supervised (or that member oversight will keep them sound in the absence of supervision).

Timing

The list of problems and dangers we've reviewed so far does not justify a conclusion that countries should forget about putting microfinance into a licensed environment. The question is one of timing and phasing.

We argue that most countries ought to go slow on this front. Around the world there is little experience, not just with the supervision of microfinance, but also with the long-term performance of microfinance portfolios and institutions. In such a setting, it makes sense to wait a while before casting a new legal structure in bronze. For example, in Bolivia for several years the banking superintendent supervised BancoSol by informal exception, simply declining to enforce certain banking regulations (Box 6.6). Special rules of the game for microfinance were not defined until the supervisory agency had years of practical experience monitoring a real microcredit portfolio in a solid institution.

Specifically, if the main focus is NGO microfinance, we should be inclined to wait until a few microcredit NGOs had proved for two years or so that they could manage their loan portfolios profitably enough to pay commercial costs on whatever portion of their funding the licence would allow them to leverage from outside resources. Until this happens, one must ask whether there is anything that can be licensed responsibly.

Use of an existing window: regulation by exception

As an alternative to opening a separate window, it is often possible for an NGO that is already 'licensable' to be licensed through an existing legal charter, forming a commercial bank, a non-bank finance company, or a financial co-operative. There are many cases where socially motivated MFIs have been able to use licensed structures that were not specially created for microfinance (including BASIX, India; K-REP, Kenya; BancoSol, Bolivia; Kafo Jiginew, Mali; BRAC Bank, Bangladesh).

Latin America has longer experience than other regions with regulatory windows created specially for microfinance; nevertheless the vast bulk of Latin

---

Box 6.6 Bolivian FFPs: licensing in response to demand from licensable MFIs

Bolivia's 'private financial funds' (FFPs) are often held up as a model for the regulation of microfinance, an advertisement for the creation of specially licensed non-bank financial intermediaries to provide services to the poor.

The development of Bolivian microfinance began in earnest after the economic crisis and hyperinflation of the mid-1980s. Several NGOs, among them PRODEM, FIE, and IDEPRO, were founded shortly after 1985, and were later joined by PRO-CREDITO and AgroCapital. By 1994, these financial NGOs had developed a thriving microcredit business throughout much of Bolivia, reaching about 100 000 clients out of a total estimated market of 500 000 microenterprises. Virtually all of the above-mentioned were operationally self-sufficient.

One of these NGOs, PRODEM, acquired a bank licence in 1992 and transferred its urban clients to BancoSol. By 1995, BancoSol accounted for 60 000 clients and PRODEM another 10 000. From soon after its inception, BancoSol has been regarded by the bank superintendency as one of Bolivia's best-performing banks, according to CAMEL ratings. Perhaps spurred by the demonstration effect of BancoSol, or perhaps also by news of an Inter-American Development Bank loan fund that would be available only to licensed institutions, the other financial NGOs began lobbying the Bolivian congress for a special licence in 1993. The Private Financial Fund licence was authorized in a 1993 banking law, but the superintendent and central bank waited until 1995 before approving the decree that implemented the new licence.

The FFP licence permitted a few strong NGOs to move to the next step of their development – accessing funds from the central bank, institutional investors, and time depositors. The superintendent has not yet allowed them to take passbook savings. This reluctance reflects not only the FFP's general lack of interest in such a funding strategy, but also the superintendent's perception that they do not currently possess the products, systems, or market strategy needed to handle small, liquid savings well. Even BancoSol, which has a full-service banking licence, gets relatively little of its funding from small deposits.

The FFP law and its application followed a pattern of gradualism in building a financial system for lower-income clients. The special licence was developed in response to the emergence of credibly performing financial NGOs that could afford to operate with commercial funding. The prospect of a licence motivated these NGOs to adopt the superintendency's reporting standards well before they applied for their new licences. But it was prior management orientation more than the chance to be licensed that made these NGOs sustainable.

At the time the FFP law was passed, there were dozens of other microcredit NGOs in Bolivia. Hardly any of them had an effective orientation toward sustainability. Since the passage of the law, none of them has met the requirements for licensing.

American microfinance is provided under licensing windows (bank, finance company, credit union) that existed before anyone began talking about microfinance. Banks play a major role in financing microenterprise in Chile, and are actively encouraged to do this through the Social Investment Fund (see Box 6.7).

It is often said that minimum capital requirements make a bank charter impossibly expensive for an NGO microfinance programme. This is true in some countries. But in many others, the minimum capital for a banking licence is under $10 million, often as low as $1 to $3 million. (The minimum capital for a finance company licence tends to be much lower, although most countries do not permit finance companies to offer passbook savings accounts.) In such cases, an MFI with a demonstrably reliable accounting and information system, good portfolio quality, and a profitable track record can usually raise the necessary amount. There are now a dozen international organizations prepared to invest equity capital in such MFIs; most of them face a shortage, not of money, but of strong MFIs to invest in.

Perhaps some of the regulations affecting the charter under consideration are inappropriate for a microfinance portfolio. For instance, in the Bolivian case mentioned earlier, the NGO (PRODEM) obtained a full banking licence. Banking regulations limited unsecured lending to 25 per cent of equity capital. BancoSol, the new microfinance bank, couldn't possibly comply, since nearly 100 per cent of its portfolio was unsecured at the time: its methodology relied on means other than collateral to buttress loan repayment. In addition, enforcement of the regulations concerning loan documentation would have made lending to

---

Box 6.7 The Chilean auction: minimizing supervisory problems

An innovative approach in Chile has catalysed rapid growth in microfinance services while minimizing supervision difficulties. Since 1993 the Chilean Social Investment Fund has used an auction system to subsidize the entry of commercial banks into microcredit. A fixed subsidy is auctioned off twice a year to those banks that offer to provide the largest number of microloans for the smallest subsidy. So far the value of the subsidy has fallen steadily from about $240 to $80 on loans that average $1200 (roughly 25 per cent of GNP per capita).

Several large banks with strong retail operations have responded. Today, four banks dominate the market for microcredit, reaching an estimated 80 000 active microenterprise borrowers with a total portfolio of about $100 million. About one-third of the microenterprises in Chile are customers of these banks. Chilean NGOs reach only a tenth as many clients.

The banks are big. Banco del Estado and Banco Santander have total assets measured in billions of dollars. Microcredit is not, and probably never will be, a large segment of the asset structure of any of these banks: their microcredit portfolios are only 1 to 5 per cent of assets. When microfinance is pooled in this way, with a much larger diversified commercial bank portfolio, the institutional risk posed by the microfinance assets is diluted away almost to nothing. Consequently, the Chilean banking superintendent needs to spend very little time on the microloan portfolios, whose oversight is left to the controller's office in the individual banks.

Regulating microfinance 103

BancoSol's customers impossibly expensive. The supervisor's response was to wink: he simply chose not to enforce this regulation and others for years, in view of the bank's otherwise strong performance. This sort of regulation by exception can be abused, but often it would seem to be the most efficient response to a transitional situation where new types of finance are coming into a market.

We propose a more radical approach for transitional situations. A government wanting to boost microfinance would give the supervisor explicit legal authorization to grant regulatory exceptions for a very limited number of intermediaries – new or existing ones – whose combined microfinance assets would have to fall below some modest amount that couldn't possibly affect the financial system. Eventually, of course, banking regulations will have to be changed to accommodate new microfinance methodologies, whether or not a country creates a special licence for new microfinance institutions. In most developing countries, the existing bank regulations have not been designed with character-based (i.e. uncollateralized) retail lending in mind. A detailed discussion of regulatory impediments to bank microcredit in Latin America can be found in Jansson and Wenner (1997).

Alliance with an already-licensed institution

Another alternative to special licensing of MFIs is to have unlicensed MFIs take advantage of someone else's licence. NGO MFIs have teamed up with existing banks or credit unions, in effect using the latter institution's licence to increase financial services to the NGO's target clientele. The NGO Freedom from Hunger has such arrangements with financial co-operatives or rural banks in Burkina Faso, Ghana, Mali, Madagascar, and the Philippines.

It is worth noting that the number of commercial banks interested in microfinance, while small, seems to be growing rapidly. There are at least two or three dozen commercial banks doing microfinance already in Asia, Latin America, Africa, Eastern Europe, and the Middle East (not counting those that were created for this purpose). We suspect that, in some settings, mergers and co-operative arrangements with existing licensed institutions might deserve more exploration than they are getting. From a supervisor's point of view, such an arrangement would be much easier to supervise than an undiversified institution that does only microfinance and whose owners cannot respond with quick capital in emergencies.

Non-intermediated savings

Where the motivation for licensing is to make more savings services available to poor customers, rather than to expand funding for MFIs' credit portfolios, another alternative is to allow MFIs to take savings on condition that the savings are deposited in a licensed bank as quickly as possible, and never put at risk by the MFI. Insulation from risk would involve at least two dimensions: (1) the MFI could not use the savings to finance its lending, or for any other purpose except to pay out savings withdrawals and perhaps maintain a small level of cash on hand so that it could pay out smaller withdrawals promptly; (2) depositors would have a priority claim on the bank account(s) if the MFI failed, so that these deposit claims would not be diluted to pay off other creditors.

Banking regulations may have to be adjusted slightly to permit such an arrangement. But making those adjustments should be worthwhile, given the double attraction of the arrangement: it would seem to minimize not only depositor risk but also supervisory burden. After an MFI has managed non-intermediated deposits for a few years, then it should be better situated to apply for a licence to intermediate. The MFI will have had the opportunity to prove not only that it can manage its loan portfolio sustainably but also that it can handle the systems involved in savings operations. Thus, a regime of non-intermediated deposit-taking might be a useful halfway house for transforming NGOs.

Alternative approaches to supervision

The regulation of large numbers of small non-bank intermediaries (be they specially chartered MFIs or previously unsupervised credit unions), presents supervisors with a gamut of problems already discussed. Several alternatives to direct supervision by the banking authority have been suggested and they are discussed here.

Self-supervision

Experience of self-supervision (defined here as arrangements under which the primary responsibility for monitoring and enforcing prudential norms lies with a body that is controlled by the organizations to be supervised), appears to justify a categorical conclusion. In poor countries, self-supervision of financial intermediaries has been tried dozens of times and has repeatedly proven to be ineffective (defining 'effective' as when (a) at least 80 per cent of the licensed institutions are in fact solvent, and (b) this situation stays stable over decades), even in the many cases where donors provided heavy technical assistance. The reason for the failure of the model is not hard to find. Having a watchdog that is controlled by the parties being watched presents an obvious conflict of interest. Most of the experience with self-supervision has been in federations of financial co-operatives, but it is hard to see any reason to expect better results from federations of MFIs.

In both Guatemala and the Dominican Republic, small groups of strong credit unions have formed federations whose task includes the monitoring and enforcement of prudential norms. Both these federations bring immense advantages to their task. The credit unions they supervise include only those starting out in strong financial condition. Accounting and reporting systems are not only good but also uniform. The supervisory office has strong technical staff. But despite all these advantages, staff in both federations – and many of the member credit unions as well – will admit privately that the 'supervisor' is likely to be powerless when a large member gets out of line. They don't believe that a board of directors named by the members being supervised will command credibility or stay the course in an emergency. For this reason and others, both federations have pushed strongly for their members to be subjected to the authority of the bank supervisor.

Delegated supervision

Under some proposed models, the supervisory agency maintains legal authority over – and responsibility for – the supervised institutions, but delegates regular monitoring and on-site inspection to a third party, such as an MFI federation or an independent technical entity. The role of the supervisor lies in (1) periodically testing the reliability of the agent's monitoring and inspection, and (2) intervening in problem situations.

If the agent is a federation of MFIs, then it will probably handle problem cases well only if the supervisor's oversight of the agent is active enough to give the supervisor a high degree of de facto control over the agent's operations. And though the supervisory agency may be able to delegate its monitoring, the law will usually not permit delegation of its authority and responsibility to intervene when institutions run into trouble or collapse. Thus the supervisor who accepts responsibility for new MFIs with the expectation that the agent is going to do most of the work may later find herself with serious burdens that can't be delegated.

To be successful, any agent would probably need to be better at monitoring MFI condition and risk than the typical external audit firm. As we observed earlier, external audits of MFIs have so far proved notoriously unreliable in verifying the accuracy of MFI financial statements, in particular the quality of MFI loan portfolios.

Apexes

In some countries there is an apex institution or national fund that does wholesale lending to local MFIs – typically, credit-only MFIs. As an investor, such an apex is by its nature a kind of supervisory agency. If it expects to have its loans repaid, it must evaluate and monitor the soundness of the MFIs it lends to. For MFIs that fail to meet its standards, the sanction is denial of loans.

It is sometimes suggested that apex structures be used to supervise deposit-taking MFIs, usually under a delegated supervision arrangement with the financial authority. Such an arrangement might involve potential conflicts of interest: for instance, would the apex be anxious to close down an MFI that owed it money? Some apexes have been successful at recovering their loans, but the justification for these apexes often also includes an expectation that they will catalyse significant quality improvements in the MFIs they fund. Few have been notably successful at this task. PKSF, the large microfinance apex in Bangladesh, seems to be an exception to the generally disappointing apex experience. But this apex was established *after* a critical mass of creditworthy MFIs had already developed – a situation that prevails in few other countries.

Rating agencies

Thirteen strong Guatemalan credit unions are setting up a private rating agency that will evaluate and certify their financial soundness. The crucial element is that the credit unions will not control the rating agency. The situation prompting this step is that public confidence in credit unions is so low that they have to pay 2 per cent more than the banks they compete with to raise deposits. The country's financial authorities have refused to take responsibility for supervising credit unions, so this group of strong institutions is trying a private alternative, at least as a temporary measure. The rating agency will have a large advertising budget to build public recognition of the plaque representing the agency's approval. The principal sanction for a non-complying credit union will be the (well-publicized) revocation of that credit union's plaque. Implementation has not yet begun, so nothing can be said yet about the results of this experiment. However, there are some important reasons why the rating agency model needs to be approached with caution.

The 'market' for the ratings in Guatemala is the depositors, who can use the rating to judge the safety of their deposit. In the case of non-deposit-taking MFIs, the market for ratings consists of investors – mainly donors. In Latin America and South Asia, two companies that provide ratings mainly for credit-only MFIs are finding the demand for their services from donors to be somewhat disappointing.

The Guatemalan experiment has huge advantages that are unlikely to be present in an MFI rating scheme in most countries. The participating credit unions all agree on the norms to be applied. All the credit unions have the same methodologies, accounting standards, and information system. Their competition with commercial banks for deposits provides a strong incentive to submit to supervision. Even so, it is far from clear that the Guatemala rating agency will work.

Deposit insurance

Recently there has been increased discussion of the possibility of deposit insurance for MFIs. Such insurance could be provided by the government as an adjunct to its regulation and supervision; or the insurance could be issued by a non-governmental (and perhaps donor-supported) body as a substitute for official regulation and supervision. The scheme could provide pure deposit insurance, whose only function is to reimburse small depositors in the event of failure of the depository institution, or it might operate a stabilization fund providing emergency liquidity to solvent MFIs, or capital support to MFIs in danger of insolvency who are willing to take corrective measures. In the absence of experience with such arrangements, we can only offer some general observations.

There is a respectable body of opinion that challenges the wisdom of deposit insurance, generally on the grounds that it blunts depositor oversight of institutions, encourages risky behaviour on the part of managers, and centralizes risk more than is desirable. But even for those who see deposit insurance as a good thing, deposit insurance for MFIs presents some special challenges.

A specific national insurance fund for MFIs confronts actuarial problems. Given the relatively small number of MFIs, their unsecured portfolios, and the absence of historical loss experience, how does one determine the fund size that is adequate to provide depositors with the degree of safety that is being advertised? To provide such safety, the fund would certainly have to be a much larger percentage of deposits than would be the case with a country's commercial banks.

Bank guarantees

Building on Burt Ely's work, J.D. Von Pischke has offered an intriguing proposal that non-bank MFIs be allowed to accept deposits on the condition that all such deposits are guaranteed by a bank that is licensed by the supervisor, and at least 50 per cent reinsured offshore (1998). This approach would eliminate additional burdens on the supervisor. The obvious practical question is whether banks willing to write such guarantees, and offshore markets willing to reinsure them, could be found at a price that MFIs can pay. Would a donor support experimentation along this line by temporarily covering part of the bank's risk? Time will answer these questions, if someone is willing to try.

Conclusion

At the risk of repetition, we shall underscore briefly a few points.

○ Microfinance is unlikely to achieve anything like its potential unless it can be done in licensed environments. Therefore, prudential regulation and supervision of microfinance is a topic that will unquestionably need to be addressed.

○ Nevertheless, in most developing countries today the absence of special licensing regimes for MFIs is not the binding constraint to the development of microfinance. Rather, the bottleneck is usually the scarcity of MFIs that are not dependent on the continuing availability of subsidies, and that can operate profitably enough to be able to pay a commercial price for a large proportion of their funds without decapitalizing themselves. It seems irresponsible to license MFIs to take deposits if they cannot demonstrate their ability to meet the above test.

○ The challenges facing a given country's supervisory agency need to be weighed seriously when examining proposals for the regulation of microfinance. Regulation and supervision entail significant costs, including non-financial costs like restraint of innovation.

○ Non-prudential regulation needs to be distinguished from prudential regulation, under which the supervisory agency has to vouch for the financial soundness of the supervised institutions. In some settings, reform of non-prudential regulation is probably essential to the development of microfinance – for instance where the licensed financial institutions have no interest in microfinance, but the legal regime makes it difficult or impossible in practice for non-licensed organizations like NGOs to provide credit.

○ Credit-only MFIs, including MFIs whose savings deposits are mainly compulsory compensating balances for loans, should not be subjected to prudential regulation. In addition, small community-based intermediaries – for instance small financial co-operatives – should not be prohibited from taking deposits simply because they are too small or remote to be supervised effectively.

○ The creation of special regulatory windows for MFIs is probably premature in countries where there is not a critical mass of licensable MFIs.
○ Given today's supply and demand of microfinance funding support, in most countries a solidly sustainable MFI could raise the minimum capital necessary to use an existing form of financial licence. The supply of funds available for this purpose in international organizations exceeds the demand from financially viable MFIs.
○ More attention needs to be paid to reforming regulations that make it difficult to do microfinance under existing forms of bank or finance company licences.
○ In developing countries, self-supervision, (defined as oversight of financial intermediaries by a federation or other body that is controlled by the same intermediaries being supervised) has a long history of failure, and is highly unlikely to work for MFIs.
○ Rating agencies for MFIs face serious practical obstacles.

References

CGAP, (1998), *External audits of microfinance institutions: a handbook,* Technical Tool Series 3, New York: Pact Publications.
Jansson, Tor and Mark D. Wenner, (1997), *Financial regulation and its significance for microfinance in Latin America and the Caribbean*, Inter-American Development Bank, Washington, DC.
Von Pischke, J.D., (1998), 'Guaranteeing deposits in microfinance nonbanks', unpublished manuscript.
Wright, Graham, (2000), 'Relative risk in Mt. Elgon', case study in *Paralysed by a dream: myths of regulation and supervision*, MicroSave-Africa, Kampala, Uganda.

About the authors

Robert Christen and Richard Rosenberg are senior advisers with CGAP. This paper is based on a fuller paper, to be found at http://www.cgap.org/html/p_occasional_papers.html; the descriptions of regulatory evolution in various countries have not been updated since the original paper was written in 1999. The authors received generous help from many people, especially Glenn Westley, Anne Ritchie, Graham Wright, Claudio Gonzales-Vega, Xavier Reille, Kanika Bahl, Patricia Mwangi, Jennifer Isern, Betty Wilkinson, J. Patrick Meagher, Thierry van Bastelaer, Elisabeth Rhyne, John Owens, William Steel, Hennie van Greuning, Alfred Hannig, Michael Feibig, David Wright, Tom Fitzgerald, and J.D. Von Pischke. The views expressed here, however, are the authors' alone.

7 Commercial banks and women microentrepreneurs in Latin America

GLORIA ALMEYDA STEMPER

This paper was first published in September 1996.

This paper examines the experience of a group of commercial banks in Latin America and the Caribbean in catering to microenterprise clients and to women in particular. The results indicate that a small number of commercial financial institutions are expanding the coverage and depth of financial services to these businesses, both at the wholesale and retail levels. Rather than focusing on one specific type of institution as the viable alternative, the overall supply of financial services to women microentrepreneurs – credit for enterprise and household investments, savings and payment services – should and does come from a variety of institutions including NGOs, banks, credit unions and other formal and semi-formal financial intermediaries. This variety will contribute to a larger and more efficient supply of financial services to heterogeneous groups of microentrepreneurs in the region.

MANY FACTORS contribute to microenterprise success, including access to financial services, training, technology and marketing. This paper focuses on access to financial services, and identifies different institutional options available to women microentrepreneurs in search of credit and savings services. It is based on a comparative analysis conducted by the Inter-American Development Bank (IDB) and UNIFEM of 23 formal and semi-formal financial institutions within and across six countries in Latin America and the Caribbean. Data collected through case studies conducted during 1993 of commercial banks, credit unions and non-governmental organizations (NGOs) indicate that financial services are available to women microentrepreneurs through a number of diverse institutions.

The cross-country comparisons of similar types of institutions helped to identify factors that influence the supply of financial services among different institutional models. The focus of the institutional assessment in each case was on identifying whether the institutions offer financial services deemed appropriate for low-income women microentrepreneurs.

Methodology

In order to assess the institutional features and financial technologies that provide access to women microentrepreneurs, the study addressed five research issues derived from a review of the published literature on women and financial services and microenterprise finance, and IDB project-related documents.

Institutional factors and microenterprise finance. The case studies identified a variety of institutional factors defining the extent to which these institutions provide loans tailored to women microentrepreneurs' demand (Krahnen and Schmidt, 1994). These factors include small loan size, and repayment terms in

109

relation to the nature of the sub-sectors served, i.e. trade, services and manufacturing. The studies also considered institutional factors such as mission, policies, and internal incentives, as well as external factors such as financial regulations to learn about the institutional willingness to design more efficient and viable financial instruments to serve the microenterprise sector.

Risks of microenterprise lending. The lack of adequate knowledge about the sector prevents formal financial intermediaries from evaluating adequately the risks involved. For formal financial intermediaries (FFIs), the perceived risk of financing microenterprises is particularly high because of the microentrepreneurs' lack of collateral and the absence of acceptable substitutes. Lack of collateral is one of the main barriers women microentrepreneurs encounter in accessing formal credit. To remedy this, credit programmes developed by NGOs have devised guarantees, such as those based on training courses, to screen potential borrowers and solidarity groups. The solidarity group model has proved its effectiveness in expanding credit programmes, especially among lower-income women.

The role of NGOs as intermediaries between microentrepreneurs and financial institutions. The study investigated the degree to which strengthening the relations between NGOs and formal financial institutions can improve women's access to financial services (Bennett and Goldberg, 1993). The analysis of the financial technologies of NGOs and the comparisons of the various inter-institutional arrangements help to identify the advantages, disadvantages and barriers in the provision of financial services to women microentrepreneurs.

The mobilization of savings. Savings are possible among low-income communities if appropriate mechanisms are used. Previous research has indicated that women are more inclined to save than men (Robinson, 1994). However, some research indicates that women microentrepreneurs may be less likely to rely on their own savings as a source of financing their business. This study seeks to fill the gap by analysing intermediaries that are mobilizing savings among low-income groups, with the aim of identifying which institutions have been most successful in supplying these services to women microentrepreneurs.

Characteristics of women microentrepreneurs. The social status and conditions of women influence their demand for financial services. Besides institutional factors, and the barriers that microentrepreneurs in general (men and women) face, there are cultural and social factors (such as their relative exclusion from public life) which affect women in particular. Often women microentrepreneurs regard their business as a matter of survival. In examining this issue, the study sought to identify gender-related factors that affect the demand for financial services by male and female microentrepreneurs.

Loans to microenterprise

This study found that *some* banks and the credit unions can and do provide financial services to low-income microentrepreneurs. Bank participation in microenterprise lending was significant even when compared to more advanced NGOs (see Table 7.1). Colombia's Caja Social had a microenterprise loan

Table 7.1 Estimates of microenterprise portfolio – loans of less than US$5000 (data based on outstanding loans as of December 31,1992)

Country / Metric	Banks	Credit unions	NGOs	Country indicators — (5) Per capita income (1992)	Country indicators — Women's participation in microenterprise
CHILE	BANDES (1) / BECH (2)		PROPESA / FINAM		
Loans outstanding (US$000)	$3450 / $5573		$1086 / $292	$2940	38%
Number of loans	3492 / 691		3565 / 1190		
Average loan	$988 / $8065		$305 / $245		
Ave. loan/PCI	34% / 274%		10% / 8%		
Women part. no. loans	50% / 59%		44% / 93%		
COLOMBIA	CAJA SOCIAL (3)	CUPOCRÉDITO	ACTUAR		
Loans outstanding (US$000)	$5056	$17369	$4300	$1487	42%
Number of loans	3756	25274	24685		
Average loan	$1346	$687	$174		
Ave. loan/PCI	91%	46%	12%		
Women part. no. loans	41%	44%	45%		
COSTA RICA	FEDERADO wholesale loans to credit unions	COOCIQUE	AVANCE / F. MUJER / FINCA		
Loans outstanding (US$000)		$1560	$873 / $300 / $1181	$1822	35%
Number of loans		1000	786 / 526 / 4081		
Average loan		$1560	$1111 / $570 / $289		
Ave. loan/PCI		86%	61% / 31% / 16%		
Women part. no. loans		30%	51% / 100% / 25%		
DOMINICAN REP.	BHD	SAN JOSÉ	ADEMI / FDD		
Loans outstanding (US$000)	$2000	$3000	$6900 / $1300	$709	46%
Number of loans	194	1616	9525 / 2210		
Average loan	$10309	$1856	$724 / $588		
Ave. loan/PCI	1454%	262%	102% / 83%		
Women part. no. loans	n.a.	30%	37% / 36%		
ECUADOR	PACÍFICO (4) / PICHINCHA	PROGRESO	FED		
Loans outstanding (US$000)	$2149 / $2472	$3000	$1500	$1346	37%
Number of loans	9004 / n.a.	3433	4554		
Average loan	$239	$874	$329		
Ave. loan/PCI	18%	65%	24%		
Women part. no. loans	44% / 30%	48%	56%		
JAMAICA	NOVA SCOTIA	C. OF KINGSTON	JDF / EDT		
Loans outstanding (US$000)	n.a.	$1069	$3760 / $245	$1561	31%
Number of loans		4909	n.a. / 262		
Average loan		$218	$935		
Ave. loan/PCI		14%	60%		
Women part. no. loans		37%	64%		

Source: Country studies.
Notes: (1) Microenterprise programme only. (2) Small loan programme. (3) Estimate based on borrowers with less than two minimum salaries and outstanding loans in trade, manufacturing and services. (4) Loans granted in the microenterprise programme (Community Development Programme). Includes four-year outstanding loans. (5) Source: IDB, Soci-economic data, January 1995.

portfolio of $5 million, where Actuar had succeeded in placing $4.3 million. The $3.4 million outstanding loan portfolio of Bandes is more than double that of the NGO Propesa in Chile, while in Ecuador Banco del Pacífico had placed $2.1 million where the FED had loaned $1.5 million. These results show that, contrary to widely held belief, certain banks do indeed contribute to the supply of microenterprise credit in their countries. Although loans to microentrepreneurs as a percentage of the total portfolio is quite low for most banks, the value of investment in microenterprise is comparable to or larger than that of most NGOs. Because the supply of financial services to microentrepreneurs is small vis-à-vis the demand, the current provision of credit by banks and credit unions is therefore a significant contribution to the development of this sector. In addition, their participation diversifies the sources of financial services available to a wide range of women microentrepreneurs.

Lending to women borrowers is also evident in the microenterprise loan portfolios of all the institutions surveyed (see Table 7.1). Estimates of women's share of lending, based on the number of outstanding loans, show levels of lending to microenterprises that range from 30 to 59 per cent in banks, 30 to 48 per cent in credit unions, and 25 to 100 per cent in NGOs. Estimates of women's representation in the microenterprise loan portfolio for each country across institutions suggest averages close to or higher than the estimated national average of women-owned microenterprises in all cases, except for the Dominican Republic.

The 1992 data presented in Table 7.1 help to identify the depth of coverage and relative size of loans. Outstanding loans were used as a proxy to estimate the level of coverage in each country and the level of participation of the different institutions. However, when using outstanding loans as a proxy it is important to note that banks and credit unions have longer-term loans (12 to 36 months) than NGOs, which generally make very short-term loans (one to three months). This variable highlights the area in which NGOs lead: processing short-term, smaller microenterprise loans.

Women's access to bank credit services

The case studies show that women received a share of microenterprise loans from banks similar to their share in business ownership in their respective countries. They received 44 per cent, 41 per cent and 50 per cent of the microenterprise loans made by Ecuador's Banco del Pacífico, Colombia's Caja Social and Chile's Bandes, respectively.

Because average loan sizes were larger for the commercial banks, some of the most successful NGOs – Actuar, and FED – reached greater numbers of women microentrepreneurs, especially with the smallest microenterprise loans. This may be explained by different factors. NGOs tend to specialize in smaller loans for commercial activities and to target lower-income populations more than banks, even those banks that operate in low-income sectors.

To understand bank lending better, we examined some of the features that are most relevant to access to credit for women microentrepreneurs: first, the

Table 7.2 **Distribution of microenterprise loans (number) by gender**

Range in US$	Men	Women
Range in US$	**Men**	**Women**
CAJA SOCIAL		
<$625	1%	2%
$625 – $1250	8%	14%
$1250 – $2500	23%	32%
$2500 – $3750	11%	23%
$3750 – $5000	57%	29%
	100%	100%
Participation by gender	59%	41%
BANCO DEL DESARROLLO (BANDES)		
<$1000	44%	50%
$1000 – $5000	56%	50%
	100%	100%
Participation by gender	50%	50%
BANCO DEL PACÍFICO		
<$500	38%	53%
$500 – $1000	47%	38%
$1000 – $5000	15%	9%
	100%	100%
Participation by gender	56%	44%

Source: Country Studies (Based on samples of outstanding microenterprise loans as of December 1993).

availability and distribution of small loans; and second, credit characteristics such as activities financed, repayment, interest rates and guarantees.

Availability and distribution of small loans by gender. Over 50 per cent of the total number of outstanding loans made by Caja Social, Bandes and Banco del Pacífico are under $5000. The size of loans seems to be an important factor in explaining gender differences in access to credit. After analysing the total loan portfolio of the banks, microenterprise loans (under $5000) are further classified by gender for Banco del Pacífico, Caja Social and Bandes (Table 7.2). The participation of women tends to be lower in the larger loan size ($3750–5000). For example, in Caja Social some 57 per cent of the loans to male borrowers were over $3750, while only 29 per cent of loans to women were this large.

Table 7.3 presents a comparative summary of the banks' microenterprise lending. Data pertaining to the size of small bank loans as compared to the loans of non-bank institutions were studied in order to gain better profiles of the financial services for the microenterprise sector. Bank loans (as a proportion of GDP per capita) are more comparable to NGO loans in Ecuador and Chile. In the case of Colombia, the Caja Social provides larger loans than the credit union and the NGO. The institutions studied in the Dominican Republic show a higher average of microenterprise loans to GDP per capita (the poorest country has the largest average microenterprise outstanding loans). These results help us to understand the depth of the supply of credit of each institution. Banks' credit to

Table 7.3 Average outstanding microenterprise loan comparison between banks and other institutions

	Average outstanding microenterprise loan 31-12-92 (US$)	Per capita income PCI (1992)	Average outstanding microenterprise loan as a percentage of PCI
COLOMBIA			
Caja Social	$1346	$1487	91%
Cupocrédito Credit Union	$687		46%
Actuar	$174		12%
CHILE			
Banco del Desarrollo	$988	$2940	34%
Propesa	$305		10%
Finam	$245		8%
ECUADOR			
Banco del Pacífico	$239	$1346	18%
Progreso Credit Union	$874		65%
FED	$588		24%
DOMINICAN REPUBLIC			
San José Credit Union	$1856	$709	262%
Ademi	$724		102%
FDD	$588		83%

Source: Country Studies.

microentrepreneurs varies in each country, contributing either to financial deepening or to the extent of outreach.

Credit characteristics

In addition to the size of the loans and activities financed, the following summarizes other features of the financial instruments:

Activities financed. Caja Social has about 77 per cent of its loans in personal loans. According to Caja Social, many microenterprise and small-business loans are classified under the category 'personal banking' since many of these businesses are not 'formal' or because the type of guarantee used is a savings account or a co-signer. The Chilean bank lends primarily for housing (linked to social housing programmes) and business activities.

Banks with a microenterprise loan portfolio finance all types of activities and play an important role, particularly in financing fixed assets with longer-term loans. Longer-term loans constitute a significant option in the supply of financial services, since NGOs provide microenterprises primarily with short-term loans for working capital. For example, Banco del Pacífico had about 75 per cent of its outstanding microenterprise loans primarily in manufacturing with a four-year maturity.

Interest rates. All the banks studied charged average market interest rates for microenterprise loans. These rates were lower than or equal to those of NGOs with microenterprise credit programmes. Although charging higher interest rates might have allowed them to increase financial revenues from loans, bank managers generally fear the negative publicity that could result from charging the most disadvantaged entrepreneurs rates exceeding their prevailing commercial rates. Publicized nominal interest rates (and effective interest rates) for banks in Colombia, Chile and Ecuador were more competitive than in the other countries studied. Results seem to indicate that countries with less variety and number of institutions in the supply of microenterprise credit tend to have interest rates higher than market rates. For example, in the Dominican Republic there is a broader range between the lowest and highest interest rates charged for microenterprise loans.

Guarantees. There seems to be a move toward greater flexibility in the requirements for guarantees. One of the most important features is the solidarity-group methodology as a way of guaranteeing loans and increasing coverage at a lower cost. Furthermore, use of this methodology reflects the bank's capability to reach more microentrepreneurs. Since the methodology guarantees loans by the solidarity groups, women are encouraged to participate in the loan process. Banco del Desarrollo and Banco del Pacífico emphasize the importance of having credit advisers who are responsible for searching out and screening clients. Client screening through technical assistance is a major part of risk management. These banks also offer repeat loans of increasing value as an incentive to encourage repayment.

Caja Social guarantees loans and becomes familiar with clients by reviewing their savings history. In addition, loan repayment history is used as evidence of creditworthiness for future loans, and the possibility of incremental loans is used to motivate the client to repay. Caja Social requires more traditional guarantees, such as real estate, for loans over $10 000.

None of the banks studied relied on real guarantees to grant small loans for working capital. Co-signers constituted the most generalized form of guarantee. Many of these loans are classified as personal loans rather than as business related. For these banks, the informal nature of the microenterprises makes each owner's personal credit (and savings) history as important as their financial statements.

Loan maturities and repayment schedule. Microloans and small bank loans varied from six months to four years. These terms are determined by local economic and financial environments, and according to the purpose of the loans (personal, working capital, or fixed assets). A monthly repayment schedule is the most common. Banks (and other types of FFIs) also provide loans with longer maturities and in larger amounts for fixed assets more frequently than do NGOs.

Special delivery mechanisms. Banco del Pacífico (Ecuador), Caja Social (Colombia) and Bandes (Chile) have microenterprise centres financed by the banks themselves and, in some cases, international donor funds. BECH (Chile) has a small-enterprise programme that is in the process of developing schemes for microenterprises. In addition to credit, technical assistance is one of the main activities of these programmes.

Although the banks use different approaches to reach microentrepreneur clients, they share two strategies: proximity to microentrepreneurs and decentralization of decision making. Banco del Pacífico has a microenterprise programme staff member in the main branches. By contrast, Bandes' programme functions in only one location as a platform. Caja Social uses two methods to serve microentrepreneurs. One is through a downtown Bogota agency that is completely dedicated to assisting this type of client. This office manages IDB funds (among others) borrowed for this purpose.

The rest of Caja Social's agencies lend to microentrepreneurs through 'massive banking', a system managed through a credit-processing centre, using computerized credit technology to expedite information analysis. The branch that receives the microentrepreneur loan application is responsible for collecting all the relevant data in accordance with each market segment and line of credit. The branch forwards the data to the credit-processing centre. The credit report is reviewed by a group of analysts who specialize in microenterprise credit. This group evaluates the scoring and recommends approval or denial of the loan. This system has allowed the local branches to concentrate on getting close to microentrepreneurs and collecting relevant data, and this yields a more efficient risk analysis.

Savings

The country studies have identified two distinct roles of bank savings and other types of deposit accounts. For example, for the banks in Colombia and Ecuador, accounts of under $1500 make up over 50 per cent of total savings and deposits. Competitive market interest rates are paid on savings and requirements for opening accounts are minimal ($12 in Caja Social). Being the leader in small savings accounts, Caja Social had 900 000 savers in 1993 with an average of $214 per account; 99 per cent of account holders were individuals. Further analysis of the distribution of total savings in Caja Social (available for 1991) shows that about 51 per cent of the savings accounts had a balance of less than $615. For Caja Social, savings services are also a means of establishing client history, which is taken into account when evaluating credit applications.

On the other hand, Chilean banks primarily mobilize fixed-deposit savings. In Chile, savings accounts represent 12 per cent of total savings in the country. In 1992, BECH held 90 per cent of the savings passbooks in Chile, with over six million accounts averaging savings of US$218. A small proportion of these deposits, about 10 per cent, is in highly liquid non-interest-bearing savings accounts. According to interviews with microentrepreneurs, these savings accounts are used to deposit cheques that would otherwise be difficult to cash in Chile.

Savings schemes for low-income people should ensure convenience, security, liquidity and returns (Robinson, 1994, p. 29). The savings instruments in the Caja Social have several features that match the features of services used by lower-income groups.

Our research of savings and deposit mobilization seems to indicate that those institutions that mobilize large numbers of small savers, and are more in tune with the needs of microentrepreneurs, are in Colombia, Ecuador and Chile. In countries with restrictions on the mobilization of savings (e.g. Costa Rica), or where banks have oligopolistic features (e.g. Jamaica), there might be less incentive for banks to establish closer relationships with low-income savers and borrowers, and among them, women.

Conclusions

The case studies of banks in Colombia, Ecuador and Chile reveal advances in the provision of FFIs' financial services to microentrepreneurs in general, and to women in particular. These banks play a key role in expanding the coverage and depth of financial services to the microenterprise sector both at the wholesale and retail levels, and could act as leaders in the provision of financial services to the microenterprise sector, and specifically to women entrepreneurs. This type of portfolio allocation decision will help to increase the current supply of credit to microentrepreneurs. These banks have a large percentage of their loans invested in small loans; and also derive a large proportion of their funds from small individual savings accounts. Less evidence of this profile was found in the cases of Costa Rica, the Dominican Republic and Jamaica.

In summary, the experience of Caja Social, Banco Pacífico and Bandes indicates that financial institutions wishing to improve women's access to their services might adopt the following features:

○ The identification of microentrepreneurs as clients in the bank's institutional mission.
○ The consideration of microenterprise loans as an 'investment' in future clients.
○ The allocation of bank funds (credit and human and physical resources) to this sector.
○ The acceleration and decentralization of decision making through new electronic technology.

Their credit services have the following characteristics:

○ Loans available for trade, services, manufacturing and household investments.
○ A variety of loan maturities (short-term capital, fixed assets).
○ Flexible collateral requirements for small loans (e.g. solidarity groups, personal guarantees and savings).
○ The opportunity to increase loan size upon repayment of previous loan.
○ Credit history used to assess risk.
○ A minimum size of microenterprise not required.
○ Assistance given through special microenterprise centres.
○ Training not a requirement, but provided for those who want it.
○ Ongoing available loans.

Savings and deposits services have the following characteristics:

○ Low minimum savings required to open an account.
○ Convenient location with a broad network throughout the cities.
○ Savings used as collateral.
○ Savings history that helps to build creditworthiness.
○ Competitive market rates.

The institutional mission of these banks is a key in determining their involvement in the microenterprise sector. These banks recognize that certain segments of the population are excluded from the financial services mainstream. Other banks seek a share of the microenterprise market. This is the case of BHD (Dominican Republic) and Banco Pichincha (Ecuador). Competition with other banks and the vitality of the small business and microenterprise sector led these banks to consider the viability of taking a more targeted approach for this sector.

Limitations and areas for improvement. Less flexibility was found in loan repayments for the banks studied than for NGOs. Successful NGO practices indicate that schemes adjusted to women-owned microenterprises use more frequent payments, or set payments in a more flexible way.

Only Caja Social makes use of the clients' savings history in assessing creditworthiness. Other FFIs could benefit from Caja Social's approach to evaluating credit risk. The proportional weight of savings schemes that are attractive to lower-income people in the total liabilities of the FFIs seems to be a determining factor in designing financial products and technologies to serve these clients.

One of the bottlenecks in broadening the coverage of the microenterprise sector is the relative absence of trust between banks and private or governmental institutions involved in microenterprise development. Only in a few cases have banks accepted NGOs as clients.

Banks that participated in this study identified awareness building in high-ranking executives, in addition to technical staff, as an important way to become active in microenterprise lending. An understanding of the microenterprise sector among bank staff is seen as critical to improving financial services to the sector.

Commercial private banks have expressed limited interest in governmental credit programmes because of high costs in terms of time, logistics, and risk resulting from delays in negotiations. For them this is not a lack of interest in the microenterprise sector but in the financing schemes proposed.

Recommendations

Best practices. Rather than emphasizing or concluding that 'banks tend to focus on big deposits and big loans', development practitioners should become aware of the commercial banks that are lending to microenterprises. Parallel to the recognition of a core group of NGOs successful in microenterprise finance, there is a need to focus also on the best practices of the core group of commercial banks (and other FFIs).

Specific banking industry effort. Technical seminars with a banking orientation could be sponsored among financial institutions that already have the institutional commitment and the financial capability to reach underserved populations. Until now, most microenterprise finance activities and research has been oriented to NGOs. Also, special activities targeted at bank technical staff working with microenterprises can help to raise their visibility and status within their own banks.

Savings. An institutional feature seemingly relevant to the provision of financial services to microentrepreneurs is the importance that some institutions assign to the mobilization of savings from medium and low-income groups. Institutions promoting microenterprise finance should make banks more aware of other FFIs' success in mobilizing savings among low-income groups and how to use this information to evaluate potential borrowers.

Personal banking. Banks with an interest in personal loans seem to be more adaptable to the needs of women microentrepreneurs. Their flexibility allows a consideration of additional personal information about the borrowers and acceptance of less traditional substitutes for collateral. Future research should evaluate how personal credit is used to finance business activities.

Knowledge of clients' socio-economic profile improves coverage. The knowledge of 'client profiles' and 'market niches' specific to microenterprise is only beginning to be seen as relevant to FFIs. Comparative data on clients have not been considered important or, in some cases, institutions assume that socio-economic information on clients is only marginally relevant to financial service suppliers. Institutions stipulate that they do not discriminate between women and men, confusing 'non-discriminatory' practices with not understanding the varying cultural, social, and economic practices that affect men's and women's demand for financial services.

Access to diverse financial services increases productivity. Women's household and business responsibilities place great demands on their time. In addition to savings services, paying bills (utilities and school fees), money transfers and cheque cashing are common transactions that require microentrepreneurs' time. FFIs are unaware of the importance of educating clients about different financial services available so that microentrepreneurs can make informed decisions and choose among the available options.

Financial services respond to business and household strategies. The current supply of microenterprise credit is characterized by micro-loans, primarily for working capital. Commercial banks and credit unions help to expand women microentrepreneurs' options. Among these alternatives are larger loans with longer maturities for manufacturing businesses, and smaller personal loans for housing improvements and education.

The institutional case studies confirm the conclusions of other researchers that there has been progress in the provision of financial services to microenterprises with important benefits for low-income women. Each of the spheres of financial activity we examined – formal financial institutions, credit unions and NGOs – have responded to the profiles of women microentrepreneurs. Our research confirms that some of the factors affecting women microentrepreneurs' access to credit are common to all microenterprises, but are particularly acute for women.

During the past few years, development practitioners have studied and emphasized the best practices of selected NGOs. The same approach is now being tried with FFIs and semiformal institutions such as credit unions. It is hoped that with a greater understanding of how some commercial banks have been successful in reaching women microentrepreneurs, more institutions will learn from their experience and further increase the supply of financial services to women and men microentrepreneurs in Latin America and the Caribbean.

References

The country case studies upon which this comparative study is based are indicated in the References as reports prepared for the IDB.

Bennett, Lynn, and Michael Goldberg, (1993), *Providing enterprise development and financial services to women: a decade of bank experience in Asia*, World Bank Technical Paper No. 236, Asia Technical Department Series, Washington, DC: World Bank.
Berger, Marguerite and Mayra Buvinic (eds.), (1989), *Women's ventures: assistance to the informal sector in Latin America*, West Hartford, Connecticut: Kumarian Press.
Blackwood, A. (co-ordinator), (1994), *Financial services for women microentrepreneurs: Jamaican study*, report prepared for the IDB, Mona Institute of Business, University of West Indies, Kingston, Jamaica.
Bonilla, E. (co-ordinator), B. Marulanda, P. Lizarazo and P. Rodriguez, (1994), *Servicios financieros para mujeres microempresarias: el caso Colombiano*, final report prepared for the Inter-American Development Bank, CEDE, Universidad de los Andes, Bogota.
Burbano, L.E. (co-ordinator), C. Cordova, V. Davalos, J. Gordillo, M. Montalvo and P. Valdez, (1994), *Servicios financieros para mujeres microempresarias: Ecuador*, final report prepared for the Inter-American Development Bank, INSOTEC, Quito.
Krahnen, Pieter, and Reinhard H. Schmidt, (1994), *Development Finance and Institution Building – A New Approach to Poverty Oriented Banking*, Boulder, Colorado: Westview Press.
Levitsky, Jacob, (1993), 'Credit Guarantee Funds and Mutual Guarantee Systems', in *Small Enterprise Development*, **4**(2): 4–19.
Mehech, A., V. Fuenzalida, L.A. Fuenzalida, I. Bilbao and V. Torrens, (1994), *Servicios financieros para la mujer microempresaria. Informe final del panorama chileno*, final report prepared for the Inter-American Development Bank, Santiago, Chile: Escuela de Administración, Pontificia Universidad Católica de Chile.
Robinson, Marguerite, (1994), 'Savings mobilization and microenterprise finance: the Indonesian experience', in Maria Otero and Elisabeth Rhyne (eds), *The new world of microenterprise finance: building healthy financial institutions for the poor*, West Hartford, Connecticut, Kumarian Press.
Weisleder, S. (co-ordinator), G. Monge, G. Gonzalez and P. Morales, (1994), *Servicios financieros para la mujer microempresaria: caso Costa Rica*, final report prepared for the Inter-American Development Bank, San Jose, Costa Rica: Asociación Alternativas de Desarrollo.

About the author

Gloria Almeyda Stemper wrote this paper while working as a Consultant for the Women in Development Unit of the Inter-American Development Bank (IDB).

8 Credit for the rural poor – the case of BRAC in Bangladesh

A.M.R. CHOWDHURY, M. MAHMOOD and F.H. ABED

This paper was first published in September 1991.

As the rural population of Bangladesh increases, landlessness among people once dependent upon agriculture is a growing problem. The Bangladesh Rural Advancement Committee (BRAC) has been working with the rural poor since 1972, and in 1979 it began to provide credit via its 81 branches through the Rural Development Programme (RDP). Ten years later the success of the RDP in generating incomes and employment through small businesses and building up assets has been evaluated, and this paper describes the results of the evaluation.

NINETEEN YEARS have passed since Bangladesh fought for its independence. It inherited all the complex economic, social and political problems which are typical of a less developed country. With a very high population density and rate of growth, it is the fifth poorest country in the world (World Bank, 1988). The development of manufacturing industry is taking place at a very slow pace, and the stock of mineral resources discovered so far is poor. Eighty per cent of the country's 110 million population live in rural areas, and more than 50 per cent of them have to depend on agriculture for their livelihood.

It has been estimated, however, that more than half of the rural population is functionally landless. During 1960–79, the rural population increased by 50 per cent but the number of farm households increased by only 1.9 per cent, which indicates a vast increase in non-farm households (Hossain, 1984). A number of non-governmental organizations (NGOs) are involved in the field of poverty alleviation and Bangladesh Rural Advancement Committee (BRAC) is one of the largest among them. BRAC has a long history of organizing the landless, providing them with loan and training facilities through its different interventions, particularly the Rural Development Programme (RDP). In order to assess the impact of RDP on the income and employment of its beneficiaries, the Research and Evaluation Division, an independent unit within BRAC, conducted a study in 1988, and this paper presents results from the study. Before presenting results, however, we shall try to provide an overview of RDP and indicate the methodology used for this impact study.

BRAC was started in early 1972 as a relief measure following the war of liberation. Soon it became a community development organization providing health, family planning, education and economic support to different sectors of the rural community, but with particular emphasis on the most disadvantaged, such as women, fishermen and the landless. Since 1977, however, BRAC has been working exclusively with disadvantaged sections of the community.

BRAC's initial experience with credit dates back to the early 1970s. In 1974 BRAC provided credit to the villagers in its Sulla project in Sylhet district through

121

Sulla Thana Central Co-operative Association (BRAC, 1975). In the following year, credit was advanced without interest to several landless groups; and in 1976 BRAC started providing credit to landless groups through its Manikganj project.

BRAC's Rural Development Programme

The Rural Development Programme (RDP) is one of the major programmes of BRAC. Started in 1979, RDP had grown by December 1989 into a large programme providing credit to target groups from 81 branches in 45 sub-districts of 22 districts.

The following are the major objectives of BRAC's RDP:

○ building viable organizations of the poor capable of bringing about desired changes in their own socio-economic and political circumstances
○ improving the socio-economic status of the rural poor through the provision of easy credit for income and employment generating activities, and
○ developing the managerial and entrepreneurial capabilities of the poor.

To attain the above objectives, RDP works through different components in the following chronological order:

○ Conscientization. RDP starts its operation with a conscientization programme through BRAC's functional education curriculum. Classes are held separately for men and women.
○ Institution building. The functional education classes normally lead to the formation of village organizations for men and women.
○ Training. Different types of training are organized for the members of newly formed groups. Some of these are held at BRAC's own training centres while others are held in RDP's local offices. The programme also runs a paralegal aid programme to provide legal awareness to group members.
○ Credit support. The above activities normally take approximately six months before the group members become eligible to receive credit from RDP.
○ Technical and logistical support. Some of the income generation activities may require higher-level technical and logistical support, which are provided by BRAC. Examples of such support are: vaccines for livestock and poultry, and the marketing of locally produced items such as garments.

The principles of credit under the RDP

Borrowers are expected to use the loan according to the purpose for which it was given, and no loan is given for consumption purposes. Loan repayment is started immediately and is made on a weekly basis.

Loans are given to members on recommendation from their village organizations. They are given 'on margin', which means that the borrowing organization contributes its own resources to the extent that all members have a significant stake in the venture. Each group member saves every week, and this saving is kept in the member's account.

No collateral is demanded, and hence BRAC has to enquire beforehand about the borrower's ability to carry out the proposed venture and its potential profitability. This is supplemented by continuous but supportive monitoring by BRAC staff throughout the entire life of the scheme. When a loan is given to procure an income-producing asset, however, the asset remains hypothecated to BRAC until the full recovery of the loan. In case of default, the asset is sold and the outstanding loan is recovered. Such a situation, however, seldom arises. For effective supervision of the loan from the group side, a management committee is selected by the group members.

The amount of the loan varies depending on the nature of the scheme. To date the smallest loan was for Tk.500 and largest was for Tk.1 million (the exchange rate is US$1 to Tk.35). Large loans are given for collective enterprises, such as deep tube wells, power tillers and so on, organized by several village organizations, whereas individual loans vary from Tk.500 to Tk.8000.

There are three durations for which credit is advanced to group members. Short-term credit is for a period of 12 months or less; medium-term credit is for a period greater than one year but less than three years; and long-term credit is for three years or more. On all loans, an interest rate of 16 per cent is charged.

Landlessness is not the only criterion for eligibility to RDP group membership. Households with no land may not be the poorest because they might have other substantial sources of income such as a job or a business. BRAC's target group comprises those men and women who sell their manual labour for subsistence; most of this target group, however, are found to be landless or near landless.

Each branch of RDP is headed by a manager who is assisted by four to five programme organizers. Since 1983 RDP has recruited local male and female *gram shebak* (village volunteers) to assist in the credit activities. Approximately 45–50 villages (average village population 1200) are covered through a branch and each *gram shebak* is assigned approximately 5 villages or 10 village organizations.

Until December 1989, RDP had been working from 81 centres in 45 sub-districts of Bangladesh which are scattered over 22 of Bangladesh's 64 districts. Table 8.1 shows that RDP is working in 3359 villages and that in these 65 per cent of the households belong to RDP-defined target groups, 68 per cent of whom are members of RDP groups.

Savings and credit under RDP

Through a system of compulsory individual savings, group members have saved nearly 70 million taka over the years, or approximately Tk.193 per group member (see Table 8.2). The savings are collected during the weekly meeting attended by group members and the respective *gram shebak*.

Progress in the credit operation

Between 1979 and 1989, over Tk.470 million had been disbursed. Of all the loans, 96.5 per cent have been repaid on time, a proportion which has varied between the branches. Branches that were started earlier have worse records than those

Table 8.1   Information on RDP activities (as at 31 December 1989)

Number of sub-districts in which RDP is working	45
Number of RDP centres	81
Number of villages covered	3359
Number of village organizations formed	
Male	2882
Female	3642
Total	65241
Number of households covered	202 883
Percentage of target households covered in participating villages	67.8
Percentage of target households in participating villages	64.8
Size of membership	
Male	137 736
Female	217 939
Total	355 6752

1. In some large villages, more than one group of each sex has been formed to facilitate management and discipline.
2. In the majority of cases, both husbands and wives are members of the respective village organizations.

Table 8.2   The savings and credit operation of RDP (as at 31 December 1989)

Total amount saved (in million Taka)	69
Average savings per individual member (Taka)	193
Total amount of credit disbursed (in million Taka)	473
Loans repaid on time (percentage of credit)	96.5
Average credit per group (Taka)	75 570
Average credit per individual borrower (Taka)	2297
Percentage of credit received by females	53.4

that were started later on, although the repayment record of the former branches has improved with time. Table 8.2 provides some information about the savings and credit operation of RDP.

Loans for small trading and agricultural schemes dominated the credit disbursed. Table 8.3 gives the share of each type of activity. More than half the loans were short term (less than 12 months in duration) and only 7 per cent were for long-term purposes (more than three years). Only 17 per cent of the total loans were given for collective activities and the rest were for individual activities. Repayment records were better for individual schemes (96 per cent) than for collective schemes (81 per cent) (Table 8.3).

Methods and materials for the evaluation

Although RDP has been in operation for several years, no appreciable attempt had been made previously to measure its impact on the income and employment of the beneficiaries of RDP. Because the RDP branches from which credit

Table 8.3   Share of loans for different types, duration and nature of activities (up to 1989)

Type of activities	Percentage of total credit disbursed
Small trading	53.4
Agriculture	12.1
Irrigation	7.2
Livestock (rearing and fattening)	17.3
Fish culture	1.0
Rural transport	3.2
Rural industries	5.5
Others	0.3

Duration of loans	Percentage of total credit	Percentage repayment rate
Short term (less than one year)	54.1	95.6
Medium term (between 1 and 3 years)	39.1	88.9
Long term (more than 3 years)	6.8	70.8

Individual and collective		
Individual loan	82.9	95.9
Collective loan	17.1	80.6

operations are managed were started at different times over the years, the volume and type of credit operations varied between different branches. So when the Research and Evaluation Division began to conduct its study we decided to concentrate only on the branches that started during RDP's earliest phase. Out of eight branches from this phase, four were selected at random. From each branch 50 male and 50 female members were selected at random. In the selection, it was ensured that each member chosen had been associated with an RDP-organized group for at least seven years and that all members came from separate households. This was known as the 'study group'. We were interested in knowing the overall impact on all group members and not only on those who received loans, and hence we did not concentrate only on borrowers.

For comparison we also selected a 'control' group. Within the same branch 50 males and 50 females were selected from the groups that had been organized only a short time before and had been given no credit yet. Such a selection of the 'control' ensured that the members belonged to a similar socio-economic group as the study group. The only difference between members of the control and study groups was that they had not yet been exposed to RDP credit. All the study group samples had joined RDP before 1982 and those of the control in late 1987. The survey was carried out in February 1988.

Although the ultimate samples were the individual members of the RDP groups (old and new), we collected the required information about the households they belonged to. The main instrument of data collection was a questionnaire. We sought to collect detailed information on all the conceivable sources of household income from the previous Bengali year, such as agricultural production, wage labour, service, business, fisheries, poultry and livestock, kitchen gardens, the sale of handicrafts, and so on. Information on employment, indebtedness, and the possession of assets was also collected. Income received from various sources was converted into taka equivalents using, where necessary, the existing prices. For estimating employment, the number of person-days employed for each source of income was determined. Because of the high incidence of under-employment, it is very difficult to calculate productive employment and the period of unemployment or under-employment. Therefore, such information should be taken with a pinch of salt. The methods employed for both study and control samples were the same, however, and any limitations with respect to the methodology should apply equally to both.

The difficulty of collecting reliable information on income in the rural areas, and particularly from the poor, is well recognized; however, we made every effort to identify all the possible sources of income. The interviewers who collected the data were holders of master's degrees and were extensively trained for the purpose. One of the authors was personally present in the field throughout the data collection operation and he also supervised the processing and analysis in BRAC's head office in Dhaka. An analysis of the demographic and socio-economic characteristics of the study and control samples suggested that they were closely matched.

Results

The per capita annual income in the study households was Tk.3502, which is 26 per cent higher than that of the control and the difference is statistically significant (p <0.05). In respect of average household income, the study household's was 29 per cent higher than the control group's (p<0.05).

Table 8.4 shows that the sources of income of the two groups are not very dissimilar. Trading appears to be the most popular principal source of income in both groups. When secondary sources were considered, however, cultivation took the lead, pushing trading to the second position. The proportion of households who earned some income from trading was greater in study households (34.5 per cent) than in control households (29 per cent).

If we consider wage labour (agricultural and non-agricultural), we find that 35 per cent of control households have this as their principal income source, which is higher than the study group's 21.5 per cent. On the other hand, if we consider the income sources that need some capital basis (such as cultivation, trade, cottage industry and transport), 59.5 per cent of the study sample have this as their principal source of income compared to the control's 49.5 per cent.

The table also shows the difference between the two groups with respect to the proportion of households that have more than one source of income. Among the study households, 60.5 per cent and 26 per cent had second and

Table 8.4   Proportion of households by income sources

Source of income	% of study households reporting this as:				% of control households reporting this as:			
	Principal source	2nd source	3rd source	% of hhs earning something from this source	Principal source	2nd source	3rd source	% of hhs earning something from this source
Cultivation	15.0	20.5	7.5	43.0	7.0	24.0	5.0	36.0
Agricultural wage labour	10.5	3.5	1.0	15.0	17.0	3.0	0.5	20.5
Wage labour	11.0	6.5	1.0	18.5	18.0	3.5	1.5	23.0
Trade	22.0	8.5	4.0	34.5	25.5	3.0	0.5	29.0
Cottage industry	10.5	2.5	2.5	15.5	7.5	6.0	1.0	14.5
Salaried service	6.0	7.0	3.0	16.0	7.5	4.0	1.0	12.5
Transport	12.0	3.0	1.0	16.0	9.5	2.0	0.5	12.0
Others	13.0	9.0	6.0	28.0	8.0	2.0	6.0	16.0
All occupations	100.0	60.5	26.0	186.5[1]	100.0	47.5	16.0	163.5[1]

1. The percentage exceeds 100 because a single household can be engaged in multiple occupations.

third sources of income, whereas only 47.5 per cent and 16 per cent among the control households respectively have these incomes.

Impact of RDP on employment generation

The problems of estimating employment in our rural areas has already been mentioned. We calculated the number of person-days in employment for study and control group households and found that the total amount of employment was 19 per cent higher for the study group than for the control, and that the group members in turn hired labour three times more often than the control.

With respect to the number of income earners there were 1.61 workers per household in the study samples compared to 1.38 for the control. The activity ratio (the proportion of the population of working age who are in employment) of 28.7 per cent for the study sample was higher than that of the control, which was 25.1 per cent. The average number of dependants was greater in control households.

We also investigated how men and women are employed in the study and control households. Whereas the number of person-days of employment for men was 9 per cent more in the study samples than in the control, it was 34 per cent more for females in the study samples. Also, the ratio of female to male employment was more favourable in the study samples.

Table 8.5 shows the ownership of different household goods and assets in study and control households. It shows that, except for ducks, the study households possessed more of all the selected items of assets.

Table 8.5   Assets owned by study and control households

Asset	No. of households owning		% difference of study over control samples
	Study	Control	
Cattle	184	138	+ 33.3
Goats	149	110	+ 35.4
Ducks	86	172	−100.0
Chicken	784	390	+101.0
Rickshaws	41	8	+412.5
Bicycles	22	16	+ 37.5
Agricultural machinery (per set)	56	36	+ 55.5
Weaving machines	27	15	+ 80.0
Total	1349	885	+ 52.4

Future plans

Bangladesh has inherited many complex economic, social and political problems. Over the years since independence, the overall economic situation has worsened and the poor have become poorer. The proportion of landless and those below the poverty line has increased alarmingly.

One of the causes of poverty in rural Bangladesh is the lack of access to unexploitative credit for the poor. BRAC has been experimenting with credit for the poor since 1974, and in 1979 it decided to bring credit under a separate programme structure. To provide institutional credibility, BRAC has initiated the process of 'graduating' RDP into a fully-fledged rural bank in the near future. An RDP branch will be bought over by the proposed BRAC Bank when that branch reaches a 'break-even' situation (Tk.6.4 million in outstanding credit) so as to support all costs from the interest earned. Other conditions for the transfer include a total membership of 7000 and 3400 outstanding borrowers per branch.

The target group of BRAC are those poor men and women who sell their manual labour for survival and who are landless. BRAC's Rural Development Programme has also provided the target groups with other inputs such as functional education and vocational training.

Over the years RDP has grown steadily, and by 1989 it had formed 6524 village organizations (VOs) with a total membership of 355 675, 61 per cent of whom were women. The total savings of the group members exceeded Tk.69 million. RDP has provided Tk.473 million in credit and the repayment rate has also been quite high – 96.5 per cent on time. Of the total credit disbursed, female group members received 53 per cent. RDP has an ambitious plan for growth: by the turn of the century, RDP (including the proposed BRAC Bank) will be working from nearly 400 branches in rural Bangladesh, serving a clientele of nearly three million men and women.

A comparison with other programmes

By comparison, Grameen Bank, another pioneer in credit for the rural poor, expanded more quickly than RDP. Started in 1976, GB has now nearly 700 branches serving a clientele of over 600 000 landless poor (Grameen Bank, 1990) with an excellent repayment record of 98 per cent. It may be worthwhile here to point out how RDP is different from Grameen Bank. While Grameen Bank is basically an institution to 'provide a reasonably dependable forum through which the banking system can extend credit to the landless without collateral' (Yunus, 1982), RDP is a programme for the comprehensive development of the poor. Apart from credit, the components of RDP also include consciousness raising, institution building, training, and technical and logistical support.

Even in the disbursement of credit, the principles of RDP are in many ways different from those of Grameen Bank. While Grameen credit is available almost immediately after the formation of a group, RDP takes approximately six months to develop the group to a standard considered necessary before disbursing credit. RDP forms men's and women's village organizations for exercising greater political power, but Grameen Bank forms a group with five members to receive credit, also separately for men and women. While RDP credit is strictly supervised and is intended to be used for the purpose for which it is granted, 'Grameen Bank loanees are left to their individual choices as to what to do to utilize the loans as long as they earn some income and repay the loans' (Hossain, 1984). While loans for collective activities are encouraged in RDP, most loans from Grameen Bank are to individuals.

Although RDP has been operational since 1979, there has not been any serious attempt to measure its impact. Recognizing the difficulties in measuring the impact on qualities such as awareness, we decided to concentrate initially on a few tangibles such as income, employment and assets. The measurement of these is, however, fraught with difficulties. Many authors have used different methods of measuring income and employment in rural areas. Hossain (1984) used a number of methods in the case of Grameen Bank. Rahman (1986) used a micro-level investigation to study the same institution. In our study of RDP, we used the 'control group' method to measure the impact. Because of the difficulties in collecting reliable retrospective information on income and employment, the reader should be cautious in interpreting the absolute results. However, since the same methods of data collection and analyses were used for both the study and the control samples, the differentials found between the groups should hold even if there are doubts about the validity of the absolute results.

In this paper we have presented some results from this study that have indicated that RDP has made some positive impact. The per capita annual income of the study households was found to be 26 per cent higher than that of the control households ($p<0.05$). Is this due to RDP intervention? It can be questioned whether all the increase in the study group's incomes was due to RDP intervention.

Of the sectors financed through RDP credit, trading and cultivation occupy the top positions with respect to the amount disbursed. Both study and control groups had these as their major sources of income. The proportion of households who earned some income from trading, however, was greater among study households (34.5 per cent) than among controls (29 per cent). This has possibly resulted from RDP credit, which provided 53 per cent of its total credit in this sector.

Thirty-five per cent of control households had wage labour (agricultural and non-agricultural) as their principal source of income compared to the study group's 21.5 per cent. This requires no capital and is probably the last resort of a person who has no land or other assets to start some other trade; clearly the control households without RDP credit and training services had to depend more on this. In other occupations that need some capital basis (such as cultivation, trading, cottage industry or transport), more of the RDP households (59.5 per cent) were deriving their principal income from these compared to 49.5 per cent in control households. The study households also had more separate sources of income per household than the controls.

We have also attempted to estimate the impact of RDP on the employment situation. The study households generated more employment than the controls. Because of the availability of credit, more household members, particularly women, have an opportunity for self-employment. With respect to asset ownership, the study households were consistently better off than the control households.

The samples for this study came from the earlier branches, which are not 'A' category branches in RDP's own assessment. They were the first to be started and many initial experiments were carried out with them. Punctual repayment is worse in these branches (about 80 per cent compared to 100 per cent in many others that were started later). Although the programme in these branches was started in 1979–84, not all members received a loan. Through the study we covered all member households irrespective of whether they received a loan as we wanted to get an overall picture of the impact on all members. The controls did not receive any loan from RDP but were involved with other RDP interventions such as functional education. Through such involvement, it is expected that they may have raised their consciousness, which might have helped them to increase their income even without RDP credit. Given these facts, it is probable that the impact of RDP that we have been able to measure is biased downwards. Another study that compared the income of RDP group members with a baseline found an increase of 116 per cent in real income, 84 per cent in employment and 153 per cent in the possession of assets (Ahmed et al., 1988).

Because of methodological problems, neither the cost nor the cost-effectiveness of the RDP credit has been explored through this study. Since RDP workers are also involved in activities other than credit, apportioning their time is a real problem. Future studies will look at this question.

We may now compare some of our results with those found elsewhere. We shall restrict this to those found by Hossain (1984) and Rahman (1986) in their studies of Grameen Bank. In a study involving 62 borrowers and 54 controls, Hossain (1984) found a 30.8 per cent increase in per capita income among the borrowers. We found that RDP group members had a 26 per cent higher per capita income. With respect to the generation of employment, Hossain found an activity ratio of 30 per cent for Grameen Bank borrowers and 24.3 per cent for control groups.

Compared to this we found the activity ratio of 28.7 per cent for RDP households and 25.1 per cent for control households. It seems that although the strategies of RDP differ from those of Grameen Bank as outlined above, both are having a very similar impact on their beneficiaries, the landless peasants of Bangladesh. Through Grameen Bank, a much larger number of beneficiaries are being served. On the other hand, RDP's beneficiaries are also getting benefits other than just credit, which should have a much wider and far-reaching impact. Both these interventions are showing promise for the development of the poorest sections of Bangladesh and they should be constantly monitored.

References

Ahmed, Z., et al. (1988), 'Economic empowerment of the rural poor: changes in household income, employment and resources', unpublished paper, Dhaka, BRAC.
Bangladesh Rural Advancement Committee, (1990), *Annual Report, Rural Development Programme*, Dhaka.
Bangladesh Rural Advancement Committee, (1975), *Annual Report, Sulla Project 1974*, Dhaka.
Grameen Bank, (1990), *Annual Report 1989*, Dhaka.
Hossain, M., (1984), *Credit for the rural poor*, Dhaka, Bangladesh Institute of Development Studies.
Rahman, A., (1986), *Demand and marketing aspects of Grameen Bank*, Dhaka, University Press Limited.
World Bank, (1988), *World Development Report*, Washington, DC.
Yunus, M., (1982), 'Experiences in organising grass-root initiatives and mobilising people's participation: the case of Grameen Bank Project', Society for International Development, 25th Annual Conference, Baltimore, USA.

About the authors

A.M.R. Chowdhury is Executive Director of the Research and Evaluation Division, BRAC; M. Mahmood is a former research economist, BRAC; F.H. Abed is the Chairperson, BRAC.

9 The effects of liberalization on access to bank credit in Kenya

PENINAH W. KARIUKI

This paper was first published in March 1995.

When structural adjustment policies in Kenya advocated the liberalization of commercial bank interest rates it was expected that bank credit, at realistic interest rates, would become more readily available to small businesses. This study suggests that although more businesses have become the customers of banks, the overall volume of credit has not necessarily increased. Taken together with a squeeze in demand for their products and high inflation, small businesses are not always eager for larger bank loans at higher interest rates.

INTEREST RATE LIBERALIZATION is one of the major components of structural adjustment programmes of the International Monetary Fund and the World Bank. One of the main bases on which interest rate liberalization is advocated is that it reduces the 'financial repression' of small-scale borrowers by allowing banks to cover the higher costs and risks associated with such lending. Based on the assumption that small-scale borrowers are financially constrained so that they are willing and able to borrow, this is expected to improve their access to formal sources of credit and, therefore, their use of such credit. This paper evaluates this expectation by looking at the use of commercial bank credit by a sample of small- and medium-scale industrial enterprises (SMEs) in Kenya.

The background

Interest rate policy in post-independent Kenya was fairly unchanging in the 1960s and 1970s. The government administered interest rates through a regime of fixing minimum savings rates for all deposit-taking institutions and minimum lending rates for commercial banks, non-bank financial institutions (NBFIs) and building societies. The first interest rate review in the post-independence era was undertaken in June 1974 when the minimum savings and lending rates were raised by 2 and 1 percentage points respectively. Furthermore '... it had been official policy in Kenya since independence to follow a 'low interest rate policy' in order to encourage investment and protect the small borrower' (Central Bank of Kenya, 1986, p. 54). Consequently, when adjusted for inflation, most interest rates were negative in the 1970s.

Some changes were effected in 1981. First, in April the government switched to setting maximum as opposed to minimum lending rates. More importantly, there were reviews in the level of interest rates in June and September 1981. In spite of these reviews, real interest rates remained negative, and were still negative by the time the second structural adjustment loan (SAL) was negotiated in 1982. It is, therefore, not surprising that the maintenance of positive real interest rates was specified as a policy condition in the second SAL.

A gradual liberalization strategy whereby the nominal rates were reviewed regularly was pursued until July 1981, when the rates were fully deregulated. From 1982, various reviews were made to the deposit and lending rates of commercial banks, NBFIs, and building societies. There were reviews in October 1982, June 1984, January 1988, April and November 1989 and in April 1990. Real interest rates became positive in 1983. The liberalization exercise was unmistakably justified using the theoretical arguments advanced and popularized by McKinnon (1973) and Shaw (1973). Thus, its objectives were stated as '... to encourage the mobilization of savings and contribute to the maintenance of financial stability ... and to ensure that funds flow into those areas which are most productive, and that the biases which have existed against lending to small business ... are eliminated' (Central Bank of Kenya, 1988, p. 18). To what extent, then, have these objectives been achieved?

Methodology

This study sought to evaluate the extent to which this latter objective has been achieved, by looking at the use of commercial bank credit by small- and medium-scale enterprises (SMEs) in Kenya in the 1980s. In addition to secondary data, primary information was collected from a sample of 5 commercial banks and 89 SMEs. For this purpose, SMEs were defined as formal sector firms with less than 50 employees. This is important because such firms could be expected to be big enough to use formal sector banks. In addition, the study focused on firms engaged in manufacturing and service industries. This definition allows the inclusion of firms in the 'missing middle' which has been noted to be a characteristic of the country's industrial set-up (Kilby, 1988, p. 224; World Bank, 1987, p. 222).

The sample SMEs were selected from firms operating on industrial premises owned by the Kenya Industrial Estates (KIE). This made it possible to capture a variety of sub-sectors in an easily reached but varied sample, since these premises house together SMEs engaged in diverse activities. However, it could be argued that the firms operating in KIE industrial premises are better placed than firms of similar size operating elsewhere in terms of access to services, raw materials and credit, and are not representative in this respect. Consequently, it would be naive to deny that this limits the extent to which the results can be generalized. This argument can also be used to strengthen the results, however: if the sample firms are found to encounter problems in their access to credit in spite of their relatively advantageous position, this would indeed imply that the results apply with even greater relevance to the less advantaged firms. The results of the study are reported in the following sections.

SMEs' sources of finance

The 89 entrepreneurs in the study were asked to specify the sources of their initial capital, capital for further expansion, and working capital. As regards initial capital, the most important sources among the 89 SMEs were self-finance and KIE. Fifty-two firms (58.4 per cent) had relied on their own savings, while 26 (29.2 per cent) had borrowed from KIE. Commercial banks had financed only three firms and co-financed another two with KIE. Relatively less prominent were the other development finance institutions and other organizations. The Industrial and Commercial Development Corporation (ICDC) had financed four firms, while the Small Enterprise Finance Company (SEFCO) and the Kenya Women Finance Trust (KWFT) had each financed one firm. As noted earlier, the prominence of KIE needs to be interpreted with caution, as this is basically due to the fact that the sample was selected from firms operating on its industrial premises.

How important were these institutions as sources of short-term loans for expansion and/or working capital? As regards the former, 10 firms were fairly new in operation and had not had the occasion to increase their fixed assets, while another 7 also claimed not to have increased theirs. For the remaining 72 firms, 44 (61.1 per cent) had used retained profits, while 19 (26.4 per cent) had borrowed from KIE.

With regard to working capital, the major sources were identified as savings or profits, bank overdraft, suppliers' credit and advance deposit from buyers. Relatively uncommon were export pre-shipment finance, letters of credit and foreign creditors. Indeed, only one firm relies on export pre-shipment finance, while only three have opened sight letters of credit on various occasions. Only one firm had resorted to foreign borrowing once (through the Industrial Development Bank) in 1983. However, this had resulted in a huge loss due to the foreign exchange risk and this form of credit had, therefore, been discontinued. All the firms said that they rely on self-finance and supplement it with the other types of financing. Fifty-two firms (58.4 per cent) rely on bank overdraft, either on its own or combined with the other types, while another 32 and 30 rely on suppliers' credit and customers' deposits respectively (again, on their own or in combination with other types). However, evidence regarding resort to informal sources (moneylenders) was difficult to obtain and only one entrepreneur admitted the use of such finances.

While these results provide useful insight into SMEs' sources of finance, there is a need to evaluate their access to such credit over time. The study focused specifically on credit from commercial banks.

The number of SMEs with commercial bank credit

The survey revealed that 52 firms (58.4 per cent) had gained access to commercial bank credit in the form of short-term loans or overdraft at various times. These firms were asked to state the year when they got access to the facilities for the first time. This is a measure of accessibility as it shows whether banks financed more or fewer SMEs over the years. The results show that, over the years, commercial banks have been able to finance more SMEs. The increase in the numbers financed was particularly remarkable in the latter part of the 1980s when the number of firms borrowing for the first time was double the number financed in the earlier part of the decade. This has led to increases in the proportion of SMEs enjoying commercial bank facilities over time. While 25 per cent of the operational SMEs were borrowing from commercial banks by 1970, this ratio rose steadily in the 1980s such that it was 58.4 per cent by 1991.

The volume of SME credit from commercial banks

Out of the 52 SMEs, 34 provided their annual accounts from which the volume of their borrowing from commercial banks was obtained. This was deflated to reflect the value in real terms. Annual percentage changes were calculated for each firm since the SMEs presented accounts from diverse dates.

The results do not portray a consistent trend in the annual changes in credit from commercial banks. Indeed, for 30 SMEs (88.2 per cent), increases are noted in some years and decreases in others. Furthermore, whereas no single SME sustains increases in credit over any period, two firms record annual decreases from 1987 onwards. Another two initially experience both increases and decreases until 1986, when decreases set in and are not reversed. A look at the number and proportion of firms that increased their level of borrowing from commercial banks (in real terms) on an annual basis from 1981–90 reveals that it was only in 1982–4 when more than half of the SMEs who were already borrowing actually increased their credit. Such proportions have not been achieved since. In fact, in 1990, out of 31 SMEs that borrowed that year, only 6 (19.4 per cent) realized increases in commercial bank credit.

An analysis of the trends in the average real volume of credit for the sample firms as a whole reveals some interesting developments. Increases were recorded in only three out of the 10 years under consideration. Indeed, in the second half of the 1980s (when real interest rates were positive), the average real volume of credit fell, except in 1986 when a marginal increase of 1.5 per cent was recorded.

A review of the literature on the financing of SMEs reveals that there are some factors that could deter SMEs from increasing their use of formal credit, even when access to such credit is relatively easy. Such factors include the transaction costs of borrowing and other operational constraints. In addition, the level of the nominal lending rate is important. Some evidence gathered from the survey offers an insight into these issues.

The level of lending rates

It has been argued that the level of the nominal lending rates is important due to its influence on the risk of borrowing (see, for example, Harvey and Jenkins, 1993). If positive real rates are achieved at high nominal rates of interest, then the risk of borrowing is greater. Faced with high nominal rates and high inflation, producers can certainly expect their production costs to rise with the general price level. By contrast, a rise in their sales prices is less certain, such that producers are exposed to a severe risk. Moreover, the tendency for high inflation to be more variable makes the risk even greater.

An analysis of the movements in the nominal lending rate, inflation rate and real lending rate is, therefore, in order. This reveals that there were increases in nominal lending rates from 1980 to 1983, and from 1987 to 1990. Trends in the rate of inflation generally revealed a decline between 1982 and 1986 and an increase since then. Borrowers have, therefore, faced higher nominal interest rates at higher inflation rates in the latter half of the 1980s. It can be expected that this increased the risk of using borrowed funds for all borrowers, including SMEs.

SMEs' transaction costs of borrowing

In addition to interest costs, it is recognized that there are other costs that are incurred in the borrowing process. These are referred to as transaction costs of borrowing and are defined to include explicit cash costs (for example, on travel and other expenses arising from the borrowing process) and opportunity costs of time spent applying for and obtaining the loan. These costs have been found to be surprisingly high for small-scale borrowers and to act as a deterrent to their use of formal credit (see for example Adams and Nehman, 1979; Ladman, 1984; Ahmed, 1989).

Because of limitations in the data from SMEs, it was possible to estimate only part of the explicit costs. First, it was difficult to obtain data on expenditure on travel and other miscellaneous expenses. Second, the SMEs could furnish data pertaining only to the total actual payments that they made to the banks, without disaggregating such payments into interest costs and other charges. It was, therefore, assumed that their loans were effected at the ruling maximum lending rates. The difference between this rate and that obtained by dividing the total payments by the loan amounts was taken to represent the effective explicit transaction cost of borrowing.

It is recognized, however, that this approach poses some problems. The first is that for borrowers whose total payments were less than the maximum lending rate, their other costs are indistinguishable. Second, even for those for whom it is possible to estimate other costs, the assumption that their facilities were effected at the maximum lending rate introduces a bias such that these costs are overestimated for some borrowers.

Another problem arises from the lack of data on expenditure on travel and other miscellaneous expenses. The most common method is to rely on the borrowers' recall. Although this is useful, its application is limited to the very recent past and it becomes difficult to obtain data on a trend basis. In addition, visits to the bank are usually combined with other missions such that the travel and other costs associated only with the loan become indeterminate. Furthermore, for expenditure items like bribes, it is virtually impossible to elicit any information.

The method that was used in this study was to estimate the average explicit transaction and interest costs of borrowing for the SMEs with adequate data and, consequently, their total costs of borrowing. The effect of explicit transaction costs of borrowing on the total costs of borrowing is clear. Indeed, from 1987, the results show that these two are almost perfectly correlated. Furthermore, there was a sharp increase in the transaction costs, such that by 1990 they were almost as high as interest costs. This outcome seems surprising, especially considering the fact that commercial banks were not allowed to levy other charges on their lending until 1989. However, a possible explanation is that the banks effectively circumvented the official restrictions.

These results imply that the explicit transaction costs of borrowing for SMEs are high in relation to the interest costs. This suggests that analyses that do not take these costs into consideration are incomplete, especially considering that the opportunity costs of the time spent in obtaining loans are not included.

As well as explicit travel costs, a borrower has to spend time in applying for and obtaining a loan, and thus incurs implicit costs in terms of work forgone. It follows then that the opportunity cost of borrowing depends not just on the proximity of bank services, but also on the relationship between the borrower and the banker and the procedures and requirements that the lender imposes.

In brief, the procedures that are involved in applying for commercial bank credit facilities in Kenya are as follows. The process starts with the borrower calling personally at the bank to attend an interview with the manager or lending officer. The essence of this is to give borrowers a chance to explain their investment proposals. It is, therefore, important for the borrower to be able to communicate effectively with the lender. The applicant is then required to furnish detailed financial and personal information. If this is satisfactory, the documentation of security commences – which also involves its valuation and insurance where applicable. The transaction is formalized by a letter of offer, and drawdown can start after the offer is accepted.

In this study, the ability of entrepreneurs to meet the banks' requirements was assessed by looking at their level of education, the records that they maintain and the availability of acceptable security. As regards the level of education, the results showed that all the proprietors had attained sufficient education to make them functionally literate and numerate. It was also noted during the interviews that all of them were fluent in Swahili, while 61 (68.5 per cent) were fluent in English.

As regards the maintenance of financial records, it was observed that there were considerable differences in the types of records that the SMEs maintained. While a majority of them (91 per cent) keep the very basic cash book, fewer (79.8 per cent) maintain invoice and receipt files against which entries in the cash book can be checked. Of these, 66 (74.2 per cent) utilize such records to generate the slightly more elaborate ledgers from which the profit and loss accounts and cash flow statements that are demanded by banks can be extracted. This implies that the failure to maintain adequate financial records could prove to be an obstacle for about a quarter of the firms.

Although it is often argued that unavailability of acceptable security is a major constraint to SMEs, the results suggest that this may not be the case. Among the 37 firms that had never borrowed, 30 of them (81.1 per cent) said that collateral (in the form of land or other property) would not be a problem if they needed to borrow. However, it is important to note that lack of collateral was a serious problem in areas where land has not been demarcated. This is borne out by the fact that five out of the eight entrepreneurs with no security were from a region where land titles are not yet available.

All these requirements can lead to high opportunity costs for the borrowers in terms of the time spent away from work and also in terms of unnecessary delay which could deny the borrower the chance to grasp the opportunity for which the loan was intended (Harper, 1984, p. 53). The common method used to calculate the opportunity cost is to multiply the number of days (or hours) that are actually spent away from work in connection with the loan by the estimated daily (or hourly) income (Ahmed, 1989, p. 358–9). In practice, however, it is difficult to apportion the time spent away from work on different missions which are often undertaken on the same day. This renders the estimation of the opportunity costs difficult. However, their extent can be indicated by the time it takes to get a facility approved by a bank. It can be expected that the number of visits or other contacts with the bank increases with the duration of the time taken to obtain an approval.

In order to assess the time that the approval process takes, the 52 entrepreneurs who had borrowed were asked about their very first facilities, these being important events, the details of which were less likely to have been forgotten.

The results show that most of the facilities (51.9 per cent) took about two months to approve, while five applicants had to wait for more than three months. The longest time taken was six months for one applicant, while the shortest was one week for two applicants. The delays usually arose because it took some time for borrowers to sort out the requirements, especially those regarding security and financial statements. In cases where approval was fast, this was facilitated by the fact that the borrower already had an ongoing personal facility with the bank which made some of the procedures relatively easy. In addition, the two applicants whose facilities were approved within a week of requesting them also said that they were personally known to the managers.

In all cases, subsequent facilities were granted automatically without any delay. This implies that the opportunity costs of borrowing are high for new borrowers. It also suggests that there is scope for reducing such costs through the forging of cordial working relationships with the banks. However, this itself involves time and, therefore, opportunity costs which need to be weighed against the benefits.

Other operational constraints

The expectation that SMEs would be both willing and able to borrow from formal institutions if availability of funds is assured, amounts to an assumption that other operational constraints are either absent, or that they can be solved by increased availability of funds. To test the validity of this, the entrepreneurs in the study were asked to identify their major operational problems. On the whole, demand constraints emerged as the most serious problem. This was cited as a problem by 78.6 per cent of the firms surveyed. The second and third most important problems were lack of working capital (69.7 per cent of the firms) and inadequate supplies of raw materials (47.2 per cent).

As regards the demand for SME products, some evidence was adduced which suggests that the SMEs operate in highly competitive markets. A majority of the firms (80.9 per cent) sell direct to individuals while sales to wholesalers are the second most important, providing a sales outlet for 47.6 per cent of the firms. Sales to central and local government, and exports are relatively insignificant. In addition, no evidence of sub-contracting was obtained.

In addition to the overall size of the market, it is important to consider the availability of substitutes and the possibilities for product differentiation. Some sub-sectoral examples can shed light on this. In the textiles sub-sector, for example, the major complaint was the competition from imported second-hand clothes. This was cited as a problem by 45 per cent of the firms. Severe competition from other local small firms undertaking tailoring was said to exacerbate the problem. Most of the firms had, therefore, resorted to undertaking orders whereby the clients provide the cloth. In this respect, there was little scope for improving competitiveness through product differentiation. At any rate, the nature of their operations is such that they can easily copy from each other. Two firms had tried to solve this problem by specializing in tailoring school uniforms, but they were suffering from fluctuating sales resulting from the seasonality of demand.

Most of the firms in the furniture and wooden products sub-sector experienced a low level of sales, mainly due to the homogeneous nature of their products. Except for one firm, which produced wooden clothes pegs, these firms produced a variety of household or institutional furniture, and consequently competition from other small firms was severe. Product differentiation is difficult, as the firms can easily copy designs from each other. The firm that produces clothes pegs has to contend with competition from producers of plastic pegs.

In the motor vehicle repair firms, the major complaint was the cut-throat competition from the *jua kali* (informal) mechanics. As the initial investment for starting up this business is very low, there are numerous mechanics offering this service. Some of the firms in the paper industry that were producing packaging material were facing a different kind of competition from firms producing plastic material.

As regards markets for the supply of raw materials, this involves considering the sources and availability of usual inputs, prices and methods of payment, substitutes and alternative sources. Although input requirements vary with the type, size and particular product line of the business, it can be expected that raw materials will emerge as a binding constraint if the supply is unreliable. Inputs can either be locally sourced or imported. From the interviews, it was established that only five SMEs (5.6 per cent) rely on direct imports. Although this implies that their inputs are nominally local, such inputs can have a high import content. The supply and prices of raw materials, therefore, depend on the nature of the item and the way it is produced in the country, as the following sub-sectoral examples show.

The availability of raw materials emerged as an important constraint in the food processing, paper and wooden products sub-sectors. Because of their reliance on agricultural produce, all the firms involved in food processing have to contend with fluctuations in the supply of raw materials arising from inadequate production or government interference. The bakeries experience chronic shortages of flour; the grain millers have inadequate supplies of maize; the oil miller cannot obtain enough coconut, while the sugar packaging firm does not get enough sugar. The firms producing animal feeds based on fish also face similar problems.

In the paper industry, the basic constraint was the availability of paper. This is obtained from a monopoly seller in the country and supplies are irregular. For some producers of wooden products, the availability of certain types of wood was a problem, owing to government restrictions on tree felling.

From these results, it is clear that although the constraints that SMEs face cannot be generalized, there are considerable limitations on their operations imposed by low sales and inadequate supplies of raw materials. Such problems cannot be solved by the removal of the financial constraint, as this is not necessarily the most binding constraint for most SMEs.

Conclusion

The survey results show that the use of commercial bank credit by SMEs did not increase significantly following interest rate liberalization in Kenya. The analysis reveals that there are various obstacles that could prevent SMEs from generating an effective demand for formal credit. First, there is evidence that like all other borrowers, SMEs were faced with higher nominal interest rates and higher inflation rates in the latter half of the 1980s. Consequently, the risks attached to borrowing increased.

Second, available data on the transaction costs of borrowing indicate that these rose in the 1980s, thereby increasing the total costs of borrowing for the SMEs.

Third, further evidence suggests that a financial constraint may not have been the most important constraint for some SMEs, although its existence cannot be ruled out. While the constraints that SMEs face cannot be generalized, available evidence points to considerable limitations arising from low sales and inadequate supplies of raw materials. Such problems are not solved by increased availability of funds and need to be addressed directly.

On the whole, it appears logical to conclude that while it is important to ensure the availability of funds to SMEs, it may be better to lower their costs to enable them to become creditworthy on commercial criteria. This can be done by adopting measures that improve their profitability, for example, by improving the infrastructure and by opening new markets to them. Furthermore, the fact that interest rate liberalization is undertaken in the wider context of structural adjustment underlines the need to evaluate the impact of the strategy as a whole.

References

Adams, D.W. and G.I. Nehman, (1979), 'Borrowing costs and the demand for rural credit', *Journal of Development Studies*, Vol. 15, No. 2.

Ahmed, Z.U., (1989), 'Effective costs of rural loans in Bangladesh', *World Development*, Vol. 17, No. 3.

Central Bank of Kenya, (1986), *Central Bank of Kenya: its evolution, responsibilities and organisation*, Nairobi, Central Bank of Kenya.

Central Bank of Kenya, (1988), *Economic report for the year ended 30th June 1988*, Nairobi, Central Bank of Kenya.

Harper, M., (1984), *Small Business in the Third World*, Chichester, John Wiley and Sons.

Harvey, C. and C. Jenkins, (1993), 'Taxation, risk and real interest rates', IDS Discussion Paper, No. 336.

Kilby, P., (1988), 'Breaking the entrepreneurial bottle-neck in late developing countries: is there a useful role for government?', *Journal of Development Planning*, No. 18.

Ladman, J.R., (1984), 'Loan-transaction costs, credit rationing and market structure: the case of Bolivia', in D.W. Adams, D.H. Graham and J.D. von Pischke (eds.), *Undermining rural development with cheap credit*, Boulder, Westview Press.

McKinnon, R.I., (1973), *Money and capital in economic development*, Washington, DC, Brookings Institution.

Shaw, E.S., (1973), *Financial deepening in economic development*, New York, Oxford University Press.

World Bank, (1987), *Kenya: industrial sector policies for investment and export growth*, Report No. 6711-KE, Volume 2 Main Report, Washington, DC, World Bank.

About the author

Peninah Kariuki wrote this paper while she was a Visiting Fellow at IDS, University of Sussex. She is now Senior Manager in the Research Department of the Central Bank of Kenya. The paper was based on the author's doctoral thesis.

10 'Are you poor enough?' – client selection by microfinance institutions

GRAHAM A.N. WRIGHT and ALEKE DONDO

This paper was first published in March 2001.

The debate between the proponents of maximizing sustainability, outreach and scale and thus serving many poor people (including poorer people) and the proponents of targeting 'the poorest of the poor' continues. The debate is essentially a healthy one, helping everyone involved in the industry to focus on what matters: providing financial services to poor people.

This paper argues that microfinance institution (MFI) programmes should include the 'non-poor' on the grounds that this more profitable business can cross-subsidize outreach to the poor, and because, without access to any financial services, vulnerable non-poor people are likely to be reduced to poverty when a crisis arises. Regarding 'the poor', MFIs wishing to service this group should offer savings and other innovative products, since poor people have few opportunities to utilize Grameen-type credit efficiently. Finally, the very poor or destitute may require relief services before they can use most financial products. The challenge overall is to design appropriate products, and efficient systems – and in this way both MFIs and their clients will benefit.

IN THE WORDS of Elisabeth Rhyne (1999), 'Let us begin by noting that everyone involved in microfinance shares a basic goal: to provide credit and savings services to thousands or millions of poor people in a sustainable way. Everyone wants to reach the poor, and everyone believes sustainability is important. This is not an either–or debate. It is about degrees of emphasis and what happens when tradeoffs appear.' Nonetheless, many MFIs continue to spend a great deal of time and money ensuring that the clients they are recruiting are poor enough to warrant the organization's services.

Scale and sustainability

Christen et al.'s 1995 study, building on the arguments of Otero and Rhyne (1994), concluded that, 'Some observers have argued for an exclusive focus on the poorest clients, with the objective of poverty alleviation. The data assembled here and arguments for financial leverage, suggest that mixed programmes serving a range of clients can also be highly effective in reaching the poorest. It is scale, not exclusive focus, that determines whether significant outreach to the poor is achieved.'

The demand for microfinance services is huge. In the words of Marguerite Robinson, 'Most people in the world do not have access to institutional financial services, either for credit or for savings. Despite widespread demand, it is estimated that institutional finance is unavailable to over 80 per cent of all households in developing countries. This, of course, includes nearly all the poor people in the developing world' (Robinson, 1997). Christen et al. (1995) note that for microfinance institutions (MFIs) to reach the scale at which they are going to make a serious impact on the demand for microfinance services of about 2.5 billion people or 500 million households, they will need to leverage commercial funds. 'Programmes that do not attempt to achieve large-scale outreach are simply not making a dent in the global problem... Nationally relevant scale will generally not be met without substantial leverage. The donors' role should essentially be to underwrite the commercialization of microenterprise finance and invest in specific start-up programmes' (Christen et al., 1995). The move towards using commercial funds (patient equity, loans from banks and savings mobilized from clients) is well under way in Latin America, Asia, Africa and Eastern Europe.

Targeting poverty

However, for many of the advocates of 'targeting the poorest' it is this move towards an emphasis on sustainability and commercial funding that also results in 'mission drift' and the MFIs focusing increasingly on the non-poor as their preferred clients. For example, Rene Chao-Beroff (1997) argues that, 'The fact is that if priority is given to making (MFIs) profitable as quickly as possible, then the poorest will automatically be marginalized in favour of populations that are supposed to be more creditworthy.' More recently David Hulme (Ch 12 here) notes that 'outside Bangladesh it [the microfinance industry] has not even scratched the surface of poverty'; whether nearly 15 million Bank Rakyat Indonesia clients would agree with this is, of course, subject to debate.

A polarized debate over a common goal

The polarization between the two camps of 'sustainability' and 'targeting the poorest' was encapsulated by the original positions of the Consultative Group to Assist the Poorest (CGAP) and the MicroCredit Summit. Initially CGAP focused almost exclusively on maximizing sustainability and outreach. After an introduction to CGAP, the following three technical focus notes produced by the CGAP Secretariat dealt with 'Maximizing the outreach of microenterprise finance', 'Missing links: financial systems that work for the majority' and 'Regulation and supervision of microfinance institutions: stabilizing the new financial market'. This approach was entirely appropriate at the time of CGAP's inception in 1995, when much of the industry comprised community development-oriented NGOs taking uncertain steps towards providing financial services. By the time of the MicroCredit Summit, CGAP had established a common language for the industry and had catalysed the acceptance of 'best practices' built on the principle of sustainability as a central part of any self-respecting MFI.

The MicroCredit Summit set about advocating targeting to reach the 'poorest' and finding $11.6 billion to do so. With dreams of grants of that magnitude, it is small wonder that the MicroCredit Summit felt that it could place less emphasis on sustainability (and the savings services that might well have generated a substantial proportion of this colossal sum) while still achieving outreach to '100 million of the world's poorest families'. In a recent paper for and presentation to the 1999 MicroCredit Summit Meeting of Councils in Abidjan, Muhammad Yunus, managing director of the Grameen Bank, berated the donor community for failing to 'get money into the hands of the poorest' and consultants for trying to 'convince donors to avoid or de-emphasize the poverty issue.'

By 1999 a wide, dangerous and unnecessary gap had emerged between CGAP and the MicroCredit Summit. It was, and still is, dangerous since it is likely to confuse policy makers and funding agencies. It was unnecessary since the two institutions share the same goals – much of the gap is perceived rather than real. Most of the issues that divide the institutions are relatively easy to resolve with a little thoughtful discussion; however, the two institutions often speak different languages: one technical, the other crusading (Wright, 2000). Despite this, the two institutions have played an important role in influencing one another. CGAP is moving towards placing a greater emphasis on addressing poverty and deepening outreach, and the MicroCredit Summit is moving towards placing greater emphasis on sustainability and appropriate financial discipline. Both these moves are necessary and desirable.

Probably the most considered, balanced and conciliatory perspective is outlined by Elisabeth Rhyne in the 1997 *MicroBanking Bulletin* where she notes '...reaching the poor and sustainability are in large measure complementary, and particularly that sustainability serves outreach. Only by achieving a high degree of sustainability have microfinance programmes gained access to the funding they need over time to serve significant numbers of their poverty-level clients. This image reveals that *there is in fact only one objective – outreach. Sustainability is but the means to achieve it.* Sustainability is in no way an end in itself; it is only valued for what it brings to the clients of microfinance.'

The vulnerable non-poor

Participation in MFIs' programmes is not a recreational activity. It is not an activity that people with access to alternative formal sector financial services are generally willing to undertake. The interest rates on loans are typically 2–4 times that of the formal sector. Furthermore, despite the rhetoric often heard about the social capital generated in solidarity groups, the endless weekly meetings are typically not popular: poor (and non-poor) people have better things to do with their time, like running their businesses. The presence of the non-poor seeking services from MFIs demonstrates a clear need, an absence of alternatives and a lack of access to the formal financial system, or (at the very least) lack of access to credit facilities from the formal system.

Furthermore, the non-poor often present an increased risk for MFIs, since less-poor people typically have an inferior repayment record. Indeed, it is this fact that initially formed the basis of much of the rationale for targeting the poorest (see, for example, Gibbons, 1992). If you lend to the better-off, the argument ran, they are more likely to have the political power and access to alternatives that allow them to default – an argument corroborated by the experience of badly designed agricultural credit programmes throughout the 1970s and 1980s. If this is indeed the case, then clearly MFIs have to be careful about 'upward drift' on practical as well as philosophical grounds.

It is, however, the absence of alternatives for the non-poor and their need for ongoing access to financial services that drives repayment (Otero and Rhyne, 1994; Wright, 2000). Without access to financial services, the non-poor are particularly vulnerable since they have significantly reduced opportunities for storing their wealth in good times to respond to the times of crisis. (Readers might like to reflect on how they would deal with these issues in the absence of access to formal-sector financial services: no banks, no credit cards, no pension funds, no mortgages or car loans ...) It is this vulnerability and the ever-present risk of crisis that makes poverty dynamic.

Those who criticize microfinance for 'not reaching the poorest' tend to overlook the dynamic nature of poverty (see, for example, Hulme and Mosley, 1996) and to see it as a static position. 'Non-poor' households hit by a severe crisis (fire in houses and business, natural disasters, theft of business assets and chronic illness including HIV/AIDS and many others) may be transformed into 'poorest' households with alarming rapidity. This is why microfinance's role in assisting with the development and maintenance of robust household economic portfolios is so important – for anyone and everyone who does not have access to financial services from the formal sector.

Thus access to financial services allows these 'vulnerable non-poor' to protect themselves against the risks they face and the crises that regularly engulf them (Sebstad and Cohen, 2000). This protection is essential for vulnerable people and, as the saying goes, 'prevention is better (and cheaper) than cure'. Providing financial services to the vulnerable non-poor assists them to stay out of poverty. It is a course of action that is more cost-effective for both the client and the MFI.

In most development initiatives, the more people you serve, the greater the cost becomes; with microfinance initiatives journeying to sustainability, the costs decrease. There are also institutional advantages, even necessities, which suggest that broader targeting is desirable. The very poor are unlikely to take large enough loans to allow MFIs to achieve sustainability, thus securing the long-term existence of the MFI that provides essential financial services. Furthermore, once the MFI has the infrastructure in place and the staff travelling to serve the (perhaps non-poor) clients, the marginal cost of serving poorer clients decreases. MFIs need a broad mix of clients to achieve economies of scale and allow them to cross-subsidize to deepen their outreach. (To maintain the business perspective, MFIs can usefully view these cross-subsidies as 'loss leaders' necessary to cultivate clients over time in broadly the same way that banks often provide loss-making services to students in the hope that they will one day become good, high-value clients).

Finally, some would suggest that the secondary income and employment effects of providing services to the vulnerable non-poor and the 'missing middle' helps the poorer (usually risk-adverse and non-entrepreneurial) people more effectively than requiring all to become business people. Mosley (1999) in his study of Latin American MFIs for the *World Development Report 2000/1* suggested that secondary income and employment effects were beginning to come through. Certainly there is evidence that the poorest can enjoy higher daily wage labour rates in the villages of Bangladesh as a result of MFI activities (Khandker and Chowdhury, 1995). These secondary effects are indeed of tremendous importance since many of the poor are not natural entrepreneurs, and would like to be employed in preference to self-exploitative self-employment, generating marginal returns.

The 'poorest of the poor'

Sadly, 'the poorest of the poor' has become a catch phrase that has been rendered essentially meaningless by abuse and repetition. Realistically, the 'poorest of the poor' are rarely served by microfinance institutions – even by the people who use the catchphrase so often. It is increasingly clear and accepted that the majority of MFIs worldwide are not reaching the 'poorest of the poor' even in the more microfinance-friendly and population-dense environments such as Bangladesh (Wright, 2000). This is largely a result of the dominance of the Grameen Bank/FINCA models and the often startlingly unimaginative replication of these – even by (or perhaps even particularly by) those ostensibly dedicated to reaching the 'poorest of the poor'. For the poorest households the opportunities for productive use of loans are often limited, the weekly meetings too time-consuming and the risk of taking loans that are repayable on a weekly basis are unacceptably high (Wright, 2000; Rutherford, 1998). In addition, the exclusion of the poorest is probably driven by the emphasis on credit delivery by MFIs, which pay scant attention to the needs of the poorest for somewhere safe and accessible to put their savings.

It is high time that more attention was paid both to designing products that are appropriate for poorer people and to designing systems that are more cost-effective and efficient to deliver these services. This type of innovative work should enable us to develop alternative sustainable systems that can really reach the poor on a sustainable basis. This is particularly challenging in Africa, where the majority of rural villages remain without access to financial services. Examples of such innovative products and systems in Africa include those of the *Caisses Villageoises d'Epargne et de Credit* in Mali, Burkina Faso, Madagascar, Cameroon and the Gambia; the Small Enterprise Foundation in South Africa; the Financial Services Associations that have been introduced in a variety of forms in Benin, the Congo-Brazzaville, Gabon, Guinea, Mauritania, Uganda, Kenya and South Africa; and the Kenya Entrepreneurship Promotion Programme and Partnership for Productivity initiatives centred on managing Accumulating Savings and Credit Associations. However, most of these initiatives remain small and still require ongoing subsidy.

What we should *not* be advocating is a return to perpetual subsidy for MFIs (as has been suggested by some – see, for example, Woller et al., 1999). Poor people need ongoing access to financial services and should not be left dependent on the continued beneficence of donors simply because we in the microfinance industry are too lazy or unimaginative to develop innovative products and delivery systems. In addition, it is increasingly clear that in many cases subsidies to MFIs are simply underwriting inefficient and expensive systems. And the history of agricultural credit tells us that subsidized programmes that mix grants and loans lead only to 'groans'.

Furthermore, while they are unquestionably important, financial services are probably not the highest priority for the truly 'poorest of the poor' – they need relief. And it may well be more cost-effective and appropriate to deliver relief (hand-outs) than to try to provide credit to this particularly poor part of the community. In this context, BRAC's Income Generation for the Vulnerable Group Development (IGVGD) programme is particularly enlightened and effective. The IGVGD programme provides truly poor women with wheat as payment for working on the roads and embankments of Bangladesh. At the same time BRAC helps the women save part of the funds generated when they sell the wheat and provides training in income generation schemes (typically poultry or sericulture). After three years, the women have developed the resources and skills to graduate into BRAC's mainstream rural credit programme activities. Forcing them straight into the mainstream rural credit programme would have helped neither the poor women nor BRAC as an MFI committed to sustainability.

Advocates of targeting often insist on focusing exclusively on the 'poorest of the poor' and excluding the non-poor (however vulnerable they are). This results in rather extreme positions. At one extreme those who place emphasis on serving only the 'poorest of the poor' are effectively saying: 'According to our survey, you are not-so-poor: go away and have a serious crisis in your household and come back to us when you are really one of the poorest of the poor, ideally destitute, then we will serve you'. By excluding the 'not-so-poor' from access to financial services, the advocates of targeting are making them several times more vulnerable to such crises. And so it is probably only a matter of time before they are adequately poor to be allowed into the programme, or so destitute that it is no longer useful to them. Furthermore, of course, when the vulnerable non-poor become poor enough to qualify for MFIs dedicated to targeting the poorest, serving them with appropriate products and delivery systems is much more difficult: group-based guarantee loans for enterprise repayable in weekly instalments rarely suit the needs of the poorest (Wright, 2000; Rutherford, 1998).

Focusing exclusively on the poorest could be seen as a rationale for enforced 'graduation' after a basic level of financial stability has been achieved by clients. Not only does this ignore the need for ongoing access to financial services but it also undermines the incentives to repay, and indeed the sustainability of the MFI itself, by forcing out the most valuable clients (Wright, 2000).

Conclusion

All of the above is not for one minute to suggest that poor people do not need or should be excluded from financial services – though many of the poverty enthusiasts will chose to see it as such. The poor *do* need financial services (perhaps even more than the vulnerable non-poor) and MFIs accessing public development funds should indeed seek to offer financial services to the poor and even the poorest. But the nature of the services and the products that are truly useful for the poor and the poorest are likely to differ from what is currently made available to them. In particular, savings services are likely to be more important than credit services, and credit services solely focused on microenterprise development are likely to be less useful than emergency loans. This fact is indeed an amusing irony, given the poverty-focused MicroCredit Summit's disregard for savings and emphasis on 'credit for self-employment'. This emphasis was justified at the Second Preparatory Meeting held in Washington in 1996 in terms of it being easier to explain to the general public that poor people need loans to do business: another triumph of spin over substance.

Those who are truly serious about further deepening outreach will have to look at conducting rather more careful market research to assess and understand the needs and opportunities faced by the poor. Only when this is clear are the MFIs in a position to design products that can really address the special circumstances of the poor. Targeting poor people with inappropriate products is likely to damage their interests as they join programmes hoping that they can manage their way around the product's strictures on the basis that this is all that is being offered to them. This in part explains some of the very high drop-out rates seen in many parts of the world (see, for example, Hulme, 2000 and Wright, 2000). The damage caused to very poor people by participating in inappropriately designed microcredit programmes is becoming increasingly clear.

> For the poorest households the opportunities for productive use of loans are limited, and the risk of taking loans that are repayable on a weekly basis are unacceptably high. In preference to 'targeting the poorest' and trying to persuade them to join organizations that are offering inappropriate financial services, it is the services themselves that require revision and tailoring to meet the needs of the poorest, and thus to attract them into microfinance programmes. As donors and practitioners place increasing emphasis on microfinance as opposed to microcredit, the poor are likely to join microfinance programmes in order to save. Over time the poor may also enjoy the benefits of scale that microfinance institutions' more affluent clients allow – in terms of interest on savings, a broader range of financial services and possibly even lower-cost loans (Wright, 1999).

The challenge for the future is to think beyond replicating standardized systems and products designed in distant countries for different cultures and financial landscapes. Appropriate products are more likely to assist the poor than targeting them with inappropriate services. It is essential to develop alternative appropriate systems (well beyond the Grameen/ FINCA models) to allow MFIs to reach deeper into more remote, sparsely populated areas so typical of Africa. It is for this reason that there is so much interest in the experimentation around Financial Service Associations, which may offer an alternative system that might drive the 'financial frontier' further out from the densely populated areas for which the Grameen/FINCA systems were designed.

The eventual impact of microfinance on poverty *and* the sustainability of MFIs will ultimately depend on the organizations' systems and products. The more appropriate and the higher the quality of financial services on offer, the better business will be both for MFIs and for their clients.

References

Chao-Beroff, Rene, (1997), 'Developing financial services in disadvantaged regions: self-managed village savings and loan associations in the Dogon Region of Mali', in Schneider, Hartmut (ed.), *Microfinance for the Poor?*, Paris, OECD.

Christen, Robert Peck, Elisabeth Rhyne, Robert C. Vogel and Cressida McKean, (1995), 'Maximizing the outreach of microenterprise finance – an analysis of successful microFinance programmes', *Centre for Development Information and Evaluation, USAID Programme and Operations Assessment Report No. 10*, Washington.

Gibbons, David S., (1992), *The Grameen Reader – training materials for the international replication of the Grameen Bank financial system for reduction of rural poverty*, Grameen Bank, Dhaka.

Hulme, David and Paul Mosley, (1996), *Finance Against Poverty – Volume 1*, Routledge, London.

Hulme, David, (2000), 'Is microdebt good for poor people? A note on the dark side of microfinance', *Small Enterprise Development*, Vol. 11, No. 1 (and chapter 12 of this volume).

Khandker, S.R. and O.H. Chowdhury, (1995), *Targeted credit programmes and rural poverty in Bangladesh*, World Bank, Washington, DC.

Mosley, Paul, (1999), 'Microfinance and poverty: Bolivia case study', mimeo background paper for the *World Development Report 2000/1*, UK.

Otero, Maria, and Elisabeth Rhyne, (1994), *The new world of microenterprise finance*, Kumarian Press, and Intermediate Technology Publications, London.

Rhyne, Elisabeth, (1998), 'The yin and yang of microfinance: reaching the poor and sustainability', *MicroBanking Bulletin*, University of Colorado, Boulder, July.

Robinson, M.S., (1997), 'Answering Some Key Questions on Finance and Poverty', in 'The New World of Microfinance – Conference Proceedings', *Coalition for Microfinance Standards*, Philippines, 1997.

Rutherford, Stuart, (1998), 'The savings of the poor: improving financial services in Bangladesh', *Journal of International Development*, Vol. 10, No.1.

Sebstad, Jennifer and Monique Cohen, (2000), 'Microfinance, risk management and poverty', AIMS, USAID, Washington.

Woller, Gary M., Christopher Dunford and Warner Woodworth, (1999), 'Where to microfinance?', mimeo, Freedom From Hunger.

Wright, Graham A.N., (1999), 'The impact of microfinance services – increasing income or reducing poverty?', *Small Enterprise Development*, Vol. 10, Number 1, London.

Wright, Graham A.N., (2000), *Microfinance systems: designing quality financial services for the poor*, University Press Ltd., Dhaka, and Zed Books, London and New York.

About the authors

Graham A.N. Wright is Programme Director of MicroSave-Africa (a CGAP, DFID and UNDP initiative); and Aleke Dondo is Managing Director of K-Rep Holdings Ltd. The authors thank the many reviewers who contributed to improving this article but accept responsibility for all its blemishes. The opinions expressed in this paper are those of the authors and do not necessarily represent those of their institutions or donor partners. All comments on this paper should be sent to msa@MicroSave-Africa.com

11 The holy grail of microfinance: 'helping the poor' and 'sustainable'?

CHRISTOPHER DUNFORD

This paper was first published in March 2000.

The term 'microfinance institutions' covers a broad spectrum from traditional businesses, for whom social objectives are only a by-product, to traditional social service organizations, for whom reaching the poorest is the prime objective. In between are social enterprises, which are explicitly aiming at reaching very poor people (however defined) but at the same time are aiming at sustainability. This paper takes the case of Freedom from Hunger's Bolivian counterpart, CRECER, and shows how although CRECER is making substantial progress, its success in meeting both these objectives depends on how they are defined. For example, what proportion of better-off women are allowed among the target group of poor women? And should 'sustainability' include, as well as meeting operational and financial costs, repaying the original donor for their start-up investment? It is argued that most social enterprise MFIs cannot and should not attempt to do this but should aim to provide good-value services for poor people for a very long time.

NOWADAYS THERE IS a bewildering variety of types and combinations of clients, delivery systems, and institutional structures that shelter uneasily together under the big tent known as microfinance.

It may be helpful to characterize the diversity of microfinance practitioners as lying along a continuum from traditional business (a purely financial bottom line) at one end to traditional social service (a purely social bottom line) at the other end. In the middle is the emerging phenomenon of the 'social enterprise' which manages to have a double bottom line, seeking to achieve a productive balance between business objectives and social objectives. The emergence of social enterprise can be seen in many sectors, but it may be best developed in the microfinance world.

Traditional business, traditional social service, and social enterprise

Some 'model' microfinance institutions, like BancoSol, operate as *traditional businesses*. Any social objectives they may have are assumed by-products of their financial and institutional objectives. They do not measure progress against their social objectives, and in this sense behave as if they have none at all. There is nothing wrong with that approach, as long as they do not try to attract social investors who explicitly want to pursue social objectives. These traditional business MFIs appear to address significant market failure to serve the borrowing needs of small and even micro-businesses. Only incidentally do they serve very poor entrepreneurs, as the Ohio State University Rural Finance Programme has demonstrated (Navajas et al., 2000). Serving the poor is not the objective of these traditional business MFIs, and it would be helpful to donors and practitioners alike for them to say so.

Likewise, it would be helpful for *traditional social service* providers to admit that sustainable institution building is not their objective. They and their donors would do well to acknowledge that fact by making plans for leaving a legacy to be proud of when their microfinance projects phase out, sooner or later. They can provide loans at or below market rates to the poor needing special consideration (e.g. refugees and disaster victims) and still do a good job of loan recovery and managing their costs against donor and interest revenue. I see nothing wrong in that, as long as they develop good strategies for eventually handing over their clients to more sustainable service institutions. In fact, they can serve certain market niches better than sustainability-oriented microfinance institutions. They can do a great deal of good during the 'life of the project', as long as they do not compete for clients who can better benefit from long-term micro-finance services, or put the meagre assets of the poor at risk, or use their poverty alleviation objective as an excuse for operating inefficiently and for the small scale of their outreach to the poor.

Traditional business and traditional social service approaches are familiar polar opposites, the two ends of the microfinance spectrum. What is new and interesting in the microfinance movement is the broad middle ground occupied by the emergent *social enterprises* specializing in microfinance and related services. This is where the debate over 'best practices' for combined impact and sustainability is most productively focused. The debate will improve as the different objectives are articulated and regarded as legitimate by all involved in the debate. Social enterprises have to be explicit in both their social and financial/institutional objectives. Through appropriate staff incentives for managers and service staff, they must commit themselves to managing and measuring progress towards both. To date, social enterprises in microfinance have done a very poor job of developing social impact measurement systems, much less actually measuring social impact. It is hard to do, but it has to be done, and they had better get started on it in earnest, if they are to remain credible as social enterprises and not slide inadvertently into becoming simply poorly managed traditional businesses.

Donors or investors must also clarify their own objectives and make sure these match up with the objectives of the traditional businesses, social enterprises, or traditional social services to which they donate or loan, or invest in.

For all of us involved in microfinance today, we must know ourselves and be true to ourselves. We need to be more open and honest with each other about our real objectives and our commitment to reaching them.

A Bolivian example of social enterprise – Credit with Education

The Holy Grail of Microfinance is a social enterprise that is helping the poor and is sustainable at the same time. Your chances of attaining the Holy Grail depend on how you define 'helping the poor' and 'sustainable'. I can illustrate some major issues by describing the organization I know best, Freedom from Hunger, and its programme in Bolivia, CRECER (Crédito con Educación Rural), soon to become an independent Bolivian institution.

Freedom from Hunger's and CRECER's mission is to alleviate poverty, specifically to provide very poor women with money (via village banking) and information (via non-formal adult education at the weekly village banking meetings) to overcome chronic hunger and malnutrition in their families. This mission gives us very little flexibility in the definition of 'helping the poor' – our services must enable and stimulate women to reduce chronic hunger and malnutrition in their families. Our target market is narrowly conceived as those families that are chronically hungry and have malnourished children, particularly in rural communities, where hunger and malnutrition is most prevalent. In short, we are targeting the poorest of the economically active poor women in rural communities beyond the reach and 'below the radar screen' of other microfinance providers, even those now operating in the provincial market towns. The more of these women we can reach, the better we achieve our mission. CRECER is a *social* enterprise. But the only way we can achieve our ambitious mission in Bolivia is to build CRECER into a financially sustainable, growth-oriented, impact-seeking social *enterprise*. CRECER, the institution, is the means to our end. But we are committed to CRECER becoming a sustainable means to our end.

As a social *enterprise*, CRECER is organized to be market-responsive and competitive, driven to be as efficient as possible in order to minimize or eliminate any need for donor support. This is a difficult task given that our market niche is very poor women in very rural communities. Shall we succeed?

We are seeing real progress now. As of 30 September 1999, CRECER served 18 028 members (almost all women) in 918 bancos comunales (village banks). CRECER's outstanding loan portfolio had reached US$2 623 000 with an average loan size per borrower of US$162. The operational self-sufficiency ratio for the previous six months (as defined by the SEEP Network of North American microfinance providers) had attained 101 per cent of total current financial and operating costs, including costs of education delivery, covered by the interest revenue from lending operations. Portfolio at risk was 0.56 per cent. By the end of 2000, CRECER's objective is to have 20 000 borrowers, $4 million in outstanding loans and more than 100 per cent operating self-sufficiency. How are we doing? Shall we make it to the Holy Grail?

Reaching the very poor

The answer depends, first, on whether the majority of women and families we serve were really chronically hungry and malnourished when they came on board. We do not really know for sure. Is it acceptable to our mission that a percentage of the women and families may have been better off from the start? Actually, having a good number of better-off women probably means larger loans that serve to increase our revenue even as we serve the chronically hungry poor. And the better-off are generally better educated and more worldly, which should improve the self-management capacity of the *bancos comunales* we serve.

But at what point does the proportion of better-off women to chronically hungry women become too high? We do not know yet.

What we do know from our impact evaluation work is that 90 per cent of the women surveyed before joining the programme reported their families suffered a hungry season during the year, and anthropometric measurement showed that 42 per cent of their 1-year-old children were moderately to severely malnourished. So, a significant proportion of CRECER borrowers are from the target group. Unfortunately, the evidence that CRECER is having a really positive impact on the lives of these intended beneficiaries is not as conclusive as for a very similar Credit with Education programme in Ghana (MkNelly and Dunford, 1999). The Bolivian women have significantly improved their health and nutrition knowledge and practice and significantly increased their personal savings. Their households' monthly non-farming enterprise profit significantly increased; 40 per cent reported that they had more animals since joining the programme. Yet the food security of the family and nutritional status of the young children did not improve, *except* when their mothers received good-quality nutrition education. It may be too soon to judge whether CRECER is yet offering the best product line for these women and these families.

Defining sustainability

The answer to the question 'Will CRECER be sustainable?' depends on how we choose to define 'sustainable.' Like so many microfinance practitioners, our definition has evolved. Years ago, we thought it would be a major breakthrough just to recover all the recurrent costs of field operations. Then, we set our sights on recovering all recurrent operating costs of the total CRECER institution. Then, as our loan portfolio grew with loans from the commercial bank Banco Industrial S.A. (BISA) and other lenders charging commercial and near-commercial rates, we determined that financial sustainability should mean covering all CRECER's recurrent financial and operating costs, including the hidden costs of inflation and set asides for loan loss reserves. All this made sense in terms of our understanding that financial sustainability means being able to keep on going toward our objectives without continuing donor support.

The bar keeps getting raised, however. Some among the microfinance donors and theoreticians even suggest that the 'infant industry' rationale for subsidy no longer applies, that we now have to fully pay off the costs of the initial investment to create CRECER, including a payback to Freedom from Hunger for its past technical assistance and training. Because our name is Freedom from Hunger, not Freedom from Subsidy, we have to stop a moment to think about where all this is leading us and the microfinance movement. What is most important here? Is it to build social enterprises that can last long enough to bring about major improvement in the lives of very large numbers of people? Or is it to become certified as totally subsidy free – not now, not then, not ever? I will not pretend to speak for all social enterprises, but in the case of CRECER and many other microfinance institutions, the goal is not to become totally subsidy free. That is neither necessary nor sufficient to achieve our true objectives.

The reality is that subsidy is available. Traditional businesses have thrived on it for centuries. There is a market for subsidy to traditional social services. It is called philanthropy or charity. Freedom from Hunger has more or less thrived on this market for 53 years, far longer than the average life span of a for-profit business. Since there is a developing market for subsidy to social enterprises – for start-up capital, for technical assistance, for loans at concessional rates – should not social enterprises tap that market for one-time or occasional infusions of 'social investment'? Social entrepreneurs should lose their business licences if they did not!

At this point, I do not know what 'sustainable' means. If it means 'totally subsidy free' in the sense I have just described, I would have to guess that CRECER will never be sustainable. Certainly Freedom from Hunger and its donors will never be repaid for our investment in CRECER's start-up, any more than PRODEM and its donors will ever be fully repaid for their investment in launching BancoSol. Even for 'going concerns', I would have to be convinced by really hard evidence that any social enterprise specializing in microfinance will ever be sustainable. Even traditional businesses specializing in microfinance cannot claim to be subsidy free as long as their investors have opportunities to invest more profitably elsewhere. Investor acceptance of such opportunity cost is a form of social subsidy.

Is being 'totally subsidy free' an appropriate litmus test for sustainability? Surely sustainability is too complex to be fully characterized by a subsidy index. A really good, sustainable social enterprise is not highly dependent on subsidies but also not necessarily subsidy free. What it must be is capable of consistently seizing the opportunities offered by the markets and converting these efficiently into valuable social goods and services for large numbers of people in need. It gives needy people value in exchange for value, and it can keep on doing that for a very long time. That is a Holy Grail we can realistically aspire to grasp in our own bare hands and know that it will be worth every bit of the effort!

References

Navajas, Sergio, Mark Schreiner, Richard L. Meyer, Claudio Gonzalez-Vega and Jorge Rodriguez-Meza, (2000), 'Microfinance and the poorest of the poor: theory and evidence from Bolivia', *World Development*, Vol. 28. (http://gwbweb.wustl.edu/users/schreiner).

MkNelly, Barbara and Christopher Dunford, (1999), 'Impact of *Credit with Education* on mothers and their young children's nutrition: CRECER *Credit with Education* Programme in Bolivia', Freedom from Hunger Research Paper No. 5 (Freedom from Hunger, Davis, California info@freefromhunger.org).

About the author

Christopher Dunford is President of Freedom from Hunger, California, USA.

12 Is microdebt good for poor people? A note on the dark side of microfinance

DAVID HULME

This paper was first published in March 2000.

The emphasis on loans for enterprise as opposed to general financial services means that there is a poor match between what is offered and client needs. Microfinance does not usually reach the poorest people; it is only a part of what is needed to eliminate poverty.

THIS PAPER IS NOT a polemic that argues that microfinance has failed – there is much evidence, not least from my work with colleagues, that it can help many poor people improve their lives. Rather, it is a reminder that those who provide microfinancial services (referred to here as MFIs, or microfinance institutions, but recognizing that many institutions also provide enterprise development or social development services) need to monitor carefully not only their positive impacts but also their negative effects, look to the future, and not rest on their laurels. The 'microfinance industry' needs to practise more humility about what it has achieved (outside of Bangladesh it has not even scratched the surface of poverty – for example in Kenya fewer than 70 000 people out of an estimated 9 to 10 million poor people have access to microfinance) and deepen its understanding of the financial service needs of poor people.

Microfinance, microcredit or microdebt?

Most MFIs focus on disbursing loans. Their savings services are designed as a means of collateralizing loans and providing low-cost capital: they are not designed to meet the poor's need for savings mechanisms. Such loans are usually referred to as 'microcredit' and MFIs have created the myth that poor people always manage to repay their loans because of their ability to exploit business opportunities. This is nonsense, and Pischke's dictum that we should call microcredit 'microdebt' can help us be more realistic about the different ways in which loans can impact on the livelihoods of poor people.

Microdebt can create considerable opportunities for people to utilize 'lumps' of money so that they can improve incomes and reduce vulnerability. But not all microdebt produces favourable results, especially for poor people working in low-return activities in saturated markets that are poorly developed and where environmental and economic shocks are common. Because of circumstances beyond their control (sickness, flood, drought, theft and so on), lack of skills and knowledge or taking bad decisions, a proportion of poor borrowers encounter great difficulties in repaying loans. While MFIs suggest that such problems are overcome through 'social support ' in some painless way this is often not the case

– talk to the dropouts of MFIs! Many (though presently we have little under-standing of exactly what proportion) report being threatened by group members and MFI staff or having their possessions (pots and pans, roofing iron) seized. In Bangladesh, MFI debtors have been arrested by the police (this came to light in 1997 when a police vehicle carrying such debtors crashed and the individuals concerned were killed), are threatened with physical violence (Montgomery, 1996), and the press regularly report female suicides resulting from problems of repaying loans. Many poor people are very frightened about getting into debt: this is a rational response to the dangers that arise from indebtedness to MFIs, and not a 'misunderstanding'.

Microcredit and microfinance

The emphasis that most MFIs place on microenterprise lending has led to the evolution of a microfinance industry in which services have a poor match with client needs. Clients have to pretend that they want microenterprise loans (when they need to pay school fees, cope with a medical emergency, buy food, etc) and do not have access to the types of micro-savings services that they desire. In extreme cases, such as the Kenya Women's Finance Trust and several other East African MFIs, clients who wish to stop taking loans and wish only to make sav-ings are 'balanced out' (i.e. have to leave the MFI). Whereas most banking services aimed at individuals find that demand for savings accounts is much greater than for loan accounts, the microfinance industry tries to force every saver also to be a borrower. This is often because of product design through which MFI institutional viability is dependent on expanding the loan portfolio while savings products are not designed to cover costs.

MFIs do not work with the poor and the poorest

Effective MFIs – such as those in Bangladesh – provide services that help poor people improve their prospects and reduce their vulnerability. However, the claims that microfinance assists 'the poorest' and 'the poorest of the poor' are unfounded within national contexts. MFIs virtually never work with the poorest – the mentally and physically disabled, the elderly, street children, the destitute and refugees – and many MFIs (for example, virtually all of those in Kenya and Uganda) have high proportions of clients who are non-poor, if one takes official national levels of the poverty line as the criteria. (In Nyeri, Kenya, for example, I was amazed to find that 13 out of 13 group members of a 'poverty-focused' MFI I interviewed in 1999 owned cars!)

The common assumption that microfinance is automatically about working with the poor and poorest needs to be dropped, unless MFIs can provide clear evidence that this is the case. Donors also need to be more circumspect. The grandly named Consultative Group to Assist the Poorest (CGAP) (through dis-seminating microfinance best practice) spent its first three years as the Consultative Group to Assist the Not Very Well-Off (CGANVWO) if one examines its portfolio. (To its credit, CGAP is now making serious efforts to incorporate a poverty focus into its work.)

There is no moral requirement that MFIs need to work with the poor. However, if they seek access to aid funds targeted at poverty reduction then they do need to explain what they are doing for poor people, rather than hide behind rhetoric and anecdote.

Microfinance and poverty reduction policy

MFI and donor hype has created the impression that microfinance is a cure for poverty. This is encapsulated in the work of the Microcredit Summit and the thousands of well-intentioned but misguided supporters who believe that microcredit is the answer to the problems of poverty. This is a potentially dangerous line of argument as it distracts attention from the fact that poverty reduction requires action on many fronts – social safety nets for the poorest and most vulnerable, an effective education system, low-cost and reliable health services, governments that can provide social inclusion (and thus maintain law and order) and sound macroeconomic policies, and many other issues.

Providing effective microfinance services to poor people is part of a poverty-reduction strategy – but only a part. Those who present microfinance as a magic bullet to reduce poverty provide such a simple message for policy formulation that they encourage it to be simple-minded.

Microfinance in the future

The microcredit breakthroughs of the 1970s and 1980s contributed greatly to the understanding of poverty reduction by illustrating the feasibility of creating MFIs that can approach sustainability and can provide valued financial services to poor people. However, this contribution is now being undermined by unproven claims about microfinance always helping poor people and the exaggeration of the role of microfinance within poverty reduction policies. Worse still, the microfinance industry has ossified! It promotes group-based microenterprise loan products and is obstructing the development of the full range of services and products that poor people want and need – flexible savings, contractual savings, loans for education and health, microinsurance and lines of credit.

The 1990s have been the 'Decade of Microcredit Complacency'. It is time to stocktake – to stop recycling myths and to stop copying the initial breakthrough products – and to focus on the real job in hand: developing institutions that can create and provide the broad range of microfinancial services that will support poor people in their efforts to improve their own and their children's prospects.

Reference

Montgomery, R., (1996), 'Disciplining or protecting the poor: avoiding the social costs of peer pressure in microcredit schemes', *Journal of International Development*, Vol. 8, No.2, pp. 289–305.

About the author

David Hulme is Professor of Development Studies, Institute for Development Policy and Management, University of Manchester, UK.

13 The managed ASCA model – innovation in Kenya's microfinance industry

SUSAN JOHNSON, NTHENYA MULE, ROBERT HICKSON
and WAMBUI MWANGI

This paper was first published in June 2002.

A model of microfinance has been operating in the Central Province of Kenya since the early 1990s largely unnoticed by donors. The model involves the mobilization of women into accumulating savings and credit associations by local NGOs that assist in the management of the fund in return for a management fee. The approach was developed in the early 1990s as a result of the withdrawal of donor support to traditional women's group activities, and the local NGOs are now entirely self-supporting. The outreach of the services is comparable to the main donor-funded initiatives and evidence suggests that depth of outreach to poorer people may in fact be better. This paper describes the model and explains its apparently successful performance. However, the analysis also suggests that the model has inherent weaknesses, especially in default management, that need to be addressed if its success is to continue.

MICROFINANCE ORGANIZATIONS IN KENYA, using the group-based lending model and with donor support, had reached approximately 135 000 clients by 2001. However, high operating costs, slow intake and high client exits have constrained their efforts to achieve financial and organizational sustainability. By contrast, Central Province is home to a number of local organizations providing microfinance services that are operating profitably and expanding rapidly in the same environment and without donor funding. The model is one in which management services are provided to group-based loan funds. The groups operate as Accumulating Savings and Credit Associations (ASCAs) and we have used the term ASCA Management Agencies (AMAs) to describe the service providers.

This paper describes the background to and operation of the model before analysing its performance. This performance is then explained in relation to the preferences of users before challenges facing the model are discussed.

Background

The managed ASCA model was conceived by Partnership for Productivity (PFP) based in Karatina. PFP started in Western Province in 1968 as a local programme of a US NGO providing a range of donor-funded enterprise development interventions. It moved to Nyeri in 1988 – an economically vibrant region inhabited mostly by Kikuyu who are known for their business acumen. In 1994 donors withdrew funding and the Kenyan arm of PFP decided to work with the groups that had their own funds in a revolving loan fund or ASCA. They assisted the group in the management of the fund run to a specific format for which they charged a fee. This model was not successful in Western Kenya and that part of PFP's operations closed down. Then in 1995 the training officer of PFP, who had played a key role in developing the model, decided to start his own company, the Women's Enterprise Development Institute (WEDI), opening an office immediately next door to PFP and taking some of the PFP groups with him. In January 1999 one of the WEDI staff then also broke away and started another organization called Small Enterprise Development Institute (SEDI) and, as with the earlier split from PFP, took some groups with him from WEDI. This process has continued to this day and now some eight such entities operate the Managed ASCA model in the region with an estimated outreach to over 25 000 clients. PFP, WEDI and SEDI, based in Karatina, are the focus of this study.

Central Province, where the model is mainly operating, is one of the better-off parts of the country. The Government's Kenya Poverty Assessment (1998) using 1994 data suggests that Nyeri District – the second richest in the country – does not experience absolute poverty in a year when the rains are good. Other districts of Central Province may not quite achieve this level but are not far behind.

The area is home to many, if not most, of the major financial institutions operating in the country: commercial banks, savings and credit co-operatives, government lenders. Donor-funded organizations that offer group-based lending programmes are Kenya Women Finance Trust (KWFT), K-Rep, FAULU and the Small and Micro Enterprise Programme (SMEP). These are complemented by a vibrant array of informal financial mechanisms, such as rotating savings and credit associations (ROSCAs), which are very popular and operate in both rural and urban areas.

ASCA management agencies: the model

The model involves two organizations: the AMA and the group. AMAs offer a template for the operation of the ASCAs that is almost uniform. Small differences have arisen as the organizations have formed and have given client feedback, but here we describe the core model around which variations have been made.

Members form a group and from the first meeting make a minimum monthly saving of KSh.100 (called shares) – and may save more if they wish. Savings are immediately converted into small loans at 10 per cent interest per month. This continues until the fund grows sufficiently to offer the two main loan products. One is a short-term advance (*ngumbaco*), which is usually for a month and on which a flat 10 per cent interest is paid (annual effective rate 120 per cent) and an access fee of KSh.10–20 (US$0.13–0.26). These advances may be renewed for up to three months, if the interest is paid monthly. Members are entitled to advances of up to three times their shares. There is also a longer-term loan product for up to three times shares for 10 to 24 months at 17 per cent flat per annum, repaid in equal monthly instalments. A 1 per cent application fee is levied on these longer-term loans and other family members are required to act as guarantors, or household assets have to be pledged. A grace period of one to three months is permitted on the loan.

The actual cost of borrowing is an annual percentage rate (APR) of about 68 per cent on long-term loans and 174 per cent on advances. While these figures appear quite high, they are generally lower than those of traditional MFIs due to the fact that AMA borrowers (unlike those using MFIs) receive substantial returns on their compulsory savings.

The interest paid by members on loans is paid into the ASCA, and at the end of the year the dividend is calculated. Dividends are calculated by the AMAs on behalf of the groups, and an allowance of 30 per cent of the value of the fund is made for loan-loss provision before the remaining profit is distributed as shares. In some of the organizations, the dividend to a member also comprises 10 per cent of the amount that she has paid in interest on advances. This adjustment was made as a result of feedback from members who realized that when taking advances, they were paying much more interest than those taking longer-term loans, and thought that they should therefore benefit more when the dividend was paid. A bonus or 'celebration', which is a flat payout of around KSh.500 (about US$6.40), is also paid in December. Individual dividends are either paid as additional shares or used to offset outstanding loans. In addition, the group may decide to save additional monthly contributions to fund a specific project of its own, such as to buy all members a household item, such as cooking pots, plates, mattresses or sweaters.

Savings withdrawals can be made down to KSh.1000 (US$13) if the member has no loans outstanding. Otherwise, she can withdraw only down to the value of the shares required to guarantee her short-term advance (one third the value of the advance). She cannot withdraw at all if she has a long-term loan.

A member can leave the group by giving notice and receive her shares, net of any outstanding loans, and a proportion of the accumulated profit in the fund. This calculation differs slightly between AMAs, but more importantly, if there is a significant degree of default in the group, the AMA will not usually allow the 'profit' element to be withdrawn by the member. If default in the group is very serious then even withdrawal of shares may be difficult.

The role of the ASCA management agency

The AMAs mobilize women to form groups either working with existing groups or facilitating new ones. Their experience with men has been very poor and there are now only a handful of men's groups in the programme.

The AMA field officers meet each group monthly and co-chair the meeting. At each meeting the group pays the AMA a fee, which is set at 1 per cent of the value of the group's total revolving loan fund (TRLF). During an initial three-month period the service is given free. This allows the group to build up its loan fund. As the group's total revolving loan fund grows, so the fee they pay is increased up to a ceiling of KSh.3000 per month (US$38).

Apart from the facilitation of the meeting, arbitration of disputes and the keeping of group records, the AMA has a key role in default management. Indeed, this is a key service that the group sees itself as purchasing from the AMA. When a member is in default, the onus is on the AMA to follow up and ensure that the outstanding monies are recovered. On the first occasion that a member misses a payment on a loan, the AMA staff and/or group's officials go to visit the delinquent member to establish the reason behind non-payment. If the reason is regarded as 'valid', then new terms of repayment can be negotiated with the member.

If these visits do not bring enough pressure to bear on the defaulting member, then the AMA issues a letter, summoning her to the office. If the member remains unresponsive, the Programme Manager may then begin making visits to the member. If this fails then the AMA may hire a lawyer to write a letter demanding payment and threatening legal proceedings. All the costs incurred by the AMA in recovery are borne by the defaulter. Eventually court proceedings may be taken. This is rare, but one AMA had recently pursued a defaulter to court and this had dramatically improved repayment performance in other groups.

Organizational structure: ownership, governance and management

While PFP is an NGO, the other AMAs are run as sole proprietorships with owner-managers who own the institutions and oversee their running. They recruit and supervise all staff, network with existing groups to draw in new clients, are involved in following up defaulters and make all strategic decisions. The AMAs' performance is therefore determined largely by the ingenuity and hard work of their managers.

This owner-managed and flat organizational structure allows them to respond quickly to situations on the ground. If there is potential to begin operations in a new area, they can immediately move to open an office provided they have the funds to do so. The model also operates with absolutely minimal fixed costs. Offices are rented (one does not even use electricity), all officers use public transport and the salary structure is kept low. Staff are usually Form Four school leavers or have a diploma in accounting or business. Salaries are in the range KSh.4000–7000 per month (US$50–90). It is this cost structure that makes barriers to entry very low. To start up, managers must know how to run the model, be good at dealing with people and be able to develop trust with the members.

Outreach: breadth and depth

PFP started operating this model in 1994 with some 130 groups from its previous women's group programmes. By mid-2001 the total membership of PFP, WEDI and SEDI was estimated at 855 groups with approximately 29 000 members (see Table 13.1).

In 1999, MFIs in and around Karatina had approximately 2000 members (Johnson, 2001), while the AMAs operating in a similar area had approximately 10 000 members. There has been considerable growth in membership over the past one-and-half years and the geographic coverage of these groups has spread out from the base in Karatina to stretch from Kirinyaga District to Laikipia District. During the past 18 months, fierce competition for clients has forced

Table 13.1   Numbers of groups and approximate numbers of members by organization

	Dec. 1999		July 2001		Annual growth rate
	Groups	Members	Groups	Members	
PFP	174	5742	255	8415	31%
WEDI	300	9 900	430	14 190	29%
SEDI	52	1716	200	6600	190%
Total	526	17 358	885	29 205	46%

Table 13.2   Membership and growth of K-Rep, FAULU and KWFT

MFI regional branches	1999	2000	Annual growth	2001	Annual growth
K-Rep (Mt Kenya West)	2384	2007	−16%	2769	38%
FAULU Nyeri (Mt Kenya West)	1574	1753	11%	2277	30%
KWFT (Mt Kenya region)	6922	9332	35%	11 665	25%
Total	10 880	13 092	20%	16 711	28%

AMAs to extend their reach to less populous areas away from Karatina and Nyeri. As a general rule, AMAs have extended further than the MFIs into remote rural areas in this region. During this 18-month period, growth has been about 46 per cent per year. Average group size has remained at about 33. In comparison, MFI growth in the same region has averaged about 28 per cent per year (see Table 13.2).

It can be hard to establish the status of members from AMA records, and these figures must be treated with caution. It is likely in both cases that some of the members recorded are in long-term default or no longer active. But even if members in default or dormant are estimated to be one-third of total membership, outreach of some 20 000 is still impressive.

The AMA model serves a wider client base than the mainstream donor-funded MFIs, who tend to focus their attention on micro- and small entrepreneurs, providing credit for enterprise activities. While micro- and small entrepreneurs also join, members are drawn from other socio-economic strata, including salaried workers such as nurses, teachers and civil servants as well as subsistence and semi-commercial farmers. The inclusion of salaried workers can result in ASCAs with substantial revolving funds (over KSh.1 million, US$13 000). But it is the monthly meeting, and flexibility of savings and loan sizes that is attractive to poor rural women, enabling the model to gain greater reach into the rural areas than the MFIs.

Financial performance at the group level

Internal rate of return calculations on cash flows generated by short-term loans suggest yields of between 40 and 70 per cent, which are lower than the potential maximum of 120 per cent per annum. Actual yields on long-term loans appear to be approximately 25 per cent against a theoretical yield of 33 per cent based on the interest rate. While longer-term loans are usually more risky in microfinance, the higher quality of the longer-term loan portfolio (judged by the smaller gap between theoretical and actual yields) may be explained by the dramatically lower interest rate charged, which seems to make these loans more manageable. Further evidence on these yields is from a sample of dividend payments paid to groups at the end of 1998, which ranged between 16 and 60 per cent, with an average of 34 per cent. Overall dividend yields in 2001 averaged around 20 per cent. From the perspective of a net saver in the system, this compares favourably to bank deposits, which yield about 2 per cent per annum.

Data collected from a sample of groups suggest that the total revolving loan fund (TRLF) of these groups can be estimated at KSh.155 million (US$2 million) in December 1999, increasing to KSh.215 million (US$2.75 million) by mid-2001 (see Table 13.3). Members' average outstanding advances and loans have fallen from about KSh.8000 (US$102) in 1999 to about KSh.7000 (US$92) in 2001, and this decline probably reflects the overall economic situation in which members are under pressure to draw down more extensively on their savings.

The data also suggest that these groups represent a very efficient means of intermediating savings as, on average, less than 10 per cent is banked. The system functions by attempting to re-lend as much of the money collected at a meeting as possible, with only excess funds being banked. The ratio of loans and advances to actual savings was 191 per cent in 1999 and 160 per cent in July 2001. This is due to the build-up of accumulated profits in the fund that have not been distributed as share dividends.

Table 13.3   Savings and net worth of combined portfolios of PFP, WEDI and SEDI

Financial indicator	1999		2001	
	KSh	US$	KSh	US$
Estimated total RLF (millions)	155	1.99	215	2.75
Mean savings per group (av. group shareholdings)	137 968	1769	149 308	1914
Mean savings per member	4181	54	4524	58
Mean worth of group (average revolving loan fund)	294 539	3 776	242 564	3 110
Mean worth per member	8925	114	7350	94
Average long-term loan outstanding and % of total fund	5177	58%	5596	76%
Average short-term advance outstanding and % of total fund	2767	31%	1584	22%
Average size savings held in bank and % of total fund	982	11%	170	2%

Financial sustainability of the AMAs

In addition to the monthly service fee, AMAs charge for the provision of savings books. Before loan losses are taken into account, the fee represents an annual cost of a little over 12 per cent to the group fund, which compares very favourably to the effective rates charged by traditional MFIs in Kenya, which are commonly between 50 and 300 per cent above bank base lending rates, which were about 20 per cent in mid-2001.

However, despite what would appear to be a relatively modest fee structure, these ASCA Management Agencies are proving profitable, with one of the organizations making an adjusted return on assets (AROA) of over 2000 per cent in 2000/01. This high return on assets is of course a function of the very low asset base and again illustrates the low financial barriers to entry.

Explaining performance

From these data the outreach and performance of this model appear impressive in the context of a local financial market that has an abundance of financial service providers for clients to choose between. Groups and their members perceived the advantages and disadvantages of the AMA model as follows.

Loan flexibility. In comparison to ROSCAs, ASCAs offer more flexible loan products both in terms of size and timing. Loan sizes can be larger than in a ROSCA and can be taken when they are needed. Advances can be taken for a month with an assurance that they can be rolled over if plans do not work out as intended, and the member can decide the period of a longer-term loan. Many women use ROSCAs as a mechanism to save to purchase domestic consumer items such as blankets, cooking pots and so on. In contrast, the ASCAs offer access to larger sums that can contribute to sending children to school or college, improving or building a house, constructing a water tank, or starting or expanding a business. ASCAs can also offer smaller amounts than MFIs, whose minimum loan size is usually KSh.5000, with pressure to increase loan sizes over time. This often makes them more attractive to the rural population.

Monthly repayment. Monthly repayments are often more manageable for people in the rural economy, as well as for those earning salaries, even if these are low. For those in business there is time to invest the money and make a return, compared to MFI loans that are usually paid weekly and begin the week after receiving the loan.

Repayment can be renegotiated. There is scope for negotiation over repayment if what is seen as a genuine problem arises. Unlike an MFI group, where other members are pressurized to make the repayment on her behalf to the MFI, the ASCA can allow the member to use its funds for longer. This is an important feature of user-owned group financial systems, and is particularly important at a time when economic activity is low and highly uncertain.

Access. A further feature of user-owned institutions such as ASCAs is that members are fully aware of their rights in accessing loans. As long as they have repaid without creating problems and have the right level of savings they know that their access to another loan is more or less assured. This in turn makes the group very valuable as a resource by comparison to banks or moneylenders.

Benefits of ownership. Many members of ASCAs who are also clients of MFIs expressed a preference for ASCAs for the following reasons (see also Box 13.1). First, because the interest that members pay on loans remains within the group and helps the group asset grow, allowing the members to gradually take bigger loans. Second, members receive a dividend at the end of the year that can be quite high, depending on the individual's shareholding and the profitability of the fund. By contrast, interest paid on loans from MFIs goes to the MFI and the clients therefore see themselves as 'working for' the MFI.

Support in times of need. The group and the social network it offers can be used to access or mobilize support, whether financial, material or psychological, during times of crisis or significant life-cycle events. ASCA members repeatedly echoed the refrain that they joined their respective groups to 'uplift themselves' by 'helping themselves'. Of course, groups are always diverse in the extent of their cohesion and effectiveness in operating as a group.

It appears that AMA groups are bound with a greater cohesion and sense of common identity than MFI groups as a result of group ownership of the financial resources. The considered treatment of defaulters and opportunity for loan renegotiation is a key way in which members can assist each other. Some ASCAs also operate a welfare fund (to which members make regular contributions), which is used to assist individuals in the event of crisis. Some ASCAs also have guidelines on what members would contribute on top of this to help a member to defray funeral or hospital expenses. Others have carefully defined who qualifies as 'next of kin', for those instances where it is not the member herself who is ill. However, it is not just this financial support that members value but also the social support involved, for example, in their attendance at funerals.

Key member concerns about the model. While members responded positively to the intrinsic features of the model, they (unsurprisingly) had complaints regarding the AMAs. The key concern is in the way that the AMAs carry out default management and the members' quest for value for money in paying them a service fee.

On the one hand, the AMA is asked to be tough and effective in collection; on the other hand group members do not wish to be identified as having 'set the dogs' on to their neighbour. Enforcing loan repayment is problematic (especially in the current economic climate) for the AMA, given that it does not have a clear mandate systematically to prosecute or punish defaulters. As pointed out earlier, once the initial stages are past, the defaulting member herself incurs the costs of default follow up: up to KSh.500 every time the AMA field staff or programme manager visits her. This may result in a situation where the AMA is taking whatever funds the member has available to cover its own costs rather than to make a loan repayment, and it is not surprising that members feel aggrieved at this process, since they are not regaining their funds from the member. This transfer of debt collection costs is usual in Kenya even when loans are secured with physical assets. Realizing this situation, one group stopped legal action on a defaulter and had simply attempted to keep the pressure on the member to make gradual repayments.

Box 13.1 Give me the *ngumbaco* any day!

I used to be an (MFO) client. I got a loan of KSh.10 000 and had to start paying back the money even before I had got the money out of the bank. I had to repay that loan within 3–6 months. I felt that I was working too hard and I wasn't getting anything from those people. So I decided to leave. At that time I had KSh.5000 in savings, but they only gave me KSh.3500. They told me that some money had to be deducted for the CO's fare, they said I had missed a meeting and therefore had to pay a fine … at that point I was so upset I didn't even want to listen to the reasons they were giving me. I just wanted to leave and never return again!

Ruth Waeni, Gatunai Adult Women's Group

Helping Kamau rebuild his business

A calamity befell Kamau, a carpenter and member of Nyeri Mwanjo group. The day before his group's scheduled meet date, a fire started up in the kiosk next door to his, where the proprietor ran a food kiosk, and razed a whole line of kiosks to the ground. Kamau was able to salvage some of the timber and tools he was using in his business, but he no longer had a place to carry on his carpentry business. Kamau, through his chairman, requested an interest-free loan of KSh.10 000, which he would use to rebuild his working shed. The group agreed to alter the terms of their loan policy in light of the disaster, as a sign of support and solidarity.

Nyeri Mwanjo Group Meeting

Achievements of, and challenges facing, the model. This model has delivered impressive outreach and growth in the past few years. First, the approach mobilizes local savings and puts them into circulation within the local economy. Second, it offers a set of products whose flexibility appeals to a range of socio-economic groups beyond the microentrepreneurs at whom MFI programmes have generally been targeted. Third, it has a low entry cost, which results in strong competition among service suppliers, in turn providing pressure for improved client services. Finally, the low-cost structure provides good prospects for sustainability, both at the level of the group and the AMA.

The model offers an approach that occupies a middle ground between mainstream MFI operation and self-help group development approaches. By providing external finance to groups, MFIs have to use the group system as a means of collateral, which can create huge resentment among members when they are required to repay for others. On the other hand, NGOs have also attempted to set up and train self-help groups (SHGs) to run their own revolving loan funds – often with injections of external finance – with the intention to eventually leave them to be self-managed. This often fails as it underestimates the management skills and social cohesion required for success. The AMA model recognizes that, while group ownership of a loan fund can create a strong internal dynamic, management and arbitration is usually best provided externally. The lack of external resources available to these organizations appears to have been a favourable factor in the strength of its development.

There do appear to be problems arising: as groups mature, default is presenting more of a problem and this situation has undoubtedly worsened due to the difficult macroeconomic environment. However, further analysis of the model demonstrates that these problems arise in part from the contradictory incentives present in the way the model is structured.

Default management

In the context of debt collection, the separation of ownership of the funds from the collection service creates what is called a 'principal–agent' problem (i.e. the payment incentives are not sufficiently well aligned, or supervision is inadequate, to ensure that the agent delivers services as defined by the principal). The AMAs earn a fixed fee from the group and therefore in order to maximize their own returns wish to minimize the time and effort they spend pursuing defaulters. The fact that they can pass on costs of follow-up to defaulters could be seen as an added incentive not to deal with them effectively. Moreover, since loans are not written off at the group level, the value of the fund on which the AMA levies its fee does not fall when arrears build up. The model does not therefore reward the AMA according to its ability to manage the default problem.

In practice, however, group members are well aware of the amount of money that is collected at a meeting from savings and repayments, and as this amount starts to fall, may negotiate with the AMA to reduce the service fee. But since this is not a feature of the model, it is likely to be exercised with differing degrees of effectiveness depending on the strength of a group's negotiation powers.

As repayment problems in the group increase they can create a vicious spiral as remaining members may fail to get the loan they wanted that month. This in turn can reduce their incentive to repay, and once this spreads to a critical mass of members the group it is likely to become dormant. Once this situation occurs it is difficult to revive the group, as there is no mechanism through which to force members out or replace them. Nor is there a clear means through which a group can be liquidated. A member cannot leave as she may not be able to withdraw the value of her shares, and hence is locked into the group. Nor are there rules about how the group can liquidate itself or de-link itself from the AMA. Some groups may feel strong enough to do this, but many may not. In part, this reflects the lack of an adequate written service agreement between the two parties that clearly defines exit options.

The AMAs' response to falling service fees is to create new groups that can replace the revenue lost from groups in difficulties. This in part explains the heavy rate of AMA expansion in the past two years. There is a danger that if this situation continues it could produce a more generalized backlash against the model as members become disaffected with it. While programme managers are aware of the extent of this problem and the importance of default management, they do not currently have clear strategies to deal with it.

Moreover, attempts by AMAs to pursue default more severely may be resisted by groups. Groups have the ability – and the right – to determine the default management regime and some groups will wish to be stricter than others. The ability of members to negotiate conditions of repayment is a key feature of a user-owned service. AMAs therefore need to be able to work more effectively with groups in deciding the strategy, rather than taking full responsibility for default management.

Ways in which this situation might be improved are:

o The responsibilities of the group in relation to default management should be more clearly defined. Since the group members own the funds, this is the only way in which the principal–agent problem can effectively be solved.
o Written service agreements could be introduced to address explicitly the roles of the different parties in relation to default management.
o Ways to link the AMA's fee to its success in recovery could be explored.
o Service agreements should clarify how members and groups might exit the service.
o Strategies could be developed with the AMAs to address the revitalization of groups that have significant default problems.

Constraints to the growth of existing AMAs

Further expansion of the AMA model is potentially limited by the existing organizational structure in which field officers report direct to owner-managers. Under this structure, direct supervision by the programme managers of an increasingly dispersed field team becomes problematic given the difficulties of communication and cost of transport. This is no doubt exacerbated by the risk that field officers, given a degree of autonomy in an area, will themselves split off from the original AMA, so undermining any investment that the owner-manager may have made in this expansion. The most recent case of splintering involved a loan officer taking about 13 groups with him. For this reason, among others, programme managers try to maintain their own personal relationship with all members and often rotate field officers to prevent the development of strong relationships between clients and loan officers.

Alternatively, given the relatively low start-up costs to this system, it may be that an organizational structure of a programme manager and a number of field officers is in fact the most appropriate, and that further expansion through breakaway staff is, in fact, the most viable one. The challenge would then be to find means of creating a more positive environment in which 'splintering' could occur.

Further development of products and services

As they currently operate, the AMAs provide a template for the services that the group offers. Strong groups are able to develop their own additional activities, such as mutual support mechanisms for unforeseen circumstances, or they may change the rate of interest or adapt loan sizes and so on. In general, the AMAs do not operate in a manner that is intended to build the capacity of the group to manage its own affairs. This is again one of the conflicts of interest that can arise.

To an AMA a good group is one that is easy to run and which the AMA wishes to carry on deriving revenue from, in part to subsidize the provision of service to new groups. However, some groups are strong enough to learn the system and eventually to take it over. An approach by AMAs that sought to improve the skills of the groups and offer an alternative service, which involved for example, the provision of a supervision or audit function to groups on an intermittent basis might be a new service for the AMA to offer.

While the products that currently exist appear to satisfy the needs of a variety of socioeconomic profiles, developing these products and services further, and improving the transparency and accountability with which they are delivered, is likely to be costly for organizations such as these, especially in the current economic environment. While modifications to services have occurred on account of feedback from members, there is currently limited capacity within the AMAs to respond to member needs systematically. Improving the AMAs' financial management systems is critical to the overall development of the service. Indeed, some relatively simple modifications and the introduction of systems for cross-checking could better ensure the quality of the product to clients.

Conclusion

The experience of the AMAs in Central Kenya shows how innovation can be stimulated when donors withdraw. The model that has evolved occupies an interesting middle ground between self-help group models and externally funded MFI approaches. While SHG models may make too strong assumptions about the capacity and willingness of local people to manage them effectively, MFIs providing external funding may make too strong a demand on the groups themselves to pursue defaulters. However, the way in which the AMAs have adopted the role of default collection has created an incentive problem that must be resolved through a clearer division of responsibilities and the adoption of service agreements.

While there is still much that can be improved in the model, it does appear to build on the local popularity of user-owned finance groups whose benefits are well understood by users, and contrast with those offered by the more mainstream MFI model. Perhaps dropout rates in MFIs (Hulme, 1999) can be better understood when the characteristics of their services are compared to those of these user-owned institutions: especially the social safety net features which clearly reduce the risks to poor people of entering the capital market. A key question for donors is whether they should shift their focus to reconsider supporting models of promotion of user-owned services, in addition to the core 'provider' model that currently dominates the industry.

References

Government of Kenya, (1998), *First report on poverty in Kenya*, Nairobi, Ministry of Planning and National Development.
Hulme, D., (1999), 'Client drop-outs from East African microfinance institutions', MicroSave-Africa.

Johnson, S., (2001), 'From fragmentation to embeddedness: towards an institutional analysis of financial markets', www.devinit.org/findev, Finance and Development Research Programme Working Paper No. 32.

About the authors

Susan Johnson works at the Centre for Development Studies,University of Bath, Nthenya Mule is with K-Rep Advisory Services, Nairobi, Robert Hickson is with AFCAP, Nairobi, and Wambui Mwangi with K-Rep Advisory Services, Nairobi. We are grateful to MicroSave-Africa who funded this study.

14 Empowered to default? Evidence from BRAC's microcredit programmes

SHAHIN YAQUB

This paper was first published in December 1995.

This paper investigates whether the acquisition of greater skills, resources, confidence and social position through repeated microcredit borrowing might reduce the effectiveness of mechanisms that promote repayment. The idea is motivated by new data from BRAC's (Bangladesh Rural Advancement Committee) Rural Development Programme, in which repayment appears to decline with repeated borrowing. In lending without physical collateral, group-based finance (GBF) uses alternative 'collateral', such as obligation to peers, which is socially based. GBF relies partly on high administrative inputs (for group formation, and for weekly visits by fieldworkers), and substantially on the borrowers' lack of alternative sources of credit and social powerlessness. If so, repayments will be undermined if repeated borrowing empowers by enriching and individualizing borrowers (through 'individual empowerment'), or improving access to alternative credit (through 'social transformation'). This is particularly important where groups have been formed simply to supply cheaper credit. The BRAC experience suggests that a microcredit intervention, based strongly on incentives for individual self-enrichment alone, eventually undermines the social forces inducing repayment by changing the incentives and costs associated with honouring the financial contract.

EXPERIENCE WITH RURAL CREDIT has shown both the public provision of subsidized credit and private provision in liberalized financial markets to be problematic. Group-based finance (GBF) is presented as a practical solution to some of these problems: however, the limits and complexities of this relatively new innovation are gradually being explored.

Lenders are said to face 'screening problems' (appraising potential borrowers), 'incentives problems' (making borrowers' behaviour consistent with repayment) and 'enforcement problems' (forcing borrowers to repay). The joint-liability feature in GBF allows lenders to use a borrower's peers to monitor and enforce the loan contract. Peers undertake monitoring and enforcement roles to avoid the choice arising from a default by a peer: either repaying a peer's loan or accepting the penalty of being denied access to credit. The choice would depend on the relative demerits of the two costs. Free-riding in joint liability (i.e. making a peer repay a loan which could have been repaid by the borrower) is mitigated by the large peer-imposed social penalty. Joint liability maintains constant peer pressure, thus reducing the temptation for a borrower in a cash crisis to forfeit his or her access to future credit by defaulting on the repayment of an instalment, which might be a rational strategy in a physically uncollateralized loan. 'The existence of the group thus acts like a collateral for a bank loan' (Hossain, 1988, p. 26).

The screening process, such as the use of landlessness as a programme eligibility criterion, ensures that participants in microcredit are likely to respect these borrower/peer roles. Under this screening process, applicants may be considered 'acceptable risks' even if they have previously defaulted on a formal loan, as long as they are thought to be likely to honour joint liability (with the associated behavioural response) and be susceptible to the monitoring and enforcement activities of fieldworkers. Thus GBF ameliorates strategic default, a problem encountered in some public lending programmes, and thereby offers an opportunity for the poor to access cheaper donor funds.

This discussion highlights that the effectiveness of GBF repayment mechanisms depends fundamentally on how borrowers perceive certain 'costs' and 'benefits' to programme participation (i.e. the 'group game'). Arguably we should not expect the effectiveness of incentives and costs to be constant for all people and all time, for they surely depend on a person's particular context at a particular time (e.g. a person's lack of alternatives). This is simply stating the obvious: the outcomes of objectively determined incentives and costs (say a penalty imposed by a bank for default) are conditioned by subjective appraisal of those incentives and costs by the players involved in the game, and this is contextual. Of course, considering the rapid expansion of some GBF programmes (e.g. Grameen and BRAC), with experience this subjective appraisal is to a large extent initially predictable for members of the target population.

However, transformations in rural sociology arising from programme intervention may open up alternative supplies of credit for a programme participant, and changes in individuals, arising from the repeated borrowing experience, may be associated with a reduced identification with the 'group game'. Without further technical definition, as a shorthand we apply the term 'empowerment' to refer to these effects. Thus we suggest that although longer participation may increase the chances of repayment (through greater experience, etc.), more contentiously, it may also decrease repayment through an 'empowerment' effect.

Since microcredit projects aim to change poor people's lives economically and socially, using 'socially constructed collateral', this paper makes the logical next step of hypothesizing that such changes over time may alter the behaviour of participants of group finance. In particular, does the 'empowerment process', widely accredited to repeat borrowing, lead to some erosion of the effectiveness of mechanisms that promote repayment in GBF? This paper explores whether repeat borrowers with BRAC behave differently (in subsequent loans) to first-time borrowers, owing to their having acquired greater skills, resources, confidence and social position through participation in microcredit projects.

Puzzles from BRAC's Rural Development Programme

The puzzle revealed by BRAC's data is that repayment rates appear to decrease with increasing borrowers' experience. This point is initially demonstrated with a small survey of RDP (Rural Development Programme) borrowers in which 'repeated borrowing' and 'longer programme participation' are both linked to lower repayment rates. Further evidence appears at a programme level where borrowers in RDP have different repayment rates according to when their villages joined BRAC.

Individual level. This section uses data from programme records and a 1991 survey of 122 randomly selected male borrowers under one BRAC office. Regression results show that a borrower's repayment rate significantly decreases with the borrower's length of membership of BRAC in months. Second, repeat borrowing, age of village membership of BRAC, and average village-level repayment have significant negative impacts on repayment levels. This second result may be a decomposition of the first into the three processes to be described later in this paper: the first variable captures an 'individual-level empowerment effect', the second captures a 'social transformation effect', and the third a 'demonstration effect'. Clearly there is more to explaining variation in repayment levels than just these three variables; however, other variables that might have been relevant to repayment, such as household assets and borrower's skills, were found generally to be not significant.

Programme level. Analysis of repayment of 17 323 RDP loans in 1989 shows that grouping RDP borrowers according to their previous experience of programmes in BRAC gives significantly different repayment performance between groups.

Before RDP, BRAC experimented with three other programmes: the Integrated Development Programme (IDP), Outreach, and the Rural Credit and Training Programme (RCTP), each with a different programme content. 'Outreach was established to test the limits of what the landless could accomplish using only their own resources, and whatever support they could find from local and government sources ... RCTP was established to test the idea that with adequate local organization, credit and self-employment activities the poor could become more independent of local élites for loans, employment and the resolution of conflict' (BRAC, 1992). This two-way response in 1979 emerged from BRAC's experience with the IDP, which was introduced in 1976 on a small experimental scale to explore the foundations of conscientization, institutional, economic, health and education intervention. All three programmes were replaced by the RDP (introduced in 1986), which also incorporates elements of both conscientization and income generating approaches. Thus although currently under the same lending methodology, some RDP borrowers have been in BRAC considerably longer and have been exposed to rather different development philosophies and assumptions, and presumably hold different perceptions of BRAC as a lending institution. Of the four, Outreach was more socially radical, RCTP was economically or credit oriented, IDP was intensive, experimental, and action–research oriented, and RDP was a more mature and socially conservative version of IDP.

When RDP borrowers are grouped according to which programme they initially joined (IDP, Outreach, RCTP, or RDP), each group has significantly different repayment behaviour to the other three (see Table 14.1).

For example, those RDP borrowers who joined BRAC under the RCTP programme (1979–86) showed an average repayment rate of 70.5 per cent (using the definition:

$$\text{repayment rate} = \frac{\text{amount realized}}{\text{overdue} + \text{amount realized}} \times 100$$

Table 14.1 **Repayment rates for borrowers who joined at different times under different programmes**

Repymt rate %	'*'= pairs different at 5% sig. Brwr Exper	RCTP	Out	IDP	Yr of origin	Programme characteristics
70.5	ex-RCTP				1979	basic organization, emphasis on credit and economic action
79.9	ex-Outreach	*			1979	group development, social mobilization, collective action
95.6	ex-IDP	*	*		1976	intensive, action research, conscientization, group development, credit
97.5	RDP-only	*	*	*	1986	similar to IDP mix, larger and rapidly expanding, better defined, relatively stable

This result holds across gender and economic sectors.

Worldwide group-lending experience is mixed (see Devereux and Fishe, 1993), due to a variety of factors such as organizational commitment and methodology. Yet it is surprising to obtain such clearly non-random repayment rates within the same programme, RDP. (Unfortunately it was not possible to make any allowance for branch-level effects along the lines of Khandker and Khalily (1995, p. 75). Regional distribution of loans may have important effects, through variations in agriculture, climate, and supply of other sources of finance.) These results might be in concurrence with a 'repeat borrower thesis', in that borrowers who have been in BRAC longer have lower repayment. This idea is also mentioned in some of BRAC's internal documents (e.g. Ahmed, 1992), and also in conversations with field staff.

Each of the programme categories (IDP/Outreach/RCTP/RDP) represent different proportions of repeat borrowers and first-timers (since they have been operating for different lengths of time), with consequent effects on repayment. The central contention is that in BRAC repeat borrowers respect the 'group game' less than first-timers, because of an 'empowerment–repayment' effect associated with repeated borrowing.

Importantly, the data also reveal that programme content and philosophy may affect how repeat borrowers evolve. Stearns (1991) finds that image and lending philosophy were important in programmes in Latin America, particularly as regards default. We do not argue that the 'repeat borrower/empowerment thesis' is inevitable, to be observed everywhere. We suggest that BRAC's data might indicate that credit programmes that pay close attention to group formation and cohesiveness (IDP rather than RCTP) may result in more resilient lending groups.

Repayment and empowerment: any links?

Empowerment may be thought to result from changes occurring at a wider social level and at a narrower individual level. 'Some see empowering as the development of skills and abilities to enable poor people to manage better and to have a say in or negotiate with the existing delivery system, while to others it is more fundamental and essentially concerned with enabling poor people to decide upon and to take the actions that they believe are essential to their development' (Westergaard 1992, p. 1). An empowerment–repayment link is considered theoretically plausible, since empowerment should alter borrowers' appraisal of costs of the bank penalty (usually the denial of future credit), the social penalty and other opportunity costs of non-participation. The following three mechanisms will be discussed more fully in the next sections.

o Cross-sectionally, those who are more socially powerful (as indicated by wealth, income, education and status) empirically have lower repayment; and repeated borrowing in GBF is thought to improve wealth, income, education and status.
o Wider social transformation may improve access to credit; and prolonged GBF interventions are thought to make structural transformations in rural society in favour of the poor.
o 'Demonstration effects', or 'learning to cheat effects', may be experienced with repeated borrowing.

Effects due to individual empowerment through repeated borrowing

Regression and discriminant analyses have isolated certain (often puzzling) socio-economic factors and behavioural proxies indicating 'good repayers'. Generally, these studies do not distinguish repeat versus first-time borrowers. Importantly, no studies exist on ex-borrowers who are denied credit due to past default. These studies are therefore cross-sectional, whereas ideally we should like to observe the financial behaviour of a panel of borrowers and non-borrowers over time, particularly as their social and economic characteristics change. These cross-sectional studies show that inverse relationships exist between repayment and: income and wealth; education; and social status (particularly gender).

Income and wealth. Several studies have shown that, paradoxically, repayment decreases with greater land ownership and wealth. Mohan, Veerasamy and Sivaraman (1985) find that larger landownership, income and consumption expenditures all implied greater chance of wilful default in their 1981 study of co-operatives in Tamil Nadu. Similar evidence is found in Uttar Pradesh (Singh and Jain, 1988, p. 424), Rajasthan (Dadhich, 1971, p. 586), in the Indian IRDP (Gupta, 1987, p. 161), Ethiopia (Lele, 1974, p. 422), and Bangladesh (Chowdhury, 1992, pp. 335–6). The direction of these correlations with repayment seem counterintuitive in terms of economics, except when some notion of 'empowerment' is included in the explanation.

Education and experience. Some studies have linked default to higher education levels: 'this implies that the literate were capable of evading repayment by taking advantage of loopholes in the loan administration' (Mohan, Veerasamy and Sivaraman, 1985, p. 555); similar evidence appears in Rajasthan (Dadhich, 1971, p. 586), Nepal (Agricultural Development Bank, 1987, p. 98), India (Gupta, 1987, p. 172), and Bangladesh (Chowdhury, 1992, p. 328).

Education displays strong correlations in other areas of development research; e.g. in fertility studies small levels of female schooling raise fertility, while higher levels reduce fertility. Education imparts knowledge and (arguably) the ability to make independent life-decisions, which is often linked to notions of 'empowerment' (Batliwala, 1993, p. 11). It is thought that fertility rises because a little education improves knowledge about nutrition, hygiene, bottle-feeding (thus reducing postpartum infecundity) etc., but higher levels of education actually empower women to make their own fertility decisions and delay marriage. 'Education strengthens the bargaining position of the woman as a mother ... Girls' education also ... reduce[s] population pressure via delayed age of marriage' (Hansen, 1994, p. 337).

Could education have effects on repayment, parallel to that observed on fertility? Certainly education, literacy, skills, and experience are different things, but without other direct evidence we generalize the education relationships presented above. Repeat borrowing probably improves skills and experience, and BRAC's child and adult education interventions raise household education and literacy levels over time. Thus we hypothesize that repeat borrowers may be better able to take independent decisions, and these may include behaving in ways that undermine repayment mechanisms, such as not respecting monitoring or enforcement. 'Empowerment also means having choices, and ... [the] ability to make choices *which the activist/change agent may disapprove of*. But it means the exercise of informed choice within an expanding framework of information, knowledge and analysis of the options available ... choices can only be made within the menu of known or experienced possibilities' (Batliwala, 1993, p. 11, emphasis added).

Social status. Puzzlingly, lower status and lower caste are frequently associated with higher repayment (Mohan, Veerasamy and Sivaraman, 1985, p. 555; Dadhich, 1971, p. 586; Chowdhury, 1992, p. 329; Gupta, 1987, p. 155). One author writes: 'Our field visits reveal that non-repayment of amounts due to governmental agencies is considered as a symbol of power and influence in the villages' (Gupta, 1987, p. 160). Perhaps the clearest evidence for the 'repayment–disempowerment' link is the very robust result that poor women show the best repayment in microcredit all over the world (e.g. Ahmed, 1992, for BRAC). This is particularly puzzling since generally women have less access to markets, fewer economic skills, fewer resources, and often greater nutritional deprivation.

Is the explanation women's lower levels of power? Are men more easily empowered by microcredit projects than women? Goetz and Gupta (1994, italics added, p. 6) observe that women may be preferred to men as participants in microcredit programmes because '... women are seen to be more reliable and *tractable*, and are easier for fieldworkers to access. Unlike men, who may be involved in rural markets or wage labour during the day, women tend to be found at home, and are more available than men for daytime group meetings as well as visits to monitor loan use and repayment.' GBF may be particularly effective with 'disempowered' women since non-compliance involves: greater objective costs (i.e. women are more available to be monitored and pressured); and greater subjective appraisal of costs (i.e. alternatives to the microcredit may be non-existent).

The idea that men may be more easily empowered than women arises because repeat borrowing increases the likelihood of female-to-male loan diversion (for Grameen, Hossain and Afsar 1988; for BRAC, Goetz and Gupta 1994, p. 16). For example, in Grameen, female first-time borrowers used 88 per cent of loans themselves, compared to only 57 per cent for those who received four or more loans. Hossain and Afsar speculate that women '... allow other members to utilize the money, so that their work involvement in economic activities does not increase' (p. 54). This argues that beyond certain loan sizes women are unable to expand their paid work due to the demands of household work on their time. Yet certain activities undertaken by women exhibit sufficient time-economies of scale to question this argument. For example, rearing 100 chicks rather than 50 chicks is not likely to be much more time-consuming regarding feeding time, cleaning time, and visits by the para-vet. Furthermore, since female projects (especially first-time borrowers) nearly always have perfect repayment rates, the incentives for the household should be to expand female projects, rather than divert resources into male hands.

Goetz and Gupta (1994) focus more closely on gender power relations, and taking control over the use of a loan may be a way of strengthening male control over household resources. It may take a few repeat (and larger) loans for men to perceive potential shifts in intra-household gender power due to credit, and also to work out that it is perfectly possible to take control over women's credit without jeopardizing household access to that resource. Thus women's control over credit decreases with repeat borrowing. 'Poor men are almost as powerless as poor women in terms of access to and control over resources. This is exactly why most poor men support empowerment processes when they enable women to bring much-needed resources into their families and communities, and/or challenge power structures which have oppressed and exploited poor men as well as women. The resistance, however, comes when the same women begin to question the power, attitudes or behaviour of men in the family' (Batliwala, 1993, p. 9).

Effects of sociological gains through programme intervention

It is often contended that microcredit improves the status and power of the poor within rural society. The idea is drawn out clearly in the debate between the relative merits of the 'minimalist credit interventions' versus the 'credit plus conscientization' approaches. We argue that if such shifts in social power balances occur, the importance of future credit as a sanction (and collateral substitute) could be eroded accordingly, since alternative sources may be more favourably arranged than before the intervention. The strength of respect for the joint-liability clause depends in part on whether there exists a positive value to sourcing credit from the microcredit programme, rather than elsewhere.

Devereux and Fishe (1993) make a similar point, except they incorrectly reduce the whole issue to interest rate differentials. There may be non-interest costs associated with microcredit (e.g. attending weekly meetings, accepting different ideology and social practice, joint liability, losing autonomy, accepting the authority of a fieldworker, and so on), and non-interest benefits to borrowing from informal lenders (e.g. through interlinked markets to marketing and production, social protection, and so on). Montgomery (1995) suggests that BRAC borrowers may turn to informal lenders simply for weekly repayments, due to the absence of supporting mechanisms from BRAC. Arguably, when left with the choice between repaying both a formal and informal debt, informal debts would be considered superior since informal penalties are higher and more difficult to evade. All things considered, the formal–informal interest rate differential (the main reason for accepting joint liability) may not be regarded by some microcredit borrowers to be that great. In certain contexts informal lenders may have only to drop interest rates relatively slightly to become attractive to microcredit borrowers. This drop may be induced by shifts in social power (increasing the bargaining position of the poor) and greater credit market competition.

Rahman and Wahid (1992) claim that '... the Grameen Bank brought a silent revolution in the century-old patron-client relationship in rural Bangladesh' (p. 303). Based on interviews of 49 'patrons', they provide evidence to say that GB intervention has decreased sharecropping, increased agricultural wages, and reduced patrons' quasi-judiciary powers (under *salish*). All of these may be taken as signs that 'rigidities' in rural credit markets, particularly those associated with patron–client power asymmetries, have been decreased with microcredit intervention, and thus suppliers of financial services are being exposed to greater competition.

Indeed, based on a national survey of 2912 households, Iqbal (1988) finds that moneylenders in India drop their interest rates in response to increased formal interventions, and developments that reduce risk (e.g. Green Revolution technology). Importantly, greater land ownership and education implies lower informal interest rates (by 0.16 per cent per hectare and 0.83 per cent per schooling year, respectively): 'the effect of education is particularly revealing and indicates that moneylenders view progressive attitudes and human capital with considerable favour' (p. 373). Further, 'our results constitute strong support for the view that ... rural income growth and prospects of income growth ... tend to lower the margin of risk in general' (p. 373) (and therefore informal interest rates).

Risk reduction from repeat borrowing (via human capital improvements, assets accumulation, diversified household incomes, and increased new technology adoption), combined with the fact that repeat borrowers are already 'screened' and have demonstrated creditworthiness, allows us to argue that informal lenders might prefer to lend to repeat borrowers. This suggestion is confirmed by 'patrons' in Rahman and Wahid's (1992) study. Thus microcredit may be 'moving the frontier outward' for repeat borrowers.

In summary, microcredit intervention may improve the poor's bargaining position with informal lenders by altering rural power and increasing competition among service providers, and second may make the poor more attractive to informal lenders through pre-screening, increasing debt capacity, and reducing risk. This reduces the cost to a group member of losing access to microcredit.

The demonstration effect

Gibbons and Kasim (1991) give good descriptions of a Malaysian Grameen replication project in which a 'demonstration effect' was thought to have contributed to a spread of poor repayment. '... Delinquency is contagious. It has a tendency to spread and worsen, leading to high levels of default, unless it is aggressively controlled ... Clients within the same area tend to hear about who pays loans back on time, who does not, and what happens to those who do not' (Stearns, 1991, p. 30, p. 34). Demonstration may affect the credibility of a lender and sanctions. We argue that with time a similar process occurs in which a repeat borrower witnesses cumulatively several peers defaulting in the village. Ideally this should not make a difference since the borrower's contract with BRAC and the group should remain unaffected. We have already argued that the ideal game may be undermined with repeated borrowing. Further, Montgomery (1995) shows that in BRAC peer pressure is not from the group but from the village as a whole.

Conclusions

The thesis of this paper is rather simple: in lending systems where social collateral replaces physical collateral, repayment may be affected if with time the lending process changes the initial social conditions upon which the social collateral is based. Over time, in different social contexts, agents revalue (and are revalued by) various service suppliers and their financial contracts. The first part of this paper showed that, in BRAC, prolonged participation in microcredit is associated with failing repayment. The second part showed how changing social conditions might reduce the effectiveness of social collateral to induce repayment. Thus an 'empowerment–repayment' link was hypothesized. In other credit programmes, repayment was found to be lower among wealthier, more educated, and high-status borrowers. Repeated borrowing in GBF increases incomes and wealth (thus sanctions may be better absorbed), education and experience (thus monitoring and enforcement may be less respected), and status (thus alternatives may be found). GBF interventions may also improve the provision of informal credit. Additionally, borrowers gradually learn from other borrowers the consequences of default.

In a poverty alleviation context, microcredit should not be considered solely in financial terms. Yet the pressure for NGOs to think in these terms is great, arising from the weight of past collapses of programmes through high default rates, and second and very powerfully, through the prerogatives of justifying rapid programme expansion to donors by proving financial sustainability. Exclusive concern with financial criteria may mean that both donors and NGOs fail to recognize important aspects of group dynamics.

NGOs may fail to realize that forming groups solely to channel credit is not sufficient to sustain non-opportunistic behaviour and curtail privately optimal short-sighted behaviour among participants. Groups that are formed solely to channel credit may encourage an individualistic ethos, in which 'learning to cheat' becomes a rational (and fulfilled) pursuit. The BRAC data suggest that close attention is needed to form groups in ways in which members sufficiently identify with the collective, and continue to feel ownership over the 'social collateral' as their situation changes. Two features are particularly instructive here: (1) the resilience and high repayment of groups formed from ex-IDP members (intensive, experimental, action–research oriented); (2) the different performances of borrowers with Outreach experience (collective-action oriented) and RCTP experience (simple credit-oriented), which are both of the same age. Creating durable groups is tricky. NGOs must encourage members to identify with the group for solidarity and constructive monitoring (such as skills transfer), as well as for the credit. In addition to developing group ethos, NGOs must build rewards into their programmes so as to elicit long-term commitment from borrowers as their financial experience grows. In this vein, interestingly, Grameen attempts to make members 'stakeholders' in GB by selling shares. Clearly, group formation is an important investment.

This fact may escape donors focusing strongly on financial criteria. Along the lines of this article, repayment rates may represent greater empowerment and freedom for some poor borrowers. Some commentators would be horrified by this, and insist that attaching 'social' considerations to credit has destroyed many financial systems around the world. Yet some grassroots practitioners involved in mobilizing the poor may be more sympathetic, since they see poverty as rooted in immiserizing social structures and therefore 'socio-political'. Until ways are suggested to tackle structurally regenerated poverty, which can be implemented on a national scale (other than suggesting revolution), microcredit remains a powerful tool. If this course of action is accepted then credit and social goals are intertwined, and demanding a divorce of the two is false in terms of poverty alleviation. Thus donors must accept that they will have to subsidize microcredit projects, and that complete financial independence may not be desirable.

References

Agricultural Development Bank, (1987), *Loan delinquency of ADB*, Evaluation Division, AgDB, Nepal.
Ahmed, Z., (1992), 'Loan recovery performance for rural poor', mimeo, RED, BRAC.
Batliwala, S., (1993), *Empowerment of women in South Asia*, FAO, Delhi.
BRAC, (1992), *BRAC at 20 Years*, BRAC, Dhaka.
BRAC, (1992b), *RDP Phase 11 Report*, BRAC, Dhaka.
Chowdhury, O.H., (1992), 'Credit in rural Bangladesh', *Asian Economic Review*, Vol. 34, No. 2.
Dadhich, C.L., (1971), 'Wilful default of co-operative credit in Rajasthan', *Indian Journal of Agricultural Economics*, Vol. 26, No. 4.
Devereux, J. and R.P.H. Fishe, (1993), 'An economic analysis of group lending programs in developing countries', *Developing Economies*, Vol. 31, No. 1.
Gibbons, D.S. and S. Kasim, (1991), *Banking on the rural poor*, University Sains, Penang, Malaysia.

Goetz, A.M. and R.S. Gupta, (1994), *Who takes the credit? Gender, power and control over loan use in rural credit programmes in Bangladesh*, Working Paper 8, Institute of Development Studies, Sussex.

Gupta, S.C., (1987), *Development banking for rural development*, Deep and Deep, New Delhi.

Hansen, S., (1994), 'Population: its challenge to economic and social scientists', *International Social Science Journal* No. 141 (UNESCO).

Hossain, M., (1988), *Credit for alleviation of rural poverty: The Grameen Bank in Bangladesh*, International Food Policy Research Institute (Report 65), Washington.

Hossain, M. and R. Afsar, (1988), Credit for women's involvement in economic activities in rural Bangladesh, BIDS, Dhaka.

Iqbal, F., (1988), 'The determinants of moneylender interest rates: evidence from rural India', *Journal of Development Studies*, Vol. 24, No. 3.

Khandker, S.R. and B. Khalily, (1995), *Designing a sustainable poverty alleviation program: the BRAC strategy in Bangladesh*, Education and Social Policy Department, World Bank.

Lele, U., (1974), 'Role of credit and marketing in agricultural development', in N. Islam (ed.), *Agricultural policy in developing countries*, Macmillan, London.

Mohan, T.C., T. Veerasamy and S. Sivaraman, (1985), 'Bayesian analysis of crop loan overdues in Tamil Nadu', *Indian Journal of Agricultural Economics*, Vol. 40, No. 4.

Montgomery, R., (1995), *Disciplining or protecting the poor? Avoiding the social costs of peer pressure in solidarity group micro-credit schemes*, CDS, Swansea.

Rahman, A. and A.N.M. Wahid, (1992), 'The Grameen Bank and the changing patron–client relationship in Bangladesh', *Journal of Contemporary Asia*, Vol. 22, No. 3.

Singh, S.P. and A.K. Jain, (1988), 'Study of overdues in Uttar Pradesh', *Indian Journal of Agricultural Economics*, Vol. 43, No. 3.

Stearns, K., (1991), *The hidden beast: delinquency in microenterprise credit programs*, Discussion Paper 5, ACCION, Washington.

Yaqub, S., (1994), *On empowerment and peer monitoring in micro-credit programmes: some anomalies from BRAC*, Paper presented at UK Development Studies Association Conference, Lancaster.

Yaqub, S., (1993), *A review: Philippines rural credit study*, AG1, Asian Development Bank, Manila.

Yaqub, S., (1992), *Impact of BRAC's programme strategy on credit performance*, RED, BRAC, Dhaka.

Yaqub, S., (1992), *Repayment in RDP*, RED, BRAC, Dhaka.

Yaqub, S., (1991), *Study of BRAC Habigonj-1*, RED, BRAC, Dhaka.

About the author

Shahin Yaqub wrote this paper while he was a researcher at the Poverty Research Unit, University of Sussex, UK. He acknowledges the advice of M. Lipton, M. Fontana and I. Matin, as well as the institutional support of BRAC, Asian Development Bank, Institute of Development Studies (Sussex) and Melvilla.